The Kabbalistic Scholars of the
Antwerp Polyglot Bible

Studies in the History of Christian Traditions

Founded by

Heiko A. Oberman†

Edited by

Robert J. Bast
Knoxville, Tennessee

In cooperation with

Henry Chadwick, Cambridge
Scott H. Hendrix, Princeton, New Jersey
Paul C.H. Lim, Nashville, Tennessee
Eric Saak, Indianapolis, Indiana
Brian Tierney, Ithaca, New York
Arjo Vanderjagt, Groningen
John Van Engen, Notre Dame, Indiana

VOLUME 138

The Kabbalistic Scholars of the Antwerp Polyglot Bible

By

Robert J. Wilkinson

BRILL

LEIDEN · BOSTON
2007

On the cover: Matthew 21:1–5 from the *Antwerp Polyglot Bible.*

Brill has made all reasonable efforts to trace all rights holders to any copyrighted material used in this work. In cases where these efforts have not been successful the publisher welcomes communications from copyrights holders, so that the appropriate acknowledgements can be made in future editions, and to settle other permission matters.

This book is printed on acid-free paper.

A Cataloging-in-Publication record of this book is available from the Library of Congress.

ISBN 978 90 04 16251 8

For Kathleen

uxori carissimae
sine qua non

CONTENTS

INTRODUCTION

The *Antwerp Polyglot Bible* is one of the great monuments of sixteenth-century typographic and scholarly achievement. It is surprising then that it lacks a worthy treatment in depth in any language, though there are several important works and articles that provide essential orientation. Predictably much of the secondary literature has been produced either around the Plantin Museum in Antwerp or in Spain. With significant exceptions the earlier Spanish work tended to be celebratory and patriotic as Spanish scholars have in the past shown themselves eager to claim the Antwerp Polyglot, or the *Biblia Regia*, as the culmination of the great Spanish tradition begun at Alcalá, and to see Montano, the Spanish king's project director, very much as the channel through which the tradition was transmitted to Antwerp. Things look somewhat different from Belgium where the magnificent resources of the Plantin Museum and specifically Plantin's correspondence have enabled scholars to produce fundamental works of scholarship and to emphasise the contribution of North European scholars to the project.[1]

I shall not deny below the continuities that the *Biblia Regia* shows with the Spanish tradition—indeed I shall be concerned to bring certain features of the tradition into sharper focus—particularly in the personal contributions of Montano, nor shall I underrate him as a capable diplomat who had the challenging task of getting approval

---

[1] Controversial but stimulating has been a work with which we shall frequently be engaged: B. Rekers, *Benito Arias Montano (1527–1598)* (E. J. Brill, Leiden 1972). The article of P. Theunissen "Arias Montano et la Polyglot d'Anvers" Les Lettres Romanes (Louvain) XIX/3 (1965) pg 231–246 responded to Rekers's perspective with a thorough knowledge of Plantin's letters. A balanced account in English is given in C. Clair, *Christopher Plantin* (Cassell, London 1960). Basic are M. Rooses, *Chr. Plantin, imprimeur anversois* (Brussels, 1883 chapters IV and V); L. Voet, *The Golden Compasses* Vol. II, pg 44–60 and A. F. G. Bell, *Benito Arias Montano* (OUP, Oxford 1922) which follows *Colección de Documentos inéditos para la historia de España* (Codoin) tom. 41 (1862) pg 127–418 very closely. Rekers discusses the Bible, *op. cit.*, pg 45–69. In Spanish there is P. Dominico Ramos Frechilla "La Poliglota de Arias Montano" Revista Española de Estudios Biblicos III (1928) pg 27–54; and two lectures given at the Fourth Centenary of the Bible: F. Perez Castro and L. Voet, *La Biblia Poliglota de Amberes* (Fundacíon Universitaria española, Madrid 1973). We shall refer later to F. Secret "Documents pour servir à la histoire de la Bible d'Anvers" Revista da Sefarad XVIII (1958) pg 121–128. Bibliography given below on Montano is, of course, often relevant.

for the bible that has also been named for him as the *Biblia de Montano*. The fact remains however that much of the work for the bible had been completed before the arrival of Montano in the Netherlands and that the inspiration for that work had nothing to do with Spain, but was a continuation of the work of the small group of northern oriental scholars who previously worked on similar biblical projects. It is the purpose of the present work to establish the contribution of these scholars to the Antwerp Polyglot.

The scholars in question—Andreas Masius, Guillaume Postel, Jean Boulaese and Guy Lefèvre de la Boderie are, I believe, most helpfully described as Christian kabbalists. That is to say they are interested in reading not only Hebrew, but also other oriental languages like Syriac, in a mystical fashion to discover deep hidden truths. Though their methods and notions were derived from Jewish Kabbalah, the hidden truths they uncovered, it must be admitted, are generally no more than Christian orthodoxies.[2] However, in the mind of Postel and to a lesser extent those who followed him (Boulaese, Guy Lefèvre de la Boderie) the final synthesis of their mystical imagination so far exceeded the contemporary boundaries of tolerable theological innovation as to attract the attention of the Inquisition. Postel was confined as a madman for much of the period under discussion in this book, yet this did not prevent his notions in some part from both instigating and informing the bible project, nor his eschatological timetable from driving the work on.

Similar kabbalistic notions informed the reception of Syriac and subsequently other oriental languages in the West at the time of the Fifth Lateran Council (1513–1515). An important and innovative figure then was the Cardinal Egidio da Viterbo, but the approach was maintained by Teseo Ambrogio, Johann Albrecht Widmanstetter and again Masius and Postel. In a previous work I have shown the importance of Christian kabbalistic notions in the production of Widmanstetter's

---

[2] Such verbal manipulations may be thought to fall well below the complexity and sophistication of Jewish kabbalah. I have briefly defended my unexceptional use of the term Christian kabbalah in the introduction to my *Orientalism, Aramaic and Kabbalah in the Catholic Reformation* where there is also an indicative bibliography of Christian kabbalah. That work also relates more substantially to some of the work of Gerhom Scholem, the master of Jewish kabbalah research whose influence remains central though his legacy is currently being reassessed.

1555 *editio princeps* of the Syriac New Testament.[3] The present work will demonstrate that the continued influence of these ideas, particularly in the person of Postel, was significant in the promotion of the Antwerp project, explains several features of that great bible, and also helps to account for the problems the bible had with the Inquisition.

The particular prominence given to Syriac rather than Arabic or Armenian or any other oriental language as a carrier of mystical meanings is not accidental nor merely a function of my own scholarly interests. Arcane significance was indeed found in the script and etymologies of these languages. Syriac, however, was considered to be the language of Christ, and, like Hebrew, it was therefore particularly efficient in conveying spiritual truths, and its script was early discovered to carry occult significance like the letters of the Hebrew alphabet. Moreover it was easier to print than Arabic and scholars actually had editions of the Syriac New Testament to present and explain. As we shall see they continually lamented the absence of a printed Arabic New Testament. Had one been produced, and Postel written the preface, that would no doubt have been as illuminating as the comments which, as it turned out, can only be found in the introductory or explanatory material published with the Syriac editions.

One has of course to beware of single explanations and simplistic characterisations of what was itself a very complicated project, executed collaboratively and at a time of great political and ideological disturbance. This present work, alas, is not the multi-faceted and encyclopaedic synthetic account of the Antwerp Polyglot Bible that is still awaited. I hope, however, to be able to bring together previous (often excellent, but necessarily partial) accounts to stress the continuity of this bible with work of the earlier Catholic kabbalistic oriental scholars in Northern Europe and to give due weight to those elements in the Spanish tradition which (though in some ways distinctive) may similarly be helpfully defined as kabbalistic.

Once again I must express my gratitude to my teachers, the late Dr Trevor Johnson (University of the West of England) and Dr Sebastian Brock (formerly of Oxford University) and to the helpful staff of Brill.

---

[3] R. J. Wilkinson, *Orientalism, Aramaic and Kabbalah in the Catholic Reformation. The first printing of the Syriac New Testament* (E. J. Brill, Leiden 2007).

CHAPTER ONE

THE SPANISH TRADITION:
THE NOTION OF A POLYGLOT

Properly to locate the production of the Antwerp Polyglot within
Spanish traditions of scholarship we shall need first to consider several
things: the previous Alcalá Polyglot; the person of Arias Montano as a
scholar, as representative of Spanish biblical scholarship, and possibly
as a member of the Family of Love; the discussion and ruling of the
Council of Trent on bibles; and the Inquisition and censorship. We
shall then hope to be able to appreciate which Spanish elements of
this bible were controversial and why, and the extent to which those
elements may be considered kabbalistic. Subsequently in later chapters
we shall set this Spanish tradition to one side and argue that motivation for the Polyglot came also from Guillaume Postel and his friends
who were instrumental both in completing much of the work before
Spanish control in the person of Montano arrived, and in seeking
Philip II's sponsorship for the bible. But first we must describe the
Spanish tradition.

Our primary aim throughout is to establish the continuity between
the Antwerp Polyglot and the northern scholars who had been involved
in the production in Vienna of the 1555 *editio princeps* of the Syriac
New Testament and who are most helpfully characterised as Christian
kabbalists. Our intention is to show that the edition of the Syriac
New Testament in the Antwerp Polyglot in particular was the product
of the same type of kabbalistic orientalism as the 1555 *editio princeps*,
and that this northern tradition was more influential in shaping the
Polyglot than the Spanish antecedents. A detailed examination of the
Antwerp edition itself and the other Syriac materials that appear in
the Antwerp Polyglot will demonstrate that this is the case, and will thus
be a convenient index for us as we trace the kabbalistic notions of its
scholars. We shall also examine some of the controversy to which the
Polyglot gave rise and attempt to reconstruct the *censura* of the inquisitor Juan de Mariana.

Finally, in the last chapter, we shall consider the extension of these
traditions of kabbalistic scholarship beyond the Antwerp project. Here

our focus will fall upon the later work of Guy Lefèvre de la Boderie
and in particular his 1584 Paris edition of the Syriac New Testament,
a final monument to the particular type of Christian kabbalism that
characterised the northern Catholic orientalists we are pursuing.

The Notion of a Polyglot[1]

Turning first to the Spanish antecedents of the Antwerp Polyglot,
the immediate model was the magnificent Alcalá Polyglot or *Biblia
Complutensis* produced in Alcalá by Cardinal Jiménez (Ximenes) de
Cisneros printed 1514–1517 and published in 1520.[2] However, before
we examine that revolutionary book, it will be instructive to consider
an earlier polyglot.

The Psalter of Agostino Giustiniani was the first European humanist
polyglot to be printed, though its production overlapped with that of
the *Biblia Complutensis*. Giustiniani was a Genoese patrician who entered
the Dominican Order (for the second time) in 1488 and was Bishop of
Nebbio in Corsica. He published his psalter in 1516 in Genoa.[3] The
psalter has eight columns across each opening of two pages: the Hebrew
text; a Latin translation thereof; the Vulgate; the Greek Septuagint; an
Arabic text; the Targum, printed for the first time; a Latin translation
of the Targum; and a column of copious scholia.

This remarkable book, dedicated to Leo X, was printed by a Milanese
printer lately from Turin, Paulus Porrus whom Giustiniani had brought
to Genoa, and went on sale in the house of Nicolas Giustiniani. There

---

[1] A good general introduction is G. Bardy "Simple remarques sur les ouvrages et
les manuscrits bilingues" Viver et Penser III (1945) pg 242–267.

[2] Aldus had conceived of a polyglot even earlier before the end of the fifteenth
century. In the preface to his Greek Psalter (1497?) he promised a triglot Old Testament. In a letter of July 1501 he wrote: *"Vetus et novum Instrumentum graece, latine, et
hebraice nondum impressi sed parturio."* A. A. Renouard, *Annales de l'Imprimerie des Alde* (2nd
ed. 1825) pg 44–45 and 273–274 gives a facsimile of a specimen sheet preserved in the
Bibliothèque nationale Paris giving the first few verses of Genesis 1 in Hebrew, Greek,
and Latin columns. (A privately printed English version of this work by E. Goldsmid
appeared in Edinburgh in 1887.)

[3] *Biblia Polyglotta Psalterium Hebraeum Graecum Arabicum & Chaldeum cum tribus Latinis
interpretatibus & glossis [Edidit Aug. Iustinianus Genuensis Praedicatorii ordinis episcopus Nebien-
sis] Genua impressit Petrus Paulus Porrus, in aedibus Nicolai Iustiniani Pauli 1516.* 4to. See:
J. Balagna, *L'Imprimerie arabe en occident (XVI, XVII, XVIII siècles)* (Maisonneuve et Larose,
Paris 1984) pg 20–23.

were two thousand copies, and fifty on vellum.[4] The preface further promised the whole bible in polyglot format and claimed that the New Testament had been completed in manuscript, but of this nothing now is known.

This Genoa Psalter is the first polyglot edition of part of the bible printed with exotic script. The Hebrew type is a little clumsy, not only because this is the first Hebrew printed in Genoa, but also because it was made by Gentiles. No Jews took part in the production of the book: the Doge was expelling them from Genoa at the time.[5] The Arabics, however, are of particular interest. They are only the second produced after those of the 1514 prayer book of Fano (of which only nine copies are now known).[6] Arabic script posed particular problems for printers using moveable type because of its ligatures and early printed books where they do aspire to Arabic characters usually have woodcuts or even leave blank spaces for the characters to be written in by hand. The Arabics which Guillaume Postel used for his *Linguarum duodecim* of 1538 are woodcuts, those of his slightly later *Grammatica Arabica* (c.1539–1540) were moveable but without ligatures. The Genoa Psalter thus represents a considerable achievement in this respect and its role in spreading knowledge of Arabic was considerable: both Nicolas Clénard (1495–1542) and Wolfgang Musculus (1497–1563) used it.[7] By contrast, neither the *Biblia Complutensis* nor the Antwerp Polyglot had Arabics. We shall see that it was a particular concern of Postel and others involved with the Antwerp Polyglot that it should include an Arabic version. They achieved the addition of a Syriac version which was lacking in the *Biblia Complutensis*, but failed ultimately to include an Arabic version after the fashion of the Genoa Psalter.

---

[4] R. Smitskamp, *Philologia Orientalia III* # 236, pg 231–235. Also: D. W. Amram, *The Makers of Hebrew Books in Italy* (Holland Press, London 1963) pg 225–229.

[5] *Op. cit.*, pg 227.

[6] *Septem horae canonicae, a laicis hominibus recitandae, iuxta ritum Alexandrinorum seu Jacobitarum Alexandrino Patriarchae subditorum Arabicae, editae a Gregorio Georgio Veneto, sub auspiciis Leonis X Pontificis Maximi in urbe Fano.* See: C. F. de Schnurrer, *Bibliotheca Arabica* (Halle, 1811) pg 231 #235; G. Galbiati "La Prima Stampa in Arabo" in *Miscellanea Giovanni Mercati* vol. VI (Studi e Testi 126, 1946) pg 409–413. The prayer book was produced for the Melchites (Egyptian Jacobites).

[7] Briefly: K. H. Dannefeldt "The Renaissance Humanists' knowledge of Arabic" *Studies in the Renaissance II* (1955) pg 96–117 pg 113–115. For an appraisal of Agostino himself as an Arabist: H. Bobzin "Agostino Giustiniani (1470–1536) und seine Bedeutung für die Geschichte der Arabistik" in eds. W. Diem and A. A. Falaturi, *XXIV Deutscher Orientalistentag* (Köln 1988) (Stuttgart 1990) pg 131–139.

The column of scholia in the Genoa Psalter is also interesting. It has long quotations from rabbinic and midrashic material, but more particularly shows the kabbalistic interest characteristic of the early Catholic orientalists and which we shall find also motivating the scholars of the Antwerp Polyglot. Thus, for example, on page X2 Giustiniani quotes from the *Cabbalistica Fragmenta* he published in woodcut in 1513—itself taken substantially from Reuchlin's kabbalistic *De Verbo Mirifico* and in turn to be taken up by Petrus Galatinus in *De Arcanis*. Secret describes these notes by saying *"fourissent toute une littérature kabbalistique"*.[8]

Both Giustiniani's Psalter and the Complutensian Polyglot were ultimately inspired by Origen's great Hexapla and were intended for scholarly rather than practical use.[9] Earlier diglot or triglot manuscripts are not uncommon. Far rarer however are the true polyglot manuscripts (with four or more languages), and those that are found usually have a liturgical function, though Sebastian Brock has published a most instructive exception to this rule in Cambridge Or. 929.[10] We shall investigate the intended scholarly use of the Complutensian Polyglot below in the context of the questions it raised about the authority of the Vulgate. When, however, we subsequently turn to the motivation of Postel and his friends in wishing to produce polyglot bibles, and in particular the Antwerp Polyglot, we shall find them quite different.

The Complutensian Polyglot

The immediate model for the Antwerp Polyglot, as we have said, was the *Biblia Complutensis*.[11] This revolutionary book was the product of

---

[8] For this and comments on both Giustiniani and on Galatinus see F. Secret, *Kabbalistes chrétiens de la Renaissance* (Dunod, Paris 1964) pg 99–106.

[9] On the Hexapla, see: D. C. Parker s.v. in *The Anchor Dictionary of the Bible* (Doubleday, New York 1992) Vol. III pg 188–189; P. M. Bogaert "Origène et les Hexaples" in *Dictionnaire de la Bible*, Suppl. fasc. 68 (1993) pg 568–573; and N. Fernández Marcos, *The Septuagint in Context* (E. J. Brill, Leiden 2000) pg 204–222 with up-to-date bibliography.

[10] S. Brock "A Fourteenth-Century Polyglot Psalter" in eds. G. E. Kaddish and G. E. Freeman, *Studies in Honour of M. R. J. Williams* (Publications of the Society for the Study of Egyptian Antiquities, Toronto 1982) pg 1–15. This polyglot manuscript, perhaps from the Syrian monastery in the desert of Sketis, seems to have had as its purpose the correction of the Syro-hexapla from the Hebrew.

[11] *Biblia sacra, hebraice, chaldaice et grace cum tribus interpretationibus latinis: de mandato ac sumptibus Cardinalis D. F. Francisci Ximenez de Cisneros.* Alcalá 1514–1517. There is a re-impression by the Fundación Biblica Española y Universidad Complutense de Madrid

the progressive school of Hebrew at the university that the powerful reforming Cardinal Cisneros had established at Alcalá.[12] The Constitution of the University provided for the teaching of oriental languages as required at the Council of Vienne: the Polyglot, the eventual fruit of this scholarly commitment, was produced at a time when Erasmus and Hebrew studies had not yet become suspect in Spain.[13]

(1984) together with *Anejo a la Edición facsimile de la Biblia Poliglota Complutense* (Fundación Biblica Española, Valencia 1987). Only a selective bibliography can be given here. The best introduction remains that of M. Bataillon, *Érasme et l'Espagne* (1st ed. 1937: reprinted Droz, Geneva 1998) pg 1–75. A corrected and augmented Spanish second edition appeared from Fondo de Cultura Económica, Mexico/Buenos Aires in 1966. The relevant pages are 1–71. Thereafter a very large three-volume Spanish edition with additional essays etc. was edited by D. Devoto and Ch. Amiel (Droz, Geneva 1991). The reference on pg 42 of the French edition to *"text syriaque"* is in error as there is none. The Spanish version has *'caldea'* and the reference is to the Aramaic Targum. B. Hall, *Humanists and Protestants 1500–1900* (T&T Clark, Edinburgh 1990) pg 1–51 has an excellent English introduction with good modern bibliography. See also his earlier *The Trilingual College of San Idelfonso and the Making of the Complutensian Polyglot* (E. J. Brill, Leiden 1969). J. H. Bentley "New Light on the Editing of the Complutensian New Testament" Bibliothèque de Humanisme et Renaissance XLII (1980) pg 145–156 makes use of manuscript annotations in the Archivo Historico Universitario, Madrid (AHU ms 117–Z–1). See also his *Humanists and Holy Writ New Testament Scholarship in the Renaissance* (Princeton UP, Princeton 1983) pg 70–111. Á. Sáenz-Badillos, *La Filologiá Biblica en los primeros helenistas de Alcalá* (Editorial Verbo Divino, Estella (Navarra) 1990) now replaces previous work on the Greek scholars. N. Fernández Marcos writes on Greek text in "El Texto griego de la Biblia Políglota Complutense" and E. Fernández Tejero on the Hebrew Text in "El Text hebreo de la Biblia Políglota Complutense" in their joint collection *Biblia y humanismo Textos, talantes y controversias del siglo XVI español* (Fundación Universitaria Española, Madrid 1997) pg 219–228 and 209–218 respectively. The latter provides a summary of previous work by *inter alios* F. Delitzsch, *Studies on the Complutensian Polyglot* (S. Bagster, London 1872) and *Complutensische Varianten zum Altest. Text. Ein Beitrag zur Biblischen Textkritik* (Leipzig 1878). For a fuller bibliographic description see T. H. Darlow and H. F. Moule, *Historical Catalogue of the Printed Editions of Holy Scripture in the Library of the British & Foreign Bible Society* (London 1903) Vol. 2 pg 2–6.

[12] V. Beltrán de Heredia "Catedráticos de Sagrata Escritura en Alcalá durante el siglo XVI" Ciencia Tomista XVIII (1918) pg 140–155 and XIX (1919) pg 49–55 and 144–156.

[13] It is not possible to review the enormous question of Erasmus's influence in Spain, for which Bataillon, *Érasme et l'Espagne* remains the essential introduction. Many Spanish intellectuals were eager for change in the early days of the European Reformation. New horizons were opened up when Antonio de Nebrija returned from Europe to his chair in Salamanca in 1505, and Cisneros, Archbishop of Toledo from 1495 and Inquisitor General from 1507, laid the foundations for humanistic study in his University at Alcalá. His professors included humanists like Nebrija, but also conversos like the brothers Juan and Francisco de Vergara—the latter perhaps the greatest Classical scholar in Spain (Ángel Sáenz-Badillos, *La Filologiá Biblica en los primeros helenistas de Alcalá*, pg 321–378: for Francisco de Vergara pg 367ff). The accession of Charles I to the imperial throne as Charles V seemed to ensure the inclusion of Spain in Europe's Humanism. Cisneros even tried unsuccessfully to have Erasmus himself come to Spain in 1517. The future Inquisitor General, Alonso Manrique, was an enthusiastic supporter of Erasmus and

There are regrettable gaps in our technical knowledge of the production of this bible: the intellectual trajectory, the precise division of
labour, and the working methods of the scholars and the textual basis
of their labours all remain somewhat opaque.[14] There is no question
however of the excellence of their achievement. The *Biblia Complutensis*
remains a truly outstanding book. The Old Testament has the Vulgate
together with Septuagint and Hebrew text with interlinear gloss. The
Pentateuchal Targum is given with columnar translation.[15] The New
Testament gives Vulgate with glossed Greek. The glosses, numbered links
between words in the text and the glosses, and the isolation of Hebrew
'roots', together with the Apparatus in the last volume, offer the facility
for precise (word for word) comparisons between versions and also an
effective way for scholars to learn or improve their Hebrew or Greek
through use of the Bible. The layout is magnificent, the typography

---

Erasmus's *Encheridion* appeared in Spanish in 1527, published by Miguel de Eguía
printer to the University. Juan de Vergara spent two years with Erasmus from 1520.
Yet the admiration was not universal. We shall see in our text below that differences
of opinion arose over the Reformer's attitude to the Vulgate, translations and other
Biblical matters, and Erasmus did display some unsettling resemblances to Luther. A
conference at Valladolid in 1527 of representatives of the Mendicant Orders under
the presidency of Manrique, however, failed to determine conclusively on Erasmus.
The first Inquisitorial prosecution for Erasmian ideals was that of Diego de Vieda
in 1528: he had spoken too freely about Luther! The Inquisition increasingly found
Lutheran ideas everywhere, even among the *alumbrados*. Juan de Vergara was arrested
in 1530 and had to abjure Lutheran ideas amongst others at an *auto* in Toledo 21
December 1535. Juan de Valdés published his *Dialogue of Christian Doctrine* in 1529 that
was based upon some early Luther. He was obliged to flee to Italy. Subsequently Miguel
de Eguía printer to the University was imprisoned for Lutheranism in 1531, though
he was absolved and released in 1533, the year Erasmus died. Rather awkwardly for
scholars, Erasmianism became linked with Lutheranism. The reality is however that
before 1558, when there was a notorious Protestant scare in Seville, less than fifty
cases of alleged Lutheranism came to the notice of the Inquisitors and in most it is
difficult to identify specifically Protestant beliefs (H. Kamen, *The Spanish Inquisition An
Historical Revision* (Weidenfeld and Nicolson, London 1997) pg 91. I have used Kamen
pg 83–102 for this summary). See also: J.-P. Dedieu "Le Modèle religieux: Le Réfus de
la Réforme et le contrôle de la pensée" in B. Bennassar, *L'Inquisition espagnole XV–XIX
siècles* (Hachette, Paris 1979) pg 263–304.

[14] See: M. Welte "The Problem of the Manuscript Basis for the earliest Printed Editions of the Greek New Testament" in eds. P. Saenger and K. van Kampen, *The Bible
as Book The First Printed editions* (British Library, London 1995) pg 117–123. The search
for manuscript exemplars of the Complutensian New Testament continues.

[15] Cisneros had the rest of the Targum translated into Latin and deposited in the
University Library as he tells us in the Preface to Vol. 1 (f. IIv).

clear, and Arnon Guillén de Brocar's Greek, which has no ligatures, is simply a delight.[16]

The Authority of the Vulgate

It is important to appreciate Cisneros's attitude to the traditional Scriptures of the Church that distanced him from contemporary scholars such as Antonio de Lebrixa and Antonio de Nebrija.[17] Cisneros could agree the Hebrew and Greek versions should be a guide to choosing between variants in Latin Vulgate manuscripts, but unlike those scholars he was not prepared to correct the Vulgate text by those versions.[18] Rather, he likened the (Old Testament) Vulgate text laid out on the page between the Hebrew and Greek text to Christ on the Cross between the two thieves (representing on the one hand blind Jewry, and on the other the schismatic Greek Orthodox). That is to say: the bible of the Roman Church alone preserved truth: *"reliquis a recta Scripturae intelligentia quandoque deviantibus"*.[19]

---

[16] On the printing now see: J. M. Abad "The Printing Press at Alcalá de Henares" in eds. P. Saenger and K. van Kampen, *The Bible as Book The First Printed editions* (British Library, London 1995) pg 101–115. Astonishingly the printer noted a mere fifty errors.

[17] Á. Sáenz-Badillos, *La Filologiá Biblica en los primeros helenistas de Alcalá* (Editorial Verbo Divino, Estella (Navarra) 1990) pg 381–453 offers a significant contribution on this issue. There is also a good description of Nebrija's *Apology* pg 96–100. On the technical linguistic aspects of Nebrija's work: K. W. Percival "Antonio de Nebrija and the Dawn of Modern Phonetics" Res Publica Litterarum V (1982) pg 221–232. On the important figure of Antonio de Lebrixa see Bataillon, *Érasme et l'Espagne* pg 26–38. Also V. Baroni, *La Contre-Réforme devant La Bible La Question biblique* (Imprimerie de la Concorde, Lausanne 1943) pg 43.

[18] In his Prologue dedicated to Leo X (f. IIIa) he writes: *"Accedit quod ubicumque latinorum codicum varietas es…ad primam Scripturae originem recurrendum est: sicut beatus Hieronymus et Augustinus ac coeteri ecclesiastici tractatores admonent: ita ut librorum Veteris Testamnti synceritas ex Hebraica veritate: Novi autem ex Graecis exemplaribus examinetur."* Pedro Martínez de Osma (c. 1430–1480) the teacher of Nebrija had attempted some correction of the Vulgate from the codices.

[19] Prologue f. IIIb: "…whenever the others deviate from the true understanding of Scripture." Jerome's translation from the Hebrew, he held, had been accurate: the Jews subsequently corrupted the Hebrew text. (Here one might compare: K. Reinhardt "Hebraische und spanische Bibleln auf den Scheiterhaufen der Inquisition. Texte zur Geschichte des Bibelzensur in Valencia im 1450" Historisches Jahrbuch CI (1981) pg 1–37. See pg 10–11 and 21–24 for the relevant parts of this interesting Latin text.) The 'schismatic' Septuagint, similarly held to be corrupted, had previously however found its first defender in Johannes Crastonus in his Greek and Latin Psalter (Milan 1481) where he had corrected the Latin from the Greek (W. Schwarz, *Principles and Problems of Biblical Translation Some Reformation Controversies and their Background* (CUP, Cambridge

Cisneros thus took care to offer no competitor to the Vulgate. In this respect he was quite different from Erasmus whose New Testament edition of 1516 was controversial, not because it offered a Greek text, but because it offered a completely recast translation of the Greek into a very different Latin to compete with the Vulgate. The Vulgate itself was not even included in the volume! Thus Stunica, López de Stuñiga, the competent editor of the Alcalá New Testament Greek text, could go on to achieve notoriety for the vigour of his attack on Erasmus's *translation*.[20]

Cisneros not only preserved the Vulgate from the criticism of the other versions but, his philological learning notwithstanding, continued to read Scripture with the traditional four-fold exegesis, quoting in his Prologue (IIIb) the famous text of Nicolas of Lyra in *Postilla Literalis in Vetum et Novum Testamentum: "Littera gesta docet: quid credas allegoria: moralis quid agis: quo tendas anagogia".*[21] Far from being contradictory, this hermeneutic approach in fact formed the basis for his interest in the

---

1955) pg 105–106. Cardinal Cisneros's position we shall see maintained through Trent and beyond. Thus Bellarmine's *De Verbo Dei scripto et non scripto* (*Disputationes* 1st ed. Ingolstadt 1586) accords to the true originals of the Hebrew and Greek Bible texts the status of pure sources, but then argues their current tendentious corruption has deprived them of authority. The Vulgate is the authentic Scripture of the Holy See. Bellamine accepts recourse to Hebrew and Greek where there is a copyist's fault in a Latin manuscript, where there are several Latin readings, where the Latin phrase is ambiguous, or where it is necessary to recover the real meaning of some difficult Latin words. See Baroni, *La Contre-Réforme devant La Bible* pg 152–159.

[20] *Annotationes contra Erasmum Roterdamum in defensionem translationis Novi Testamenti* (Alcalá 1520). Bataillon, *Érasme et l'Espagne* pg 43. H. J. De Jonge *"Novum Testamentum a nobis versum*: the essence of Erasmus's edition of the New Testament" Journal of Theological Studies XXXV (1984) pg 394–413 especially pg 405, 410. De Jonge describes how an attack on the phraseology of a version fundamental to the Western study of philosophy, law and theology might appear as an attack upon society itself. For more nuanced remarks: M. A. Screech's introduction to ed. A. Reeve, *Erasmus's Annotations on the New Testament The Gospels* (Duckworth, London 1986). The edition also of course enjoyed annotations and other material indicative of Erasmus's evangelical doctrines. On the relationship between Erasmus's manuscripts and the printed text, A. J. Brown "The Date of Erasmus's Latin Translation of the New Testament" Transactions of the Cambridge Bibliographical Society VIII/4 (1984/5) pg 351–380 is decisive. For Stunica's attack on Jacques Lefèvre d'Etaples for the same reasons, see: R. Cameron "The Attack on the Biblical Work of Lefèvre d'Etaples" Church History XXXVIII (1969) pg 9–24.

[21] "The Literal teaches what happened, the Allegorical what you believe, the Moral how to behave, and the Anagogic about the Last Things". W. Schwarz, *Principles and Problems of Biblical Translation Some Reformation Controversies and their Background* (CUP, Cambridge 1955) pg 45–60; M. E. Schild, *Abendländische Bibelvorreden bis zu Lutherbibel* (Gerd Mohn, Heidelberg 1970) pg 135–7.

ancient versions. For, as Cisneros explained to Leo X in the Prologue of the Complutensian Polyglot, though the Vulgate text preserved its authority against the Hebrew and Greek where they disagreed with it, they were still Scripture—albeit corrupted in places. Access to them gave, in turn, access to the manifold richness of their significance that inevitably had been narrowed by the process of their translation into the authoritative Vulgate. The traditional hermeneutic exposed the many layers of meaning found in the Vulgate Scriptures. Cisneros was displaying a yet greater richness and laying out the whole wealth of the biblical textual tradition in its several versions for meditation. This did not compromise the authority of the Vulgate.[22] Cisneros's view of the relationship between the Vulgate and the other versions commended itself, as we shall shortly see, to the Council of Trent.

Just as Cisneros's work stands in sharp contrast to Erasmus's with respect to the authority of Vulgate, so the difference between their attitudes to the Old Testament and Hebrew Studies was similarly pronounced. Though insistent upon the importance of original languages for the study of Scripture, Erasmus had little or no Hebrew, nor much time for it. His discovery of the *Adnotationes* of Valla on the New Testament which he himself subsequently published in 1505 confirmed his sense of the importance for the exposition of the Gospel texts of both the study of Classical literature and the use of an idiom freed of the clutter of Scholasticism.[23] On the other hand Erasmus did not care much for the Old Testament, wished that the Church would pay less attention to it, and referred to Jews and Judaism in generally pejorative terms.[24] His philosophic Christ was derived very much from the New

---

[22] Occasionally he had to fudge it. The *Comma Johanneum* (1 John 5. 7, the verse about the Three Witnesses which is not found in any Greek manuscripts nor any Vulgate manuscripts before the eighth century and was in fact added at the time of the Arian Crisis) he retroverted from the Latin into Greek without a note: Bataillon, *Érasme et l'Espagne* pg 45. Cisneros thus avoided the troubles caused for Erasmus here.

[23] For all Erasmus's biblical annotations: E. Rummel, *Erasmus's Annotations on the New Testament From Philologist to Theologian* (Toronto UP, Toronto 1986).

[24] Erasmus sets out his views in the three linked Introductions to his New Testament: *Paraclesis ad lectorem pium, Methodus,* and *Apologia.* On this generally J. H. Bentley *Humanists and Holy Writ New Testament Scholarship in the Renaissance* (Princeton UP, Princeton 1983) pg 112–193. On his attitude to Jews: G. Kish, *Erasmus's Stellung zu Juden und Judentum* (Tubingen 1969) based upon Erasmus's correspondence. There is a response in S. Markish, *Erasmus and the Jews* (Chicago UP, Chicago 1986) with a contrary Afterword by A. A. Cohen. Erasmus's dislike of Kabbalah is discussed in W. L. Gundersheimer "Erasmus, Humanism, and the Christian Cabala" Journal of the Warburg and Courtauld Institute XXVI (1963) pg 38–52. M. A. Screech in ed. A. Reeve, *Annotations on*

Testament. By contrast the Spanish scholars at Alcalá had a decided interest in the Old Testament, a particular emphasis that arose from the distinctive traditions of biblical scholarship in the peninsula.[25] Most strikingly one notices the presence of converso scholars working on the Alcalá team—principally Pablo Coronel working on the Hebrew text. The inclusion of the Pentateuchal Targum and the Hebrew Grammar found in Volume VI of the Complutensian Polyglot betray the same emphasis.[26] Important also are the influences of Jewish mysticism and Kabbalah upon Spanish biblical scholars in the context of the Inquisition's anxieties about conversos.[27] In particular we shall be inter-

---

the New Testament The Gospels (Duckworth, London 1986) pg x notes some interesting evidence from the Annotations for a softening of Erasmus's attitude.

[25] I here draw upon N. Fernández Marco and E. Fernández Tejero "Biblismo y erasmismo en La España del siglo XVI" in their joint collection *Biblia y Humanismo Textos, talantes y controversias del siglo XVI español* pg 21 (Fundación Universitaria Española, Madrid 1997) pg 21. Jewish traditions of scholarship were of course important: for the specifically philological, see: C. del Valle Rodríguez "Die Anfänge der hebräischen Grammatik in Spanien" Historiographia Linguistica VII: 2/3 (1981) pg 389–402. There were vernacular bibles made from Hebrew before the sixth century and the Castilian vernacular bible of Alfonso el Sabio anticipated Luther by two hundred and forty years. See: M. Morreale "Vernacular Scriptures in Spain" *The Cambridge History of the Bible* (CUP, Cambridge 1963) vol. II pg 465–491 and also "Spanish Versions" vol. III pg 125–129. See also S. Berger "Les anciennes versiones espagnoles et portugaises de la Bible" Romania XXVIII (Jan.1899) pg 306–408. We shall see that the Inquisition subsequently took steps against unauthorized bibles with Paul IV's Index of 1559. Important here is G. la Fragnito, *La Bibbia al rogo. La Censura ecclesiastica e i volgarizzamenti della Scrittura (1471–1605)* (Il Mulino, Bologna 1997). Also on this question: G. Bedouelle "Le débat catholique sur la traduction de la Bible en langue vulgaire" in eds. I. Backus and F. Higman *Théorie et pratique de l'exégèse* (Droz, Geneva 1990) pg 39–59.

[26] Reprinted as: *Introductiones Artis Grammaticae Hebraicae nunc recenter editae in Academia Complutensi Alcalá* (Eguía) 1526 (in Madrid: BNM R.18.844). This was the work of Alfonso da Zamora, the father of the Spanish school of Hebraists. Important for orientation is: F. Pérez Castro, *El Manuscrito Apologetico de Alfonso da Zamora (Sepher Hokmat Elohim)* (CSIC, Madrid 1950). He discusses Montano's use of his works and library pg xxxii; his biblical and targumic works pg xxxiv–lx (with a list of targumic manuscripts thereafter); and the letter mysticism in his work pg lxxvi–lxxxviii. For the possible identification of Zamora's Hebrew manuscripts in the Escorial: G. de Andres "Historia de las Procedencias de los codices hebreos de la real biblioteca de el Escorial" Revista da Sefarad XXX (1970) pg 9–37, pg 15–17. L. Díez Merino is producing an edition of Zamora's Latin translation of the Complutensian Targum after manuscript Villa-Amil 5 of the Biblioteca de la Universidad Complutense, *Job y Proverbios* (Madrid 1984) and *Qohelet* (Madrid 1987).

[27] In essence the converso problem may (from the point of view of the Inquisition) be divided into two stages. Before the Expulsion, there was worry that the Jews were seducing their converted brethren back again from their new faith, and the answer was to expel the Jews. After the expulsion, the anxiety was rather that the Jews who had converted rather than face expulsion, and their descendants, were judaising or secretly living as Jews. (Whilst the Inquisition had no legal jurisdiction over Jews, who were not

ested in their influence upon Arias Montano, Philip II's representative who was sent out to oversee the production of the Antwerp Polyglot. Nonetheless there is no reason to believe that any of the scholars of the Antwerp Polyglot were aggressively eager to replace the Vulgate, as Erasmus was, or unwilling to accept it as the bible of the Church. Cisneros's approach was adequate and peaceable.

The fate of Cisneros's great Complutensian bible was cruel.[28] Scarcely had the printing been completed when the Cardinal died, and that before he had obtained the Pontiff's authorisation for his work. A dispute broke out over the Cardinal's estate at the same time as civil war amongst the communes of Castile. Not until after a *motu proprio* of Leo X 22 March 1520 was the Bible authorised to be put on sale and then not until 1522. By this time, of course, Erasmus had produced three editions of his New Testament. But there was worse: the scholarly group at Alcalá was dispersed. The printer, Arnao Guillén de Brocar, disappears from our view without us knowing what became of his type. Six hundred copies of the Complutensian Polyglot were sold off cheaply, and some of these were lost at sea *en route* for Italy.

Christians, it did have jurisdiction over converts who lapsed.) There were mediaeval Inquisitors in Aragon from 1232 as part of the Crusade against the Cathars, but their activities had lapsed and there never had been Inquisitors in Castile. However it was as a result of the perceived converso threat and after a Bull of Sixtus IV 1 November 1478 that commissions for Castilian Inquisitors were issued 27 September 1480 and the Spanish Inquisition came into effective existence. A Bull of 17 October 1483 made Torquemada Inquisitor General of Aragon, Valencia and Catalonia, thus uniting the Inquisition under one head under the Crown. In the years before the Expulsion both Jews and conversos suffered a rising tide of anti-semitism. The Expulsion seems to have been a decision of the Crown and apparently made for religious reasons alone as directed by the Holy Office. Perhaps about half the Jews in Spain preferred conversion to expulsion. To whatever extent the converso problem before the expulsion was the product of clerical imagining, it took on real proportions afterwards. Subsequent anxieties tended to focus around issues of geneology: *limpieza* was purity from Jewish origins. On the Expulsion and the origins of the Inquisition, see H. Kamen, *The Spanish Inquisition An Historical Revision* pg 8–65; B. Netanyahu, *The Origins of the Inquisition in Fifteenth-Century Spain* (American Academy for Jewish Research, New York 1995) On Marranos: C. Roth, *A History of the Marranos* (Jewish Publication Society of America, Philadelphia 1932. Reprinted: Arno Press, New York 1979); J. Friedman "Jewish Conversion, the Spanish Pure Blood Laws and the Reformation: a Revisionist View of racial and religious Anti-semitism" Sixteenth-Century Journal XVIII/1 (1987) pg 3–29. D. M. Gitlitz, *Secrecy and Deceit The Religion of the Crypto-Jews* (Jewish Publication Society, Philadelphia 1996) is massively documented and has a useful survey of historiographic controversies pg 73–96.

[28] On what follows: Bataillon, *Érasme et l'Espagne* pg 46–47.

Soon it was impossible to find a copy to buy. The subsequent Antwerp Polyglot, therefore, met a real need.

The Council of Trent

Cisneros's position on the authority of the Vulgate was broadly confirmed by the Council of Trent.[29] The biblical question was discussed from 8 February until 8 April 1546 in the context of both the Protestant Schism and papal determination to maintain the supremacy of the Holy See over the Church. Debate was heated and the wide range of views expressed gave an indication of the variety of positions held.[30] The papal legates, however, were eager to avoid theological debate upon the authority of the Church, though this was, of course, a necessary context for the discussion of the authority of Scripture. For

---

[29] L. B. Pascoe "The Council of Trent and Bible Study: Humanism and Scripture" Catholic Historical Review LII (1966) pg 18–38.

[30] See Baroni, *La Contre-Réforme devant La Bible* pg 60ff. That theologians are above mere Grammar was the argument of Jacques Masson (Latomus) in *De trium linguarum et studii theologici ratione dialogus* (Antwerp, 1519). He, of course, was Tyndale's Inquisitor. See R. J. Wilkinson "Reconstructing Tyndale in Latomus: William Tyndale's last, lost, book" Reformation I (1996) pg 252–285. For the *De trium linguarum et studii theologici ratione dialogus* see: J. H. Bentley "New Testament Scholarship at Louvain in the early Sixteenth Century" Studies in Mediaeval and Renaissance History (n.s) II (1979) pg 53–79, pg 60–62. A position not too distant from that adopted by Trent can be found in another Louvain scholar Jean Nijs (Driedo) in his *De ecclesiaticis scripturis et dogmatibus* (1533). A similar resistance to humanist scholarship was found in Paris, at the Sorbonne. Noël Bédier (Beda) set himself against Erasmus, Lefèvre d'Étaples, and Luther, as did Pierre Couturier (Sutor) (Baroni, *La Contre-Réforme devant La Bible* pg 63–65). On the other hand Sante Pagnino had produced his word for word translation in 1527 and his *Isagogae*—a sort of dictionary of mystic meaning—in 1536 (T. M. Centi "L'Attività Letteraria di Santi Pagnini (1470–1536) nel Campo delle Scienze bibliche" Archivum Fratrum Praedicatorum XV (1945) pg 5–51). Isodorus Clarius had brought out a Latin version in Venice in 1542, *Sacrae Scripturae versionem vulgatam permultis locis mutatem cum brevibus adnotationibus* (also 1557 and 1564) correcting the Vulgate from both Latin and Greek. Paul IV put this on the 1559 Index. Vatable had also brought out his Bible in 1545 with Robert Estienne. Augustin Steuchus, the Vatican Librarian, defended both the Vulgate against the Greek as a translation of the Hebrew and Jerome's own accuracy. This however was not good enough, and led to violent attacks upon him at Trent by Dominique Soto. Cajétan, the General of the Dominicans, held to a liberal and critical view of the tradition. Richard Simon (cited Baroni, *op. cit.*, pg 70) conjectured that his views might have provided the basis for agreement on biblical studies between Catholics and Protestants. Cervini's desire for a new Latin version and a reorganisation of biblical studies (Baroni, *op. cit.*, pg 114 and 117) will not surprise us in the light of his sponsorship of oriental editions: see R. J. Wilkinson, *Orientalism, Aramaic and Kabbalah in the Catholic Reformation. The first printing of the Syriac New Testament* (E. J. Brill, Leiden 2007).

them it touched too closely upon the question of the authority of the Pope *vis-à-vis* the Council. Similarly, though the exegesis of a scholar like Cajétan might well have provided a broad *rapprochement* with the Protestants, such possibilities were subordinated to considerations of doctrine and discipline.

The Council proceeded to consider the canon; the authority of the biblical books with respect to the wider tradition; the text of Scripture; and the question of biblical interpretation. The Decrees of the Council uphold the Vulgate canon and the interpretive traditions of the Church, though they generally avoid argument or justification.[31] In a sense it is remarkable just how little they do say. In the matter that concerns us in particular, that of the text of Scripture, the Council decreed that the Vulgate be held as authentic in disputes, preaching, exposition and public reading—and that no one should be so rash as to reject it. There was no doubt a certain wisdom in such a sparse formulation, but, as we shall see in the case of the Antwerp Polyglot, what was in fact tolerable continued to be debated.

In the last period of the Council under Pius IV, a Commission was nominated by the decree *De delectu librorum* 26 February 1562 to consider rules for the censorship of books. As the Commission did not complete its work during the Council, the matter was referred to the Pope himself, together with the supervision of the publication of the Catechism, Missal, Breviary and a new edition of the Vulgate.

Censorship

The censorship of books in Rome was not new and with the spread of printing numerous popes had sought to control the content and circulation of books.[32] Paradoxically even Leo X himself, a great patron of letters, biblical and oriental scholarship (to whom we have seen both Agostino Giustiniani's Genoa Psalter of 1516 and the Complutensian Polyglot were dedicated) felt the need for pre-publication vigilance which he expressed in the Bull *Inter sollicitudes* of 4 May 1515 that arose from the tenth session of the Fifth Lateran Council and granted bishops the power to license books for printing. By the Bull *Exsurge Domine* of 15 June 1520 Leo also banned Luther's work. The problem however

---

[31] Baroni, *op. cit.*, pg 92–132.
[32] Baroni, *op. cit.*, pg 178–179.

did not go away and Cardinal Carafa, the future Paul IV, sought to reorganise the Roman Inquisition on the model of the Spanish Inquisition and to extend its authority as a universal tribunal, not only over the Estates of the Church but over all Christianity.[33]

In September 1557 Paul IV drew up a list of prohibited books that was published in 1559 as the *Index Librorum prohibitorum*. Lists of this sort were again not new, though they had previously been envisaged as local measures. They had appeared at Lucca in 1545, Venice in 1549, Florence in 1552, and Milan in 1554. The Sorbonne issued indices first in 1542, then in 1544, 1547, 1555, and 1556. Charles V also had demanded such a list from the University of Louvain. Paul IV's list included not only notorious heretics but also unauthorised Bibles. There were forty whole bibles, twelve New Testaments and all non-authorised vernacular versions.

It was subsequently Pius IV who brought out 24 March 1564 the list which the decree *De delectu librorum* of 26 February 1562 at Trent had anticipated. It was carefully drawn up and less severe than Paul IV's list. Certain works were prohibited only *donec corrigatur*.[34] The rules of the Index that were in fact to remain in force until 1897 were given. Subsequently, Pius V, seeking to relieve the Congregation of the Inquisition of the time-consuming work of censorship, established the Congregation of the Index. It is, however, to the Indices of the Spanish Inquisition, and to other more general features of that institution that we must turn to establish the specific context of the suspicions and debates aroused by the Antwerp Polyglot.

The Indices of the Spanish Inquisition[35]

Printed books seem to have been burned in Salamanca in the 1480s. In 1502 a pragmatic of Ferdinand and Isabella required licences for the printing or import of books and bishops had been given power to license books, as we have seen, at the Fifth Lateran Council of 1515 and at Trent in 1564. Post-publication censorship appeared after the Protestant Scare in 1558 when all printed books introduced into Spain

---

[33] Baroni, *op. cit.*, pg 181–214 for what follows.
[34] "…until corrected".
[35] H. Kamen, *op. cit.*, pg 103–136 for the following.

without a licence from the Council of Castile were banned.[36] This was effective, if at all, only in Castile, and most Spanish authors published outside Spain.

Valdés, Spain's Inquisitor General, produced an index in 1551 that was based upon that of Louvain in 1550, with an appendix of Spanish books. This was modified in 1551–2 and issued by local tribunals banning the works of the leaders of the Protestant Reformation and laying down principles for bibles and books in Hebrew and Arabic. The Inquisition began to censor bible editions and collect up copies of prohibited editions until they had a huge collection. Valdés issued a general censure of bibles and New Testaments in 1554 and identified sixty-five editions from Paris, Antwerp and Lyons for correction. The emergency laws of 1558 after the Protestant Scare confirmed the Inquisition as the producer of indices. Valdés and his fellow Dominican, Melchor Cano, proscribed all heretical books and all vernacular bibles, listing some seven hundred books from the lists of 1551 and other indices from Portugal, Louvain, Paris and Venice. Many of these were foreign books, and may not even have reached Spain. Books were again burned.

The Spanish Index of 1559 set out to identify unacceptable books, which were mostly foreign, and simply to prohibit them in Spain. However, when Philp II arranged for the Tridentine Index to be published in Flanders in 1570, he sponsored Arias Montano to prepare an expurgatory index that appeared in 1571. The principle here was of merely crossing out offending words from otherwise orthodox books, an innovation that subsequently became the model for all Spanish indices produced in peninsular Spain as well. This rather more liberal innovation was the work of the man who would be sent to oversee the Antwerp Polyglot.[37] There is then considerable irony in the fact that

---

[36] H. Kamen, *op. cit.*, pg 97–98. Inquisitor General Valdés wrote in 1558 to Philip II in Brussels detailing a wave of problems with Moriscos, Judaisers and Protestants. The Protestant threat he represented as so severe that he effectively asked for the whole country to be put into the hands of the Inquisition, for special tribunals and pre- and post-printing censorship to become the responsibility of the Inquisition. The King took little notice.

[37] Kamen, *op. cit.*, pg 114–115 discusses the educative policy behind the censorship of both Montano and Mariana. Also J. M. de Bujanda, *Index des Livres interdits, Vol. VI Index de l'Inquisition espagnole 1583, 1584* (Droz, Geneva 1993) pg 55–63.

his own bible project ran into difficulties with the Inquisition and that eventually his own work ended up on the Index.[38]

Peninsular Spain's response to the innovation of an expurgatory index in Flanders was a little slow, not least because of the arrest in 1572 of several professors at Salamanca whose fate was closely connected to the difficulties the Antwerp Polyglot was to encounter. Plans to produce a new index were resumed in 1578 under the guidance of Juan de Mariana. The resultant two volumes of prohibited and expurgated books that were issued respectively by Inquisitor General Gaspar de Quiroga in 1583 and 1584 contained some 2,315 prohibited items, including a wide trawl of European classics. It was Juan de Mariana who was the eventual censor of the Antwerp Polyglot.

The Inquisition and the Spanish Hebraists

The Inquisition was not without its effects on scholarship and on occasions it served the interests of University rivalry.[39] As early as 1504 Inquisitor General Diego de Deza had confiscated the papers of the humanist Nebrija who had dared to declare that as a philologist he was as capable as a theologian like de Deza of determining the text of Scripture. Nebrija was fortunate in the patronage of the powerful Cardinal Cisneros, editor of the *Biblia Complutensis*, and was subsequently able to accuse de Deza of seeking to destroy the study of the two biblical languages.[40]

Even more notoriously, in December 1571 Léon de Castro and a Dominican friend Bartolomé de Medina laid accusations of heretical scriptural study and theology against three professors at Salamanca: Luís de Léon, Gaspar de Grajal and Martín Martínez de Cantalapiedra.[41]

---

[38] But not all of it, Kamen, *op. cit.*, pg 335 n 97 *contra* Rekers.

[39] Again, I have made general use of H. Kamen, *op. cit.*, pg 103–136. Kamen is justifiably at pains not to overestimate the effects of the Inquisition on Spanish learning and culture. However he concedes that the few really notorious cases are those that concern precisely the issue of biblical studies that interests us. The dispute may have arisen as a scholarly contest but became very dangerous with the involvement of the Holy Office. Nevertheless the attacks upon the Hebraists appalled many. Kamen quotes (pg 126–127) Juan de Mariana's own statement of outrage.

[40] In his *Apology*: Kamen, *op. cit.*, pg 123.

[41] See M. de la Pinta Liorente "Fr. Luis de Léon y los hebraístas de Salamanca" Archivo Augustiniano XLVI (1952) pg 147–169 for a description of the charges. The article is based upon the author's larger works: *Proceso criminal contra el hebraísta salmantino Martín Martínez de Cantalapiedra* (CSIC, Madrid 1946) and *Procesos inquisitoriales contra*

Fray Luís de Léon, a distinguished theologian and poet, professed into the Augustinians in 1544 in Salamanca, had been given a chair at the youthful age of thirty-four. His rivals supposedly discovered converso descent. He was subsequently said to have questioned the accuracy of the Vulgate and to have claimed that a better vernacular version could be made; he had translated Canticles as a profane love-song rather than as befits Scripture; his exegesis was rabbinic; he had little time for allegory; and he considered Scholasticism of little help in the study of Scripture. Grajal was arrested first on the same count on 22 March 1572. Five days later Luís de Léon and Martín Martínez de Cantalapiedra were taken. Fray Luís de Léon was imprisoned for four years, eight months and nineteen days. During that time he was mercifully allowed to read and to write his work *De Los Nombres de Cristo*.[42] Restored eventually to his chair, he is said to have begun his first lecture with: *"As I was saying last time…"*

Fray Luís de Léon was summoned again in 1582 to answer for rash propositions, but this time Quiroga intervened on his behalf and he got off with a warning. Gaspar de Grajal however died in his cell. Professor of Hebrew, Martín Martínez de Cantalapiedra, endured until his release in May 1577 but failed to regain his chair. Predictably, converso origins had been insinuated in his case too. Léon de Castro was also responsible for the death in the Inquisition's cells of another scholar of converso descent, Alonso Gudiel, Professor of Scripture at Osuna.

---

los catedráticos hebraístas de Salamanca: Gaspar de Grajal (CSIC, Madrid 1935) where full documentation is given. Martín Martínez de Cantalapiedra had defended the utility of the Hebrew text and had championed it against charges of corruption. N. Fernández Marco "Censura y Exégesis: las Hypotyposeis de Martín Martínez de Cantalapiedra" in *Biblia y humanismo Textos, talantes y controversias del siglo XVI español* (Fundación Universitaria Española, Madrid 1997) pg 27–33 shows very clearly what the censors deleted from his work. Charges against Fr. Luís de Léon are also discussed in Alexander Habib Arkin, *La Influencia de la Exegesis hebraea en los Comentarios biblicos de Fray Luís de Léon* (CSIC, Madrid 1966) pg 191–198.

[42] Ed. F. de Onís, *Fray Luis de Léon De Los Nombres de Cristo* (Espasa-Calpe S.A., Madrid 1956). N. Fernández Marco "De *Los Nombres de Cristo* de Luis de Léon y *De Arcano Sermone* de Arias Montano" in *Biblia y humanismo Textos, talantes y controversias del siglo XVI español* pg 133–152 rejects direct literary dependence of Fray Luís de Léon upon Montano in this work (which is chronologically possible and given their friendship even likely) as *'not proven'*, but draws attention to their similar concepts of the significance of proper names, Hebrew, the arcane meanings of Scripture etc. She is content to say that Fray Luís knew Kabbalah and did not condemn it, but used it discreetly in his theological arguments, but apparently does not feel confident enough to call him a kabbalist. His usage certainly seems veiled and allusive, but it is surely not hard in the circumstances to see why.

It was precisely at the time of the arrest of Luís de Léon and Martín Martínez de Cantalapiedra that Pope Pius V refused to issue a privilege for the Antwerp Polyglot. After his successes against the Spanish Hebraists, Léon de Castro subsequently turned his attention to Benito Arias Montano and mounted a hostile attack upon the Antwerp Polyglot.

CHAPTER TWO

THE SPANISH TRADITION:
HEBREW STUDIES AND KABBALISTIC INFLUENCE

The extreme hostility we have seen directed at the Salamanca Hebraists (Cantalapiedra tells us that his opponents considered the Hebrew
bible worse than the Qur'an)[1] prompts us to consider the extent of
their dependence upon Hebrew scholarship and more particularly
upon kabbalistic notions. Such influence that we shall find will appear
somewhat pale when set in comparison, say, with Postel's own editing
of kabbalistic texts. It should be moreover born in mind that Christian
kabbalistic scholars did not see themselves as enemies of the Church
and that the mysteries they sought to uncover were generally Christian
ones. This statement is true even after the qualifications necessary in
the extreme case of Postel. The intense suspicions of their enemies are
nonetheless beyond question. Their frequent abuse of the Salamanca
Hebraists as conversos may well indicate the real and markedly Spanish
reason for the hostility to scholarship which was felt to be unaccept-
ably judaising. This hostility was materially to affect the reception of
the Antwerp Polyglot and will provide the background to the work of
Benito Arias Montano in Antwerp.

Early Interest in Kabbalah

In considering the antecedents in Spain of the Christian kabbalism that
is a clear feature of Fray Luis de Léon's work and that of the other
unfortunate Hebraists, we may conveniently begin with Ramón Martin.[2]
His *Pugio Fidei* of 1280 used rabbinic commentaries themselves to refute
Judaism in the hope of converting the Jews. He offered a trinitarian
explanation of the divine name YHWH, associating Christ with the
letter yod as a sign of the future age. This was to become a common

---

[1] M. de la Pinta Liorente "Fr. Luis de Léon y los hebraístas de Salamanca" Archivo
Augustiniano XLVI (1952) pg 147–169, pg 163.
[2] C. Swietlicki, *Spanish Christian Cabala: the works of Luis de Léon, Santa Teresa de Jesús
and San Juan de la Cruz* (University of Missouri Press, Columbia 1986) pg 3–8.

type of argument. Peter Alfonso, a converted rabbi, had also used the spiritual meaning of Hebrew letters against the Jews. His *Dialogus* gave a kabbalistic proof of the Trinity based on the three (different) letters of the Tetragrammaton. Arnold of Villanova (1235?–1313?), Martin's pupil, and author of the *Allocutio super Tetragrammaton* again offered a proof of the Trinity from the Divine Name.[3] By contrast, an unusual Jewish initiative in the matter of Kabbalah is represented by Abraham ben Samuel Abulafia (1204–1284) who personally set off to convert Nicolas III to Judaism by kabbalistic proof. Alfonso the Wise also showed interest in these matters but himself sought translations of kabbalistic books.[4]

Others were not sympathetic. Pedro Ciruelo published a refutation of Christian use of the Kabbalah in 1538 at Salamanca. Ciruelo had been a collaborator of Alfonso de Zamora on the Complutensian Polyglot and probably felt moved to resist what he saw as the kabbalism of the New Christians associated with the project.[5] His work shows knowledge of Christian kabbalistic writing in Germany and Italy and is thus a very useful indicator that these books were known in Spain.[6]

---

[3] See here: J. Carreras Artau "La 'Allocutio super Tetragrammaton' de Arnaldo de Vilanova" Revista da Sefarad IX (1949) pg 75–105 and E. Colomer "La Interpretación del Tetragrama bíblico en Ramón Martí y Arnau de Vilanova" Miscellanea Mediaevalia XIII/2 (1981) pg 937–945.

[4] F. Secret "Les Débuts du Kabbalisme chrétien en Espagne et son histoire à la Renaissance" Revista da Sefarad XVII (1957) pg 36–48 pg 38.

[5] Alfonso de Zamora worked under Pedro Ciruelo on the Hebrew and Aramaic texts for the Complutensian Polyglot as we have seen above. They produced the interlinear Latin gloss of which there are two manuscript copies in the Alcalá and Salamanca and the Hebrew Grammar in Volume VI that was printed again in 1526. Zamora's preoccupation with kabbalah has been noted by F. Secret, "Les Débuts du Kabbalisme en Espagne et son histoire à la Renaissance" Revista da Sefarad XVII (1957) pg 36–48 pg 41 and F. Pérez Castro, *El Manuscrito Apologetico de Alfonso da Zamora* (*Sepher Hokmat Elohim*) (CSIC, Madrid 1950) pg xxviii–xxxii and F. Secret "Pedro Ciruelo: Critique de la Kabbale et de son Usage par les Chrétiens" Revista da Sefarad XIX (1959) pg 48–77.

[6] It is possible that Egidio da Viterbo's visit to Spain as Papal Legate 1518–1519, the year after the publication of his first kabbalistic work, *Libellus de litteris sanctis*, was not without influence. Fray Luis de Léon was numbered amongst the Salamancan Augustinians after the reform and visit of Egidio. J. W. O'Malley, *Giles of Viterbo on Church and Reform* (E. J. Brill, Leiden 1968) pg 173: "There were certainly instances of his encouraging friars in the study of Cabala and *Caldeas litteras*". Galatinus's *De Arcanis* was certainly known in Spain (*"entre toutes les mains"*, according to F. Secret "Les Débuts du Kabbalisme chrétien en Espagne" pg 45). K. A. Kottmann, *Law and Apocalypse: The Moral Thought of Luis de Léon* (M. Nijhoff, The Hague 1972) pg 130–133 has tabulated all the parallels between that work and *"Pimpollo"* from *Los Nombres de Cristo*.

An important scholar, falling between the generation of the Complutensian Polyglot and that of the Antwerp Polyglot, Fray Luís de
Léon, and the Salamanca school of Hebraists, was Cipriano de la
Huerga (1509/10?–1560).[7] He was Abbot of the Cistercian monastery
of Nogales (Léon), Rector of his order's college at Alcalá and holder
of the chair of biblical studies there after 1551 until his death. During
his time there he enjoyed several students who would become distinguished *alumni*: Fray Luís de Léon, B. Arias Montano, and Juan de
Mariana S.J.—the last two being respectively the King's overseer and
the censor of the Antwerp Polyglot. Cipriano de la Huerga enjoyed
in his formation the whole Alcalá heritage: the philological tools in
the last volume of the Complutensian Polyglot, Alfonso de Zamora's
Hebrew Grammar of 1526, and Zamora's translation of the Targumim
of the Prophets and Hagiographa that would ultimately appear in the
Antwerp Polyglot. It is, of course, quite possible that as a student he
had known Zamora. It is evident that he used Zamora's translation in
his Job commentary.

Cipriano de la Huerga wrote commentaries on Psalms 38 and 130
(Alcalá 1555), Nahum (Lyons 1561) Job and Canticles (Alcalá 1581).
His commentaries are literal. He offered a new version of Job ("*noster
versio*"), and cites the Psalms *iuxta Septuagintos et iuxta Hebraeos*. In his
Nahum commentary he refers to readings of Aquila and Symmachus.
He cites the *prisci theologi* in addition to the targumim, Kimchi, Ibn Ezra,
Rabbi Abbah, Rabbi Yonah and Reuchlin.[8] Generally his method is a
rigorous comparison of the Hebrew and the versions with the citation
of parallels from elsewhere in Scripture. Nonetheless after extensive
citation and the weighing of opinions, he is capable of admitting he
does not know the answer. Like Cisneros he did not see the Hebrew as
an opponent of the Vulgate.[9] He shows a sharp awareness of Hebrew
idiom and a detailed interest in biblical *realia*. In these two respects

---

[7] The project to publish Cipriano is led by G. Morocho, but the various volumes of
the complete works, *Humanistas españoles: Cipriano de la Huerga,* have different editors. For
bibliography: K. Reinhardt, *Bibelkommentare spanischer Autoren (1500–1700)* vol. I (Madrid
1990) pg 214–217. See also: N. Fernández Marco and E. Fernández Tejero "El Ex Libris
de Cipriano de la Huerga" *Biblia y humanismo Textos, talantes y controversias del siglo XVI
español* pg 47–56; "Desentrañando el Comentario de Cipriano de la Huerga al Salmo
130", *op. cit.,* pg 57–64; and N. Fernández Marco "La Exégesis bíblica de Cipriano de
la Huerga", *op. cit.,* pg 65–82. I have relied extensively upon this latter article.

[8] For the *prisci theologi,* see D. P. Walker, *The Ancient Theology* (Duckworth, London
1972).

[9] L. Díez Merino, *Job y Proverbios* pg 234–236.

Cipriano's work clearly anticipates that of Montano in the Antwerp Polyglot where his controversial treatises in the Apparatus deal precisely with these matters. This insistence upon a literal non-allegorical reading of the text with its concomitant emphasis upon the archaeological *realia* of biblical referents may seem to us initially quite incompatible with any kabbalistic interest in the text, but the cases of Cipriano and Montano warn us against such a simplification.

Fray Luís de Léon

We have already met Fray Luís de Léon (1527?–1591). Thorough and fundamental studies have established his dependence upon Jewish exegesis. A. H. Arkin has examined in detail Luís's debt to the literal Jewish commentators of the High Middle Ages in his translations *Cantar de los Cantares* and *Libro de Job*.[10] Arkin contextualises his findings within a more general but distinctive *hermenéutica española* that drew upon Hebrew sources[11] (pg 11–34). He points out that the ordering of books in medieval Spanish bibles is often that of the Hebrew bible (Torah, Prophets, Writings), and that Hebrew words and Hebrew forms of proper names proliferate in them; that numerous Hebrew texts of all sorts were turned into the vernacular for Church scholars in the thirteenth and fourteenth centuries; and particularly, as we have said, that the emphasis of the later Jewish scholars upon literal rather than allegorical exegesis is also characteristic of Fray Luís de Léon and the Salamanca school of Hebraists. Arkin finds Luís de Léon particularly comparable to Ibn Ezra.[12]

An important interpretive study by K. A. Kottmann appeared in 1972 which places Luís de Léon in what he reconstructs as a typically converso reading of the Thomist tradition of understanding the Decalogue not only as natural law but also as divine positive law for Jews (as the Old Law bound the Jews).[13] Luís de Léon, however, Kottmann

---

[10] A. H. Arkin, *La Influencia de la Exegesis hebraea en los Comentarios biblicos de Fray Luis de Léon* (CSIC, Madrid 1966). See also J. Fitzmaurice-Kelly, *Fray Luis de Léon. A Biographical Fragment* (OUP, Oxford 1921) and A. F. G. Bell, *Luís de Léon: A Study in the Spanish Renaissance* (Clarendon, Oxford 1925).

[11] *Ibid.*, pg 11–14.

[12] *Op. cit.*, pg 33.

[13] K. A. Kottmann, *Law and Apocalypse: The Moral Thought of Luís de Léon* (M. Nijhoff, The Hague 1972) especially pg 19–41.

claimed, went two stages further to assert not only that the Decalogue was divine positive law for Christians also, as well as being a command of reason, but in addition that Jewish mystical practice could be interpreted in a Christian sense and indeed was the authentic basis of that tradition in Christianity. Kottmann proceeded to show that, for Luís, church history was but an extension of Jewish history; that the end of history will be the fulfilment of God's temporal promises to the Jews after they have converted; and at that time Jewish and Christian moral practice will be identical. Kottmann claims it a strong probability that Luís de Léon was a Christian kabbalist and wishes finally to argue that Kabbalah was in fact the basis of all his moral thought.[14]

C. Swietlicki in 1986 offered a wider canvas, juxtaposing Luís de Léon with the great mystical leaders of the Carmelite Reform—Santa Teresa (whose works he edited) and San Juan (who may arguably himself have been influenced by Luís and his work when he was studying at Salamanca).[15] Swietlicki provides an overview of Christian Kabbalah in their contemporaries and also discusses converso influence upon Spanish culture at the time. Thereafter, a convenient group of previous essays on Luís de Léon appeared within a larger collection in 1997 that sought both to examine his exegesis[16] and also his links with Montano.[17]

The scholar in the Spanish tradition of most interest to us is, of course, Benito Arias Montano, the King's overseer of the Antwerp Polyglot. We shall briefly review his life here and then must digress to

---

[14] Kottmann, *op. cit.*, pg 28–29 sets out the case for this in the Commentary on Canticles. The evidence showing dependence of the Commentary in ch. V on *Idra Rabba* and the *Zohar* is set out on pg 121–129. Specifically to be noted is the proposed kabbalistic basis of Natural Science (pg 125), and Luís's devotion to the Sacred Heart of Jesus (pg 126). The quotation (pg 127) of a non-Vulgate rendering of Canticles 7.5 from his Lecture *De Fide* where he argues for an alternative translation from the Hebrew allows a mystical meaning.

[15] C. Swietlicki, *Spanish Christian Cabala: the works of Luis de Léon, Santa Teresa de Jesús and San Juan de la Cruz* (University of Missouri Press, Columbia 1986). See particularly pg 82–127 and pg 128–154.

[16] E. Fernández Tejero "Del amor y la mujer en Cipriano de la Huerga y Luis de Léon" in *Biblia y humanismo Textos, talantes y controversias del siglo XVI español* pg 85–100; her "Luis de Léon, hebraísta: el *Cantar de los cantares*" *ibid.*, pg 101–118; and also her "¿'Esposa' o Perfecta casada? Dos personajes en la exégesis de Luis de Léon" *ibid.*, pg 119–132.

[17] N. Fernández Marco "De *Los Nombres de Cristo* de Luis de Léon y *De Arcano Sermone* de Arias Montano" in *Biblia y humanismo Textos, talantes y controversias del siglo XVI español* pg 133–152. The fundamental article on this friendship is F. Cantera "Arias Montano y Fr. Luis de Léon" Boletin de la Biblioteca de Menendez Pelayo XXII (1946) pg 299–338.

consider recent debate about his association with the Family of Love.
Thereafter we may consider the treatises he contributed to the Antwerp
Polyglot and the extent to which they represent the tradition of Spanish
biblical studies that was sympathetic to Hebrew and Kabbalah.

Benito Arias Montano

Benito Arias Montano (1527–1598) was born in Fregenal in Extra-
madura into an impoverished family of the low nobility.[18] He went
to school and University in Seville. He registered at the University of
Alcalá in 1550, was introduced to the methods of biblical scholarship
we have just been exploring, and also became acquainted with the work
of Erasmus.[19] He was a friend of Fray Luís de Léon as we have seen.
After Alcalá, he appears to have travelled in Italy but spent most of his
time at his inherited country retreat in Peña de Aracena. In 1560 he

---

[18] D. T. Gonzalez Carvajal "Elogio Histórico del D. Benito Arias Montano" Memorias
Real Academia Historia VII, Madrid (1832) pg 1–199 with an appendix of documents
pg 123–199 is the fundamental work. Also A. F. G. Bell, *Benito Arias Montano* (OUP,
Oxford 1922) and essential for politics: L. Morales Oliver, *Arias Montano y la política de
Felipe II en Flandes* (Voluntad, Madrid 1927). The Revista del Centro de Estudios Extremeños II (Jan/Aug 1928) *Homenaje a Benito Arias Montano* contains important articles some
of which are referred to below, and are generally biographical. The Revista Española
de Estudios Bíblicos III (1928) was similarly devoted to Montano, though shows more
interest in his works. See also L. Morales Oliver "Avance para una biografiá de obras
impresaas de Arias Montano" Revista del Centro de Estudios Extremeños II (1928)
pg 171. Some of the letters for the period 1568–1580 appear in *Colección de Documentos
inéditos para la historia de España* (Codoin) tom. 41 (1862) pg 127–418. B. Rekers, *Benito
Arias Montano, 1527–1598. Studie over een groep spiritualistische humanisten in Spanje en de
Nederlanden, op grond van hun briefwisseling* (Groningen 1961), English edition: B. Rekers,
Benito Arias Montano (1527–1598) (Warburg Institute/E. J. Brill, Leiden 1972) contains the
fullest guide to the letters, but is controversial in its claims about Montano's adherence
to the Family of Love, and is marred by other errors. (The Spanish edition (Madrid
1973) enjoys fulsome support for its assessment of Montano in an introduction by
A. Alcalá.) In the first place see the review of B. Hall "A Sixteenth Century Miscellany"
Journal of Ecclesiastical History XXVI/3 (July 1975) pg 309–321 pg 318–320 and Ph.
Theunissen "Arias Montano et la Polyglotte d'Anvers" Les Lettres romanes (Louvain)
XIX/3 (1965) pg 231–24 and then further below. Montano's library is described in
A. Rodríguez Moñino "La Biblioteca de Benito Arias Montano: Noticias y documentos
para su reconstruccíon" Revista del Centro de Estudios Extremeños II (Jan/Aug 1928)
pg 555–598. On the biblical matters that will shortly concern us J. Conde Prudencio
"Arias Montano y La Cuestión biblica de su tiempo" Revista del Centro de Estudios
Extremenos II (1928) pg 403–498.

[19] For Montano and Humanists: see M. Bataillon "Philippe Galle et Arias Montano. Matériaux pour l'Iconographie des Savants de la Renaissance" Bibliothèque de
Humanisme et Renaissance II (1942) pg 132–160.

was admitted as a priest into the Order of Santiago at the monastery of San Marcos de Léon.[20] In 1562 Montano was sent to Trent where he delivered two speeches: one on divorce and the other on communion in both kinds. After Trent he became a King's chaplain and wrote his *Commentaria in XII Prophetas* (later printed by Plantin in 1571).[21] Though at this time without any publication to his name, Montano had established a reputation for scholarship for, in March 1568, he was sent to Antwerp to oversee the philological work on the Polyglot there being undertaken by Plantin under the patronage of Philip II. Montano's academic role appears essentially to have been to check the proofs and write several of the treatises that make up the last volume. He was at the same time invested with an inquisitorial mission (we have discussed his expurgatory index of 1571 above). During this time also he worked on translations of poetry and devotional books.

In 1571 at the end of the Polyglot project, the several volumes of the book were sent to Rome for approval. This was only granted, as we shall see shortly, after substantial opposition: 1572 was the year of Fray Luís de Léon's arrest by the Inquisition in Salamanca and there were other scholars of the persuasion of León de Castro to make life difficult for Montano. If the Spanish tradition of biblical scholarship has left its mark upon the Antwerp Polyglot, so has Spanish hostility to that tradition.

At this time Montano, though an earlier admirer of the Duke of Alba's suppression of the Revolt of the Gueux' in 1566 and the purge of the Calvinist extremists, submitted a report to the Spanish Court critical of Alba's cruel reprisals after the resurgence of the Gueux'

---

[20] Here Montano would have had to demonstrate to the order's satisfaction that he had 'no Jewish blood'. Nor was the purity of his blood seriously questioned in his lifetime. The claim however has been recently made that he was of converso stock, but the case is not proven and hangs on little better than the abuse of Léon de Castro. See A. Alcalá "Tres notas sobre Arias Montano, Marranismo, Familismo, Nicodemismo" Cuadernos hispanoamericanos CCXCVI (1975) pg 349–357. It will be evident from the following that I dissent almost totally from the estimation of Montano made in this article. For marranos in Antwerp see works cited by A. Hamilton, *The Family of Love* (James Clarke & Co, Cambridge 1981) pg 154 n 47.

[21] This is described by Rekers, *Montano* pg 187 as: 993 pages in folio with a marked preference for 'rabbinical authors, disregarding the allegorical interpretations of the Fathers'.

revolts and the Capture of the Brielle in April 1572.[22] The King evidently listened.

Six months later Don Luís de Requeséns was appointed Governor and ordered to follow Montano's advice. Montano's suggestion of reconciliatory policies was followed as he himself reported regularly to the King. Such progress however did not prevent the killing and plunder that characterised the Spanish Fury of 1576 and made Flanders a willing prey to the Calvinist forces.[23]

During these years in Flanders it is alleged by B. Rekers that Montano became (in spite of his Inquisitorial office) an adherent of the Family of Love—an allegiance that if substantiated would make a considerable difference to the way we look at the Polyglot project. We shall consider this claim below.

During this period also Montano produced in cooperation with theologians from Louvain an amended text of the Vulgate (1574), translated Benjamin of Toledo from Hebrew (*Itinerarium Benjamini Tudelensis* Plantin, 1573) and wrote the devotional work *Dictatum Christianum*. We shall make use of this work below when considering Rekers's views on Montano and the Family of Love.

In 1575 Montano went to Rome to defend the Antwerp Polyglot and to discuss the Vulgate with a Papal Commission. Thereafter in 1576 he returned to Spain where for the next decade he became Curator of the Royal Library in the Escorial. Montano corresponded frequently with Plantin during this period and Rekers claims that his letters give evidence of Montano's attempts to convert his fellow monks to the Family of Love. Certainly he sought, received and subsequently used in his own exposition the work of the Family's prophet Hendrick Jansen van Barrefelt (Hiël) and we shall shortly be at pains to assess the significance

---

[22] Montano presented a copy of the Polyglot on vellum to Alba at the King's request. The copy is in the British Library (see Darlow and Moule, *op. cit.*, pg 12) and has a printed leaf inserted: *Ex Philippi II. Catholici mandato. Illme Albae Duci Ferdinando quod compositis in Belgia belli ac pacis reb. religione instaurata bonis artibus locum servavit, Bened. Arias Montanus sacra causa legatus sanctum Bibliorum opus eadem tempestate foelicissime excusum, in aeternum pietatis monumentum optimi regis optimo ministro donum detulit. Bruxellas 1571...* This is a fascinating juxtaposition of Philip's two imperial tools: Alba and the Polyglot.

[23] On the growth of the Protestant Reformation in the Netherlands: G. Marnef, *Antwerp in the Age of Reformation Underground Protestantism in a Commercial Metropolis 1550–1577* (Translated by J. C. Grayson, John Hopkins UP, London 1996).

of this. During his stay at the Escorial, Montano enjoyed a licence from the Grand Inquisitor to classify and expurgate the volumes there.[24]

The last decade of Montano's life was spent in his house on the Peña de Aracena near Seville where he wrote his great works: the *Anima* (1593) and the *Naturae Historia* (1601: printed posthumously). Montano held an honorary post as Commander of the Order of Santiago and in 1595 he was consulted by the Archbishop of Granada on the authenticity of the ancient lead tablets that had just been discovered at Sacromonte. These were supposedly Christian texts in Arabic characters containing details from the Apocryphal Gospels. Montano denounced these as a hoax perpetrated by persecuted moriscos.[25] He died 6 July 1598.

The Roman Expurgatory Index of 1607 included Montano's works. The efforts of his friend Pedro de Valencia were successful in reducing the censored passages from forty-five in the Roman Index to nine in the Spanish. But the Spanish Indices of 1632, 1640 and 1667 indicate that Pedro's success was short lived, and the doubts entertained at Rome also resurfaced.[26]

---

[24] It later became customary to deposit prohibited books in the Escorial Library. The Prior in 1585 referred to the many prohibited books sent there by the King and stored under licence from Don Gaspar de Quiroga. Later still in 1639, the Library possessed 932 prohibited books: H. Kamen, *The Spanish Inquisition* pg 121. For the influence of Montano upon Sigüenza at the time, see: H. Kamen, *op. cit.*, pg 126.

[25] D. Cabanelas "Arias Montano y los Libros plumberos de Granada" Miscelanea de Estudios Arabes y Hebraicos XVIII/XIX (1969–1970) pg 7–41.

[26] J. A. Jones "Arias Montano and Pedro da Valencia: Three further documents" Bibliothèque de Humanisme et Renaissance XXXVIII (1976) pg 351–352; also his "Pedro de Valencia's Defence of Arias Montano: The Expurgatory Indexes of 1607 (Rome) and 1612 (Madrid)" Bibliothèque de Humanisme et Renaissance XL (1978) pg 121–136; and again his "Pedro de Valencia's defence of Arias Montano: A note of the Spanish Indexes of 1632, 1640, & 1667" Bibliothèque de Humanisme et Renaissance LVII/1 (1995) pg 83–88. Jones has also offered partial editions of manuscript material in Madrid relating to the specific criticisms of Andrés de León (1571–1642) of the Targum in the Biblia Regia: "Les advertencias de Pedro de Valencia y Juan Ramírez acerca de la impresión de la "Paraphrasis Chaldaica" de la Biblia Regia" Bulletin hispanique LXXXIV (1982) pg 328–344; "Censuras acerca de la impresión de la *Paraphrasis Chaldaica* de Andrés de León: un aspect de la amistad entre Benito Arias Montano y Pedro de Valencia" *Homenaje a Pedro Sainz Rodriguez I Repertorios, textos y comentarios* (Madrid, 1986) pg 339–348. N. Fernández Marco and E. Fernández Tejero "La Polémica en torno a la Biblia Regia de Arias Montano" *Biblia y humanismo Textos, talantes y controversias del siglo XVI español* pg 229–238 discuss this particular controversy. The same authors in the same place "Luis de Estrada y Arias Montano" pg 193–205 discuss the *Carta y Discurso del Maestro Fr. Luis de Estrada sobre la aprobación de la Biblia Regia y sus versione; y juicio de la que hizo del Nuevo Testamento Benito Arias Montano* that Luis de Estrada wrote after Montano's return to Spain.

Montano has long been known by name, but has not been studied extensively. B. Rekers's monograph attempted some sort of biographical and historical completeness, but—with the exception of its claims about the closeness of Montano's association with the Family of Love—left aside any consideration of his thought. All Montano's published works were printed by Plantin. With the exception of the *Dictatum Christianum* they have received little or no modern attention and the huge synthetic works of his last decade, the *Anima* and the *Naturae Historia* remain unread. Rekers offers several pages listing unpublished writings of Montano in various Spanish archives.[27] There are at least twenty-five works relevant to Montano's biblical studies still in manuscript and there is a reasonable expectation that there is more material to be found.

Arias Montano and the Family of Love

Montano's friendly encounter with Plantin on his arrival in Antwerp and his harmonious co-operation with the assembled scholarly team were placed in the context of his relationship with the Family of Love by Maurice Sabbe in 1926 who discussed the evidence of Montano's relationship with the sect's second prophet H. Jansen Barrefelt, otherwise known as Hiël.[28] Correspondence with Plantin after Montano's

---

[27] *Op. cit.*, pg 191–196.

[28] M. Rooses, *Correspondance de Christophe Plantin I–III* (Antwerp 1883–1911). Hereafter C.P.I–III. C.P.I pg 285; C.P.II pg 7–8, 23; C.P.III pg 110. M Sabbe "Les rappports entre Montano et Hiël" De Gulden Passer IV (1926) pg 19–43 where the correspondence and texts are given in full. For the Family of Love I follow generally the sober and convincing characterisation of Alastair Hamilton, *The Family of Love* (James Clarke & Co, Cambridge 1981) especially pg 65–82 and 94–96. Also his previous "Hiël and the Hiëlists The Doctrine and Followers of Hendrik Jansen van Barrefelt" Quaerendo VII/3 (1977) pg 243–286; "Seventeen Letters from Hendrik Jansen van Barrefelt (Hiël) to Jan Moretus" De Gulden Passer LVII (1979) pg 62–127; "From Familism to Pietism The fortunes of Pieter van Borcht's Biblical Illustrations and Hiël's Commentaries from 1584–1717" Quaerendo XI/4 (1981) pg 271–301; "The Family of Love in Antwerp" Bijdragen tot de Geschiedenis LXX (1987) pg 87–96. Hamilton has also brought out important editions of familist texts. Also J. Dietz Moss, *"Godded with God": Hendrick Niclaes and his Family of Love* (The American Philosophical Society, Philadelphia 1981). A fundamental earlier work remains F. Nippold "Heinrich Niclaes und das Haus der Liebe. Ein monographischer Versuch aus der Secten-Geschichte der Reformationszeit" Zeitschrift für die historische Theologie XXXII (1862) pg 323–402 and 473–563. On the Family of Love in France: W. Kirsop "The Family of Love in France" Journal of Religious History III (1964) pg 103–118 and J.-F. Maillard "Christophe Plantin et la Famille de la Charité en France: Documents et Hypothèses" in *Mélanges sur la Littérature de la Renaissance à la Mémoire de V.-L. Saulnier* (Droz, Geneva 1984) pg 235–253. On the

return to Spain concerns Hiël and Montano solicits his work on the first chapter of Ezekiel. Montano's own Commentary on the Apocalypse has favourable mention of Hiël in the Introduction and some dependence upon his work.[29] Sabbe's work was used by B. Rekers in 1961. He added little to it, except to claim that during his stay in Antwerp Montano was converted totally to the Family of Love and indeed that after his return to Spain he continued to teach the sect's doctrines to his fellow monks in the Escorial. Rekers further makes far reaching claims for the influence of the sect upon Montano's biblical exposition after his conversion.[30]

Rekers however claims too much. His evidence is minimal and contradicted by weighty objections. All Montano's exegesis—even that written in the Escorial or on the Peña de Aracena—is literal and not allegorical, spiritual or visionary. His library contained no works of Hiël.[31] Whilst three or four pages of Montano's Apocalypse Commentary follow Hiël, thousands of pages of biblical commentary written after 1583 do not.[32] There is a wild disproportionality between the evidence and the claim. Montano submits explicitly to the authority of the Church in his works, nor is his spirituality—to the extent that this may be said to be evident—in any way heterodox.[33] There is little in his works to support Rekers's thesis—other than the hypothesis of an improbably massive deception on Montano's part.

In this context our reading of Montano's *Dictatum Christianum* seems to me critical. The book was printed by Plantin in 1587, the year of Montano's departure from Antwerp, and deals with the steps that lead a Christian to God: fear, penance and love. It develops, no doubt appropriately for the troubled city of Antwerp, the duty of a prince

---

Family in England (without mention of the Family on the Continent): C. W. Marsh, *The Family of Love in English Society 1550–1630* (CUP, Cambridge 1994).

[29] *Elucidationes in omnia Apostolorum scripta, eiusdem S. Johannis apostoli et evangelistae Apocalypsin significationes* (4°. 484 pg. 1588). The text is quoted in Sabbe above.

[30] Rekers, *op. cit.*, pg 91.

[31] A. Rodríguez Moñino "La Biblioteca de Benito Arias Montano: Noticias y documentos para su reconstrucción" Revista del Centro de Estudios Extremeños II (Jan/Aug 1928) pg 555–598.

[32] M. Andrés Martin, *Arias Montano Dictatum Christianum y Pedro de Valencia Lección Cristiana Introducción y Edición* (Institución Cultural 'Pedro de Valencia', Valencia 1983) pg xlv–xlvii calculates this as 4/4757 pages of printed work.

[33] The dedication of the *Naturae Historia* (Plantin 1601): "*Sanctissimae Romanae Ecclesiae Matri Benedictus Arias Montanus ex Deo felicitatem et amplificationem summam…Ut summo…Deo praesente et promovente ponere et concinnae contingat, piorum et simplicium candidorumque quos plurimos sacro in gremio Ecclesia Mater alio et fores; cum primisque tuam exoptamus gratiam…*"

to God and his duty to enable his people to live together in peace
and harmony. To this end obedience is necessary, but only obtainable
because the prince has himself followed the way of fear, penance and
love. For Rekers by 'love' Montano meant *the Charity of the Familia
Charitatis i.e. an undogmatic attitude independent of any particular creed*. This is
utterly implausible in a book entirely Trentine in its doctrines: Montano
seeks a reformed clergy to be sure, but insists upon a Catholic clergy
nonetheless and his refutation of Luther's solafideism can scarcely be
described as *independent of any particular creed*.[34]

It is of course possible to claim (though Rekers does not) that Montano learned of Hiël's work only after his return to Spain. It was in
1583 that he asked for his Apocalypse Commentary and evidently liked
it enough to ask for his interpretation of Ezekiel chapter one. The reference to Hiël in the Apocalypse commentary of 1588 is undoubtedly
a great tribute: Hiël had been the first to enable him to understand
the Apocalypse and he had learnt that the book could only be understood by the pious and simple and not by those who trust too much
in human judgment. But there is no need to create difficulties here:
there is no impropriety in accepting an understanding of what the text
means from a pious and simple exegete to whose mind Providence
has brought the truth. Nor, we may add, is it possible to interpret the
Apocalypse (however literal one's reading) without explaining the sym-
bols. An inspection of Montano's use of Hiël's Commentary reveals
no passage of Montano that is allegorical, so Montano cannot be said
here to violate his normal hermeneutic, characteristic of the Spanish
exegetes we have just been examining. His comments may be merely
pious praise of the illumination of the simple godly.[35]

---

[34] Two significant recent editions of the *Dictatum Christianum* offer no support for
Rekers's view of this work. Explicitly contrary is M. Andrés Martin, *Arias Montano
Dictatum Christianum y Pedro de Valencia Lección Cristiana Introducción y Edición*, especially
pgs xxxvi–ciii, cvii–cxi. The latter passage concludes that the book is of an ecumenical spirituality based upon the Bible and traditionally Catholic in doctrine. Andrés is
equally eager to assert that the 'Erasmianism' of the work is rather the native Spanish tradition of biblical exegesis found at Alcalá since Alfonso de Zamora. See also
her article "En torno a un libro sobre Arias Montano" Arbor XXXIV 7 (1974) pg
119–123. This reading is further supported by D. Domenichini, *Benito Arias Montano
Dictatum Christianum Edizione e Studio introduttivo* (Giardini, Pisa 1984). (Incidentally, this
work has some interesting observations on biblical textual quotations in the *Dictatum*
with respect to the various texts of the Antwerp Polyglot: see pgs 57–59).
[35] Sabbe translates the relevant Latin text into French: "*J'ai appris aussi que ce livre ne
peut être entièrement compris que par ceux a qui Dieu, le Créateur de cet ouvrage, communique d'une
façon efficace le sens des allégories; et que la signification de cette transfiguration peut être démontrée*

Having considered and rejected the arguments for Montano's conversion to the Family of Love, it may be both appropriate and convenient to review here the extent of the commitment of other members of the Antwerp Polyglot project to the Family of Love. We shall be arguing subsequently that the Polyglot project was essentially the work of Plantin's scholarly team who had completed the work in most part even before Montano's arrival. In this respect we shall be claiming an essential continuity between the earlier Catholic tradition of Syriac and oriental studies, the 1555 *editio princeps* of the Syriac New Testament, and the Antwerp Polyglot. This continuity will be seen in the apparatuses and texts that are the work of Masius and Guy Lefèvre de la Boderie and his brother. Behind this tradition stands Postel. However, having made the acquaintance of Montano, and having some feel for the Spanish traditions that he represents, we shall be at pains also to recover his distinctive tradition of literalism and respect for the arcane meanings of Scripture from the Polyglot. But at this point we ask whether the influence of the Family of Love in the group around Plantin had any perceptible effect upon the scholars other than Montano who worked on the project or upon the Polyglot itself.

Masius, Postel and Plantin and the Family of Love

Though Plantin and his sons-in-law François Rephelengius and Jan Moretus were members of the Family of Love, it would be quite wrong to consider the Antwerp Polyglot—even before the arrival of Montano—as a Familist project. The technical contribution of Masius we shall see was considerable, yet his links with Hendrik Niclaes, the sect's first prophet, are tenuous. Postel, though not present in Antwerp, was in touch with the project through Guy Lefèvre de la Boderie. But

---

par les pieux etc." This translation is followed by Hamilton. A version such as this that has Montano profess to *'allégories'* and appears to equate *'le sens des allégories'* with *'la signification de cette transfiguration'* makes the latter precisely a hermeneutic shift (transfiguration) from literal to allegorical. To my view this entirely muddies the waters. I read the Latin (accessible in Sabbe) to mean that just as at Christ's transfiguration the three disciples, simple pious lovers of God, were given to know of the Resurrection (though they were to keep quiet about it until Christ was risen and not reveal it to the common herd, who rely upon human ingenuity), so Hiël similarly has been given an understanding of the Apocalypse. This understanding of the message of the symbolic text (however inspired its origin) does not make the interpretation allegorical, and is not at odds with Montano's usual exegetical practice.

it is in fact unlikely that Postel took more than a fleeting interest in the Family.

Plantin mentioned Masius in a letter to Niclaes in August 1567, but the significance of obviously critical lines in the letter—*"Je vous envoye ici les lignes de Masius pour autant qu'ils vous touchent, ainsi que vous pouvés voir"*[36]—entirely escapes us. Nothing can be built upon this.

Postel himself wrote from St-Martin-des-Champs 4 August 1567 to Abraham Ortellius inquiring about the Family of Love.[37] He sent his greeting to Plantin who was, Postel knew, leading pupils in the way of love. Postel said he was not prepared to join any society and expressed particular horror at the Davidists. Plantin replied to Postel asking what he meant and Postel replied:[38] the phrase *"notos mihi esse charitatis alumnos"* meant no more than Paul meant by *"Finis Praecepti Charitas"*,[39] and went on to criticise David Joris who he considered had hardly behaved towards his followers according to the Precepts of Love. Plantin does not seem to have persuaded Postel to approach more closely to the Family. Nor given the strength of Postel's conviction of his own mission as Angelic Pope and messianic pretender was it likely that he would have gone after Joris *"as if to a new Christ or a Great Prophet."*[40] Rather a letter to Gabriel de Zayas in October 1567 expressed Postel's satisfaction with the Antwerp Polyglot as the realisation of his own plans: God had now selected the Low Countries to accomplish His primordial purpose of gathering humanity into one fold under one shepherd and the lance and sword of victory was to be typography. Postel, with the opportunism and flexibility inevitably characteristic of every reader of the signs of the times, seems to have been prepared for the moment

---

[36] CP. I pg 160.

[37] Abraham Ortellius, cartographer and friend of Plantin. On his connection with the Family see: Hamilton, *Family* pg 70–72. More widely: R. Boumans "The Religious Views of Abraham Ortellius" Journal of the Warburg and Courtauld Institute XVII (1954) pg 374–377.

[38] CP. I pg 80–81; 82–84; 154–155 for the following.

[39] One can hardly overlook the appearance of this motto upon the end-sheet of the 1555 *editio princeps* of the Syriac New Testament. I suggest it appeared there as a favourite quotation and summative proposition of Postel.

[40] Ed. F. Secret, *G. Postel Apologies et Rétractions* (B. De Graaf, Niewkoop 1972) pg 229. On Postel's relationship with David Joris of Delft, the Anabaptist leader who had lived 1544–1556 as Johann von Brügge in Basle: R. H. Bainton "William Postel and the Netherlands" Nederlandisch Archief voor Kerkgeschiedenis XXIV (1931) pg 161–172. On Joris, Niclaes and Barrefeld: H. de la Fontaine Verney "Trois Hérésiarches dans les Pays-Bas du XVIᵉ siècle" Bibliothèque de Humanisme et Renaissance XVI (1954) pg 312–330.

to waive French claims to universal sovereignty for Spanish ones, just as earlier he had been prepared in Vienna in 1555 to find a similarly significant role for Ferdinand. But this is Postel true to form: there is nothing here to make us consider either Postel or Masius or their work as particularly associated with the Family of Love.

Plantin himself is the member of the Family of Love about whom we are best informed. Even so, it remains difficult neatly to categorise his religious life, and his correspondence to friends of different confessional persuasions does not portray a simple and straightforward picture. Plantin was ambitious and a printer: he could not afford too inflexible an approach to religion. Hamilton draws attention to the financial security the Family provided for Plantin at several turns, whilst not denying him a more general commitment to Concord beyond allegiances to visible Churches.[41] There is however nothing here to justify us considering the Polyglot in any way as a Family of Love project.

The Apparatuses of Montano in the Antwerp Polyglot

We may discount the influence of the Family of Love upon the Antwerp Polyglot project. The inspiration and instigation of the Polyglot and the bulk of the work lay with Postel and the northern scholars with whom we are about to concern ourselves. Nonetheless Montano did contribute to the project several Appendices that are found in Volume VIII of the bible.[42] The most controversial of these was *Liber Ioseph sive de arcano sermone*. Approval of the Polyglot was held up on suspicion that this essay was kabbalistic. The work belongs firmly in the Spanish traditions we have been examining and displays characteristically *both*

---

[41] A. Hamilton, *The Family of Love* (James Clarke & Co, Cambridge, 1981) pg 68–70. L. Voet had discussed the matter in *The Golden Compasses. A History and Evaluation of the Printing and Publishing Activities of the Officina Plantiniana at Antwerp* (trans. R. H. Kaye, Vangendt & Co Amsterdam 1972) Vol. I, pg 27–30. He characterises Plantin there as one who in all conscience did not wish or who was not able to chose between the two competing confessions and whose acceptance of the two religions side by side, symbolic conception of the sacraments, and tolerance were based upon the mystic idea that religious quarrels are futile because, when truth appears, all dissensions, antitheses and all that divides will be lost in the ultimate harmony. Plantin's commercial acumen is well illustrated in R. M. Kingdom "The Plantin Breviaries: a Case Study in the Sixteenth Century Operations of a Publishing House" Bibliothèque de Humanisme et Renaissance XXII (1960) pg 133–150.

[42] Conveniently listed Rekers, *op. cit.*, pg 53–54; Darlow and Moule, *Historical Catalogue*, Vol. II, pg 11 and 12.

an interest in literal idiom *and* sensitivity to arcane meanings, drawing parallels with Egyptian hieroglyphs.[43] The 122 folio pages of the treatise cite more than eleven thousand passages of Scripture and together with the treatise that follows and completes it, *Ieremia sive de Actione*, it is practically a commentary on the whole of Scripture. God has given the names to things: their essential nature is accessible through those names. Thus by examining the names of things in Scripture one can arrive at, as it were, an encyclopaedia of Creation and a grasp of the transcendental significance of all things.[44] There are also number speculations that added to the kabbalistic reputation of the treatise[45] and instances of the permutation of letters.[46] These often serve to establish closer links between the Old Testament and the New.[47]

A treatise on Biblical architecture also combines equally biblical *realia* and an appreciation of their arcane significance.[48] *Exemplar sive de sacris fabricis Liber, Antwerpiae, Anno 1572* comprises three parts: *Noah, sive de Arcae fabrica et forma; Beseleel, sive de Tabernaculo; and Ariel, sive de Templi fabrica et structura.* The interplay of text and mystic architecture is illustrated by Montano's exposition of Noah's Ark, which becomes typical of salvation: its dimensions are found spiritually to accommodate the recumbent life-giving corpse of Christ.[49] The work is of further interest because Montano's exposition of the Temple and the occult architectural principles of its design disagree pointedly with

---

[43] (From the Prologue) *"Liber itque a nobis est conscriptus, in quo non tam verborum interpretationes, quam rerum ipsarum proprietates, naturam et vim, qua potuimus et brevitate et facilitate indicavimus. Earundem vero arcanam et latentem significationem aptis et oportunis exemplis comprobatem explicavimus."*

[44] K.-O. Apel "The Transcendental Conception of Language-Communication and the Idea of a First Philosophy" in ed. H. Parret, *History of Linguistic Thought and Contemporary Linguistics* (New York 1976) pg 32–62.

[45] *Op. cit.*, pg 21, pg 23.

[46] *Op. cit.*, pg 59.

[47] N. Fernández Marcos "El Tratado De Arcano Sermone de Arias Montano" in *Biblia y Humanismo Textos, talantes y controversias del siglo XVI español* pg 177–183.

[48] In *de Arcano Sermone* (3a) Montano explains: *"Nullum enim adeo in tota illa sacra lectione, vel minimum est vocabulum quod a Spiritu Sancto non sit profectum...in nullo Sanctae Sripturae verbo, id modo si attente atque ex sui ipsius natura consideretur, summam non elucere excellentiam."* At 3b:*"Quodcirca nobis, quibus summo Deus benficio, tum arcanae illius significationis, tum etiam linguae hebraicae at que architecturae artis cognitionem impertiit (ea quam sit exigua ingenue agnoscimus) nihil non enitendum duximus quod...conferre possemus".*

[49] N. Fernández Marcos "Las Medidas del Arca de Noé en la Exégesis de Arias Montano" in *Biblia y Humanismo Textos, talantes y controversias del siglo XVI español* pg 185–191 with plate. See also: J. Bennett and S. Mandelbrote, *The Garden, the Ark, the Tower, the Temple. Biblical Metaphors of Knowledge in Early Modern Europe* (Museum of the History of Science, Oxford 1998) pg 73–102 (the Ark) and pg 135–156 (the Temple).

those of Juan Bautista Villalpando (1552–1608) whose reconstruction is reminiscent of the Escorial. Montano's *Exemplar* was republished in Leiden in 1593. The *In Ezechielem Explanationes* of Villalpando and his fellow Jesuit Hieronymo Prado (1547–1595) appeared in Rome in three volumes between 1594 and 1605.[50]

Interest in the New World is found in Montano's *Phaleg sive de gentium sedibus primis, orbisque terrae situ, liber*. Montano's thesis is that the geography of the New World may be clearly recognised in the descriptions of the world that appear in Holy Scripture.

Montano's contribution also included some technical works. *De varia in hebraicis lectione ac de Mazoreth Ratione atque usu* has recently received attention from a modern Massoretic scholar.[51] *Benedicti Ariae Montani...de Psalterii Anglicani Exemplari Animadversio* however was to give rise to an acrimonious row that further exacerbated the difficulties that beset Montano's attempts to get approval for the Polyglot. The treatise arose from the inspection of a Hebrew codex of 'the English Psalter' submitted to Montano by an Englishman called Clement—'*un cierto Clemente*

---

[50] Montano's interest in the mystical architecture of the Jerusalem Temple is the key to understanding substantial parts of his work in the apparatus: *Thubal-Cain, sive de mensuris sacris liber; Liber Chanaan, sive de duodecim gentibus; liber Chaleb, sive de terrae promissae partitione; Aaron, sive sanctorum vestimentorum ornamentorumque summa descriptio* and *Nehemias, sive de antiquae Ierusalem situ volumen*. The most helpful work is the massive and learned ed. J. Antonio Ramirez et al., *Dios Arquitecto J. B. Villalpando y el Templo de Salomón* (Ediciones Siruela, Madrid 1994) pg 94–99 ("Del Arca al Templo. La Cadena Ejemplar de Prototipos sagrados de B. Arias Montano") and pg 177–182 ("Vitruvio, La Biblia y La Polémica con Arias Montano"). Also: R. Taylor "Architecture and Magic Considerations on the Idea of the Escorial" in ed. D. Fraser, H. Hibbard, and M. J. Lewine, *Essays in the History of Architecture presented to Rudolf Wittkower* (Phaidon, London 1967) pg 81–109 (with plate IX). We cannot embark upon this enormous subject here, though its importance for a clear characterisation of Montano and his Biblical exposition is substantial. For a brief overview of Temple reconstructions from an art-historical point of view: H. Rosenau, *Vision of the Temple The Image of the Temple of Jerusalem in Judaism and Christianity* (Oresko, London 1979 esp. pg 94–95 with references to plates. On the construction of the Escorial: G. Kubler, *Building the Escorial* (Princeton UP, Princeton 1982).

[51] M.-T. Ortega-Monasterio "Arias Montani List of Qere-Ketiv-Yattir Readings" in ed. A. Dotan, *Proceedings of the Ninth International Congress of the International Organisation for Massoretic Studies 1989* 1992 pg 71–84 reports her interest in determining the manuscript origin of the Antwerp Hebrew text and whether the Massorah was used in establishing it. Her work should be compared with F. Pérez Castro "Un centenar de lecciones del texto biblio hebreo" Homenaje a Juan Prado, Miscelánea de Estudios Biblicos y Hebraicos XXIV (1975) pg 43–56. Also E. Fernández Tejero "Benedicti Montani...*De Mazzoreth ratione atque usu*" *Biblia y Humanismo Textos, talantes y controversias del siglo XVI español* pg 155–160 and further her "Dos Tratados de Benito Arias Montano" in the same place pg 169–166 which also discusses *De Psalterii Anglicani Exemplari*.

inglés de nación.[52] Wilhemus Lindanus, Doctor of Louvain, Bishop of
Rurmond in Flanders and author of *De Optimo Genere Interpretandi Scrip-
turas* was (as we shall see below) an early sponsor of Plantin's Polyglot,
well before Montano arrived from Spain. Lindanus believed that the
text of the Hebrew Bible had suffered substantial corruption and altera-
tion at the hands of the Jews. This was scarcely a new position, but
Lindanus believed he was able to offer decisive textual proof of Jewish
tinkering with the text: he claimed that a Hebrew Psalter text that he
believed to be very ancient and once in the possession of Augustine,
Archbishop of Canterbury, had escaped this corruption and was
thus of extreme value. Montano's essay in the Appendix refuted this
claim with internal text-critical arguments and external codicological
observations. Lindanus was furious. Montano wrote a mollifying letter
suggesting that Lindanus's error had arisen only because he had not
himself inspected the manuscript and had been misled by others. Not
entirely surprisingly, this only made matters worse: Lindanus replied:
"his oculis vidi librum et habui in manu."[53] Lindanus was, as Montano
indicated, ignorant and incompetent to judge but his opposition would
not help the Polyglot.[54]

Conclusion

The obvious model for the Antwerp Polyglot was of course that of
Alcalá. Though Philip II sent Montano to superintend the passage of
the *Biblia Regia* through the various storms of ecclesiastical censure, we
shall see that the Polyglot project was anticipated long before by Postel
and Masius. In the next chapter we shall hope to show that not merely
did Postel anticipate it, but that he was instrumental in winning the
patronage of Philip II for the project in the first place. Subsequently we
shall argue that the Polyglot and specifically the Syriac New Testament
are to be seen as a continuation of the type of orientalism that was

---

[52] He also contributed to the Polyglot a Greek Pentateuch once the property of Sir
Thomas More: Darlow and Moule, *op. cit.*, pg 10.

[53] "I saw the book with my own eyes and held it in my hand".

[54] E. Fernández Tejero "Benedicti Ariae Montani...*De Psalterii Anglicani Exemplari Animadversio*" *Biblia y Humanismo Textos, talantes y controversias del siglo XVI español* pg 161–167.
T. González, *Carvajal Elogio histórico del Doctor Benito Arias Montano* pg 188–193 (Document
#73) a letter from Montano 4 February 1594 to Esteban de Salazar gives an account
of the business. Rekers, *op. cit.*, pg 58 for references to letters in Stockholm.

characteristic of early sixteenth-century Catholic scholars and is marked by a developed kabbalism far more pronounced than that brought from Spain by Montano. Montano did not represent a disruption or a new Spanish initiative separate from that of our scholars. Montano himself, nonetheless, represented one of two types of Spanish scholars in the field. He had a high view of the Hebrew text and a disposition to interpret it both literally and mystically. His contributions to the Polyglot are not therefore without a natural sympathy with the work of Masius, Guy Lefèvre de la Boderie and Postel. They were however anathema to Spanish scholars like Léon de Castro, and this was to lead to difficulties: both Montano's Spanish contributions and the work of the northern scholars were to be suspected of kabbalism. But it is time now to turn to those northern scholars.

CHAPTER THREE

THE NORTHERN SCHOLARS: MASIUS

Much of the work for the Antwerp Polyglot Bible had been completed before the arrival of Arias Montano in the Netherlands. The immediate inspiration for the project had nothing to do with Spain, but was a continuation of the work of the small group of oriental scholars to whom we now turn our attention. At the beginning of this chapter we shall discuss Andreas Masius and his enthusiasm for a Polyglot—and one with Syriac too. Thereafter we shall turn to Guillaume Postel and his remarkable religious imagination, for in the miraculous events of 1566 he was to see what he called the *Beginning of the Restoration*, and the consequential need to broadcast his special message and to evangelise the Moslems. It was here that motivation for the great work lay, not only for Postel himself but also for Guy Lefèvre de la Boderie and his brother, and Postel's other pupil Jean Boulaese. The Antwerp Polyglot we shall discover was inspired not least by Postel's eschatological timetable.

Masius[1]

Andreas Maes (Masius) came from the village of Lennick to the south of Brussels where he was born on St. Andrew's Day, 30 November 1514. He studied with distinction at Louvain where he attended lectures at the Collegium Trilingue and made friendships that were to last through his life and have left their traces in his correspondence. The majority of these were with young humanists who made their way to Italy.[2] Masius left Louvain in 1537 and for the next ten years he became secretary to Johann van Wese until the latter's sudden death at the Diet of Augsburg 13 June 1548. Though the peregrinations of the court left

---

[1] I here make use of much fuller material on Masius to be found in R. J. Wilkinson, *Orientalism, Aramaic and Kabbalah in the Catholic Reformation. The first printing of the Syriac New Testament* (E. J. Brill, Leiden 2007) to which the reader is referred.

[2] Martin de Smet, Stephanus Pighius (who worked in the Vatican Library and like Masius enjoyed Cervini's patronage), John Visbroeck (Secretary to Cardinal Morone), Laevinius Torrentius etc.

Masius little time to study, he nevertheless maintained correspondence with the leading semitic scholars and his status is apparent from the accolades of that formidably learned circle: Sebastian Münster, Paul Fagius, Johann Albrecht Widmanstetter.

It was in Italy that Masius was able to meet Guillaume Postel and be instructed by him in the rudiments of Arabic. (This was the period of Postel's sojourn with the Jesuits. He had abandoned his benefice and situation in Paris and was in Rome until early 1546. He parted company with the Jesuits in December 1545 but remained in Rome for a few months more.) Not only did Postel teach Masius Arabic, he also shared with him his interest in kabbalah. Postel kept Masius informed of his own publications and their problems and at times sought his help. After leaving Rome, Postel was to continue to share his oriental researches with Masius and a letter of 1547 tells us that Postel was preparing a text of the gospels in Arabic and Syriac.[3]

This letter is important for the evidence it provides of Postel's early interest in oriental bibles, but most particularly because it clearly displays the evangelical purpose (noticeably lacking in the case of the Complutensian Polyglot) he envisaged for his versions. He intended to evangelise Moslems by gospels in Arabic. By contrast, however, the purpose of the Syriac gospels seems to have been to evangelise Jews *'in Chaldaica mutatato in linguae Adami characteres'* 'by the Syriac Version put into Hebrew characters'. This last point helps us to understand a significant feature of three Syriac New Testament editions which we shall shortly consider—their use of Hebrew type to print Syriac.[4] There was Syriac type at Antwerp and in Paris, yet in both the Antwerp Polyglot and the Paris edition of 1583 the 'Chaldaean' or Syriac text is also printed in Hebrew characters. Raphelengius's 1574 Plantin edition had *only* Hebrew script, though the house did not lack Syriac type. This, says Postel, was to evangelise the Jews. We shall take this

---

[3] Lossen, *op. cit.*, refers to the letter pg 23. It is printed in Jacques George de Chaufpié, Nouveau Dictionnaire historique et critique pour servir de Supplement ou de continuation au Dictionnaire Historique et Critique de M. Pierre Bayle. Amsterdam/The Hague/Leiden, 1750–1756 vol. III pg 219. The letter concludes with some letter mysticism.

[4] Tremellius's 1569 Heidelberg edition of the Syriac New Testament does not have Syriac characters, because none were available, and uses Hebrew. Tremellius also however envisaged the evangelisation of Jews by his edition. I have discussed this edition at length in R. J. Wilkinson, "Emmanuel Tremellius' 1569 Edition of the Syriac New Testament" Journal of Ecclesiasical History 58/1 January 2007 pg 9–25.

remark fully into account when considering the later versions because their intended evangelical function provides a key to understanding their wider purpose within Postel's eschatological framework.

Finally we should notice the remarks in that same 1547 letter of Postel to Masius about the mystical meanings of the etymologies of biblical proper names in the oriental versions. This hidden spiritual resource was greatly to interest later editors of the Syriac New Testament. The letter concludes with a passage of letter mysticism. These comments remind us again of the kabbalistic interests of these scholars. Masius was subsequently in 1549 the recipient of the Latin edition of Postel's *Candelabri typici interpretatio Venetii 1548,* a deeply kabbalistic book. He was also let into the secret of Postel's revelations concerning Mother Joanna which we shall see so revolutionised Postel's religious consciousness and programme.

Moses of Mardin

For a few months at the beginning of 1553 Masius collaborated with Moses of Mardin, a Syriac monk who had been sent to Rome in 1549 by the Syrian Orthodox (Jacobite) Patriarch of Antioch to have Gospel books printed.[5] Moses taught Masius Syriac and also helped to improve his Arabic that he had begun under Postel in 1545–1546.[6] We know about this period of collaboration from comments in Masius's subsequent publications and his correspondence, including that which he conducted with Moses in Syriac. In return for this tuition in Arabic and Syriac, Masius translated into Latin Moses's 1552 confession of faith before the Pope and Cardinals made on behalf of himself and his Patriarch[7] and also a short *Contemplatio Theologica* on the Holy Trinity

---

[5] I have discussed Moses at length in R. J. Wilkinson, *Orientalism, Aramaic and Kabbalah in the Catholic Reformation. The first printing of the Syriac New Testament* (E. J. Brill, Leiden 2007).

[6] Lossen, *op. cit.*, pg 161: 13.

[7] *De Paradiso* pg 257–262: *Fidei professio, quam Moses Mardenus, Assyrius, Jacobita, patriarchae Antiocheni legatus, suo et Patriarchae sui nomine est Romae professus anno 1552; exipso profitentis autographo syriaco traducta ad verbum per Andream Masium Bruxellanum.* Assemani, *Bibliotheca Orientalia* I pg 535 notes: *"cuius tamen fidem Ignatius eiusdem Patriarcha nequa quam ratam habuit postmodum compertum".*

that Moses had composed the previous year.[8] Masius was subsequently
to print both of these in his translation of the *De Paradiso* in 1567.
Masius was also in 1553 to meet another native Syriac speaker, Mar
Sulaqa, who had been chosen patriarch by a section of the Chaldean
Church and had come to Rome to seek consecration. Masius did
translation work for Sulaqa, as there was no one else in Rome who
could read Syriac.[9]

In 1553 an event occurred which would cast a future shadow over
Masius's reputation for orthodoxy. The Inquisition condemned the
Talmud to destruction and Pope Julius III in his bull *Cum sicut nuper*
upheld the Inquisition's decree.[10] Masius spoke out against the burning
and the view of non-biblical Jewish literature which motivated the pyres
in Rome's Campo dei Fiori. But Masius's view was not to find general
support and the subsequent election of Paul IV brought to power a
pontiff quite out of sympathy with Masius's Hebrew and Jewish studies, and, indeed, the very man who had insisted upon the burning of
the Talmud under Julius III. Masius's interests in Hebrew and other
oriental texts made him suspected of heterodoxy. Thereafter Pius IV,
one of the most severe critics of rabbinic literature, placed Masius's
Joshua of 1574 on the Index[11] and when the *Biblia Regia* was completed
in Antwerp, Masius's collaboration on the project jeopardised papal
approbation.[12]

Masius died 7 April 1573 but during the period 1560–1567 he
made his most significant scholarly contributions. Amongst these were

---

[8] *De Paradiso* pg 273–276: *Moses Mardeni Theologica de sacrosancta Trinitate contemplatio, scripta ab ipso anno 1552, et ex autographo syrico ad verbum translata per eundem Andream
Masium.*

[9] Masius, *Dictionarium* pg 54.

[10] The significance of the Burning of the Talmud for oriental scholarship is examined
at length in R. J. Wilkinson, *Orientalism, Aramaic and Kabbalah in the Catholic Reformation.
The first printing of the Syriac New Testament* (E. J. Brill, Leiden 2007). More generally:
W. Popper, *The Censorship of Hebrew Books* (Knickerbocker Press, New York 1899).
Reprinted with new introduction by M. Carmilly-Weinberger (Ktav, New York
1969).

[11] J. Perles, *Beiträge zur Geschichte der hebräischen und aramaischen Studien* (Theodore
Achermann: München 1884) pg 229.

[12] On the subsequent suspicion with which Masius was viewed: J. H. Jonkees "Masius
in moeilijkheden" De Gulden Passer XLI (1963) pg 161–168. The letter of Masius
in 1572 to Cardinal Sirleto printed there pg 164–165 is important for understanding
Masius's defence of the Talmud in passages in his Grammar and *Peculium* printed in
the Antwerp Polyglot.

of course his translations. Some were made in Rome in 1553–1554.[13] More ambitious was his translation of the *Anaphora of St. Basil*, probably undertaken in Germany and at the request of Julius Pflug,[14] Bishop of Naumbourg, and completed by 7 November 1554.[15] A revised and corrected translation that had benefited from Moses's assistance[16] appeared in print with Plantin in Antwerp in 1567.[17] Plantin also printed in the same volume Masius's most significant translation, that of Moses Bar-Cepha's *De Paradiso*.[18] Not only has the Syriac manuscript from which

---

[13] All the translations except the *Contemplatio Theologica* were dedicated to Ogier-Ghislain de Busbecq whom Masius had known in Louvain. In 1555 de Busbecq became the Emperor Maximilian's ambassador in Constantinople. Masius had written 30 November 1555 asking for Syriac books, especially works of St. Ephrem. De Busbecq wrote to Masius from Constantinople 28 May 1556 (Lossen #192 pg 260–262). Masius referred to this unsatisfied request in the *Dedicatio* to *De Paradisio* (pg 229). However Masius did finally get a fragment of Ephrem in Syriac from de Busbecq in August 1569 (Lossen #301 pg 429).

[14] *Allgemeine Deutsche Biographie* (Leipzig 1887) vol. XXV pg 688–690. Pflug played an important part in the discussions between Catholics and Protestants: *De Paradiso* pg 227. Masius visited him in September 1554 and probably gave him the translation then.

[15] Lossen #147 pg 182. A van Roey "Les Études syriaques d'Andreas Masius" Orientalia Louvenansia Periodica IX (1978) pg 141–158 and pg 147–148.

[16] Masius maintained contact with Moses after his own departure from Rome in 1553 and after the latter's collaboration on Widmanstetter's 1555 *editio princeps* of the Syriac New Testament. Their correspondence resumes in the spring of 1555. Relations between the two men deteriorated before Moses's departure for the East in 1556. Masius was to draw on this correspondence later in his *Peculium Syrorum*—a Dictionary of Syriac words not found in Jewish Aramaic included in the Antwerp Polyglot. Though some words there are noted as due to Moses's explanations, not all that appear in the correspondence are so marked. I follow here J. W. Wesselius "The Syriac Correspondence of Andreas Masius: a preminary report" in ed. R. Lavenant, *V Symposium Syriacum 1988* (Pont. Inst. Stud. Or., Rome 1990) pg 21–29 especially pg 27–28.

[17] '*Anaphora divi Basilii episcopi Caesareae Cappadociae, ex vetustissimo codice syrica lingua et caractere scripto, traducta per Andream Masium.*' *De Paradiso* pg 235–254. The manuscript itself has disappeared. It should be made clear that Masius's translations are very paraphrastic. He eliminates repetitions, overlooks precise terminology and removes every syriacism (*De Paradiso* pg 4 and 11). An estimate of this is given in H. Engberding, *Das eucharistische Hochgebet der Basileosliturgie* (Theologie des christlischen Orients 1) (Aschendorff, Munster 1931) pg lxx. After the Liturgy, Masius added a "*Precatio Divi Basilii, qua solet operatus sacris uti apud Deum, translata ex syrico...*" pg 254–256.

[18] *De Paradiso commentarius, scriptus ante annos prope septingenos a Mose Bar-Cepha Syro, episcopo in Beth-Raman et Beth-Ceno ac curatore rerum sacrarum in Mozal, hoc est Seleucia Parthorum. Invenies, lector, in hoc commentario, praeter alia multa lectu et digna et iucunda, plurimos etiam peregrinos scriptores citatos. Adiecta est etiam divi Basili Caesariensis episcopi λειτουργία sive ἀναφορά ex vetustissimo codice syrica lingua scripto. Praeterea professiones fidei duae, altera Mosis Mardenis Iacobitae, legati patriarchae Antiocheni, altera Sulacae sive Siud Nestoriani, designati patriarchae Nestorianorum. Ad haec duae epistolae populi nestoriani ad Pontificem romanum, quarum altera ex Seleucia Parthorum, altera ex Ierusalem scripta est. Omnia ex syrica lingua nuper translata per andream Masium Bruxelanum. Antverpiae, ex officina Christophori Plantini 1569.* Masius undertook the work because he was sick (*De Paradiso* pg 3). The reason why he chose

Masius himself translated the *De Paradiso* (which he bought from Moses in 1552–1553) disappeared, but all other Syriac manuscripts have also been lost. Thus Masius's Latin translation of the work is now the only witness to Moses Bar-Cepha's lost work of about 850 A.D.

Masius's translation work is of further interest as it allows us to observe the beginnings of Western knowledge of Syriac non-biblical material. In this respect the *Dedicatio* to the *De Paradiso* is of some importance. Masius's purpose was first to provide some introduction to the names of Syriac writers who are referred to by Bar-Cepha and of whom his readers would be ignorant. It cannot be said that he knew a lot about them: often he merely identifies an office or a location. Perhaps Moses had helped initially by answering questions arising from a first reading when he supplied the manuscript to Masius. He had, of course, returned home when Masius undertook the translation, and some of the information comes from the Byzantine Suidas. This is however the first listing of such names: not yet a History of Syriac Literature, but at least some famous names.[19]

---

this text was because he had it. The scarcity of Syriac texts was such as to make any manuscript inevitably an object of interest and attention. The circumstances of the work's printing have been reconstructed by A. van Roey "Les Études syriaque". As for the Syriac manuscripts none are indicated in A. Baumstark, *Geschichte der Syrischen Literatur* (Bonn 1922) pg 281. G. Graf, *Geschichte der christlichen arabischen Literatur* (Vatican City, 1947) Vol. 2, pg 229–233 indicates an Arabic translation.

[19] The mention of Ephrem (pg 7) is interesting. Masius knew of him from Jerome and Moses of Mardin. He compares his productivity to that of Augustine. Then he remarks: '*Hoc ego certe affirmare possum, nihil elegantius, nihil suavius, nihil etiam acutius, barbara illa alioqui lingua dici posse, quam ea mihi visa sunt, quae adhuc illius legi.*' This must mean that Masius had read some, though he had not yet got his fragment from de Busbecq. The terms of his praise may suggest that it was poetry, though that is not necessarily so. (It may be recalled that Widmanstetter had come across some Ephrem in Ptolemaeus's library in Sienna.) Other writers mentioned include: Jacob Orrohaisa; Philoxenus of Mabbug; Diodorus; Ioannes Monachus; Severus; Jacob of Sarrug; Jacob de Batnam; Theodorus—their inclusion being determined solely by the fact that Bar-Cepha mentions them. Masius (pg 11) allows himself to compare Syriac with Greek style, warning the readers not to expect anything ornate. The first thorough and informed History of Syriac Literature was Abraham Ecchelensis's 1653 Rome edition of Abisho of Nisibis's Catalogue of Syriac Authors, *Hebediesu metropolita Sobiensis. Tractatus continens catalogum librorum Chaldaeorum tam ecclesiasticorum quam profanorum cum versione et notis. Romae Typis Sacrae Congregationis de Propaganda Fide 1653.*

Masius and Plans for a Polyglot

Masius did not however neglect his interest in the Syriac New Testament. Already on the 9 June 1554, writing to Latinus Latinius, secretary of Cardinal Puteo at Rome, he regrets that the death of his friend the printer Bomberg in Venice had deprived him of a promised Syriac manuscript of the Pauline epistles.[20] That same letter had announced the grand project of a polyglot of the ancient versions: "I have long considered compiling and printing all the ancient biblical versions."[21] Masius clearly intended that this Polyglot should, unlike that of Alcalá, contain a Syriac version.[22]

In the same letter Masius writes of: "…a very old Syriac codex containing the Books of Kings and several other fragments with red letters saying that the Syriac version was made from a Greek codex in the library at Caesarea which had been corrected by Eusebius and Pamphilius…"[23] Masius thus gives the first notice in the West of the existence of the Syro-hexaplaric Text of which he would later make use in his edition of *Joshua.*[24]

---

[20] Lossen #140 pg 172: *"Utinam in hoc otio haberem exemplar epistolarum Pauli in illa lingua [syriaca]; non pigeret laboris, quantumvis afflictum valetudine. Et iam habiturus eram, ni fata meum Bombergum hoc autumno mihi eripuissent".*

[21] *"quod iamdudum animo verso cogitationem de conferendisque excutiendisque omnibus veteribus sacrorum Bibliorum inter[pretibus]…"*

[22] It was perhaps at this time that he consulted Vat syr 15, the text of the Four Gospels in the Vatican Library that he was to mention in his *Peculium*: Levi della Vida, *Ricerche* pg 144. A margin note in the *Introductio* to the *De Paradiso* pg 182 comments upon the Gospel text *"Ne irascaris tuo fratri gratuito".* Though Jerome and Augustine wish to omit the underlined word, Masius remarks: *"Habent tamen antigrapha* (= 'copies') *Syra quae vidi ego Masius tria quatuorve."* He clearly was deeply interested in the textual issues to which knowledge of different versions gives rise, and was looking out for new manuscripts.

[23] *'Syra lingua vetustissimum codicem, in quo sunt Regum libri et alia nonnulla fragmenta…in quo rubris elementis adscriptum repperi eam syram translationem ex graeco codice qui in bibliotheca Caesariensi erat per Eusebium et Pamphilum emendatus, factum esse.'* See now: A. Grafton and M. Williams, *Christianity and the Transformation of the Book* (Harvard UP, London 2006).

[24] The Syro-hexapla was a Syriac translation of the Old Testament made from the Greek Septuagint in the fifth column of Origen's Hexapla by Paul, Bishop of Tella in North Mesopotamia, working in a monastery near Alexandria between 613 and 617 A.D. It enjoyed considerable diffusion before losing out to the popularity of the Peshitta Old Testament. The *Dedicatio* of the *De Paradiso* (pg 7) describes this manuscript which has now been lost. Matthew Norberg, *Codex Syriaco-Hexaplaris Ambosiano-Medio-lanensis editus et Latine versus* (C. F. Berling, Londini Gothorum 1789) describes his own manuscript and refers to the loss of Masius's manuscript. The modern edition of the Greek Joshua making use of the Syro-hexaplaric material is M. L. Margolis *The Book of Joshua in Greek* (Geuthner, Paris 1931–8) that in its present form lacks the intended

In spite of these exciting discoveries, Masius still considered that his studies had been disrupted by the papal edict against Jewish books, particularly as it would seem that Syriac manuscripts were not clearly distinguished from Hebrew ones. Writing to Latinius on 13 November 1554, Masius remarks: "I wish I had at least my Syriac New Testament books to hand, but these too suffer in this calamity with the other Hebrew ones."[25] In an earlier letter of 25 February 1554 from Weingarten to the Roman prelate Octavius Panagathus, he remarks that more than the personal loss of 40 guilders, it is the perpetual shame of the impious leaders of the Church in this matter which affects him.[26] There can be no doubt of his bitterness.

---

introduction. Emmanuel Tov has provided the annotated critical text for the last portion of the book similarly incomplete at the time of the author's death. L. Greenspoon "Max L. Margolis on the Complutensian Text of Joshua" Bulletin of the International Organisation for Septuagint and Cognate Studies XII (1979) pg 43–56, pg 52 discusses Margolis's monograph on Masius. On which see now his: "A preliminary publication of Max Leopold Margolis's Andreas Masius, together with his discussion of the Hexapla-Tetrapla" in ed. A. Salvesan, *Origen's Hexapla & Fragments* (Texte u. Studien zum Antiken Judentum 58, Tübingen 1998) pg 39–69.

The *Josuae Imperatoris Historia, illustrata atque explicata*...was published posthumously by Plantin in Antwerp in 1574. The result of several years' toil, this monumental work sets out the textual evidence for the book in the versions including reference to the Syro-Hexapla and provides extensive commentary. The book presents Hebrew text, Septuagint and Theodotion with two Latin translations, and the Targum with a Latin translation. This commentary is mentioned in two letters of Plantin, 27 February 1570 (Lossen #307 pg 437–439) and 29 October 1571 (Lossen #328 pg 471–473). Other mentions in correspondence include: #319 pg 462–463; pg 511–512. Masius sent it to Rome in 1571 but was warned by friends about its contents (Lossen pg 460 for Latinus Latinius's criticisms of 18 and 20 May 1571). Pius V had not at this time approved the Antwerp Polyglot upon which Masius had collaborated and which contained his *Peculium* and Grammar. He wrote a letter to Cardinal Sirleto (no date: beginning of 1572. The text is found in J. H. Jongkees "Masius in moeilijkheden" De Gulden Passer XLI (1963) pg 161–168, pg 164–5) in which he offered a characteristic defence: *"Memini equidem me citasse Thalmudicos initio Grammaticae Syriae. Atqui id eius sanctitatem ferre aegre non existimo. Quos enim de Hebraicorum elementorum figuris disserens adhibere testes certiores potuissem quam ipsos Hebraeos? Praesertim cum per Concilium Tridentinum non sit Thalmudicis libris interdictum. Egoque alioqui adeo non probem aut defendam Thalmud, ut fortasse inter Christianos hodie pauci sint, aut nulli, in his certe regionibus, qui Thalmudicas aliasque iudaicas nugas et deliramenta tam acriter insectentur exagitentque atque ego per omnem occasionem facio. Nam si quid apud illos est, quod nostra dogmata confirmet, ipsorum convellat (ut tute scis esse plurima), cur id in nostram vertere utilitatem nefas fuerit? Cum hostem suis conficere armis sit pulcherrimum."* The pope died in May and his successor Gregory XIII gave permission to print the Polyglot. We return to these difficulties below.

[25] Lossen #150 pg 185–186. *"Sed utinam codices saltem meos syros Novi Testamenti expeditos habeam. Sed illi pariter cum aliis hebraicis calamitate premuntur."*

[26] J. Perles, *Beiträge* pg 228.

At this time, when Masius was working both on the *De Paradiso* and his biblical projects, he received a letter from the Antwerp printer Christophe Plantin[27] on 26 February 1566 on the subject of a Polyglot Bible—a project we have just seen Masius was already eager to pursue.[28] Wilhemus Lindanus, Bishop of Roermond in Limburg had suggested a polyglot and for this Plantin wanted Masius to put the Targum to the whole Old Testament into Latin which would better the Complutensian Polyglot which only had the Targum to the Pentateuch.[29] Philippe Theunissen makes the convincing point that this letter indicates that at this stage Plantin clearly envisaged Masius as the leading scholar on the project.[30] Subsequently when Plantin was obliged to seek the patronage of Philip II, Masius retreated into the background and produced mainly linguistic tools—a Grammar and a Lexicon—for the Polyglot. No doubt this was so that the suspicions of his orthodoxy we have been considering would not prejudice the success of the project.

Fascinatingly Plantin, in the same letter, tells Masius how he had consulted Immanuel Tremellius upon his return from England in December 1565 about a Syriac New Testament and learned that he had already translated three Gospels and the letters of the Apostle Paul that would eventually appear in his 1569 edition.[31] Though, in

---

[27] Bibliographic material on Plantin is enormous. Relevant works are cited below in connection with the Polyglot or at appropriate places. Basic but essential orientation to the Library and Archives of the Plantin-Moretus Museum are found in F. De Nave, *Het Museum Plantin-Moretus Te Antwerpen I: De Bibliotheek & II De Archieven* (MPM/PK, Antwerp1985). Turning to the text above, A. van Roey "Les Études syriaques" pg 152 somewhat discounts Postel's influence here on the ground that Masius had previously cherished the idea. As we know they had met as long ago as 1545 in Rome, shared their knowledge and kabbalistic interest, and were corresponding by 1547 about producing the Gospels in Syriac and Arabic (Chaufpié III pg 219), it seems pointless in this respect to set them in competition.

[28] Lossen #259 pg 362–364. Also eds. M. Rooses and J. Denucé, *Correspondence de Christophe Plantin* (Vereeniging der Antwerpche Bibliophilen, Antwerp 1883–1920. Reprinted: Kraus-Thomson, Liechtenstein 1968) Vol. 3 pg 1 # 333. The date is wrongly given as 1565. It should be 1566: A. van Roey "Les Études syriaques" pg 152 n 65.

[29] P. Theunissen "Arias Montano et la Polyglot d'Anvers" Les Lettres Romanes (Louvain) XIX/3 (1965) pg 231–246 pg 234 emphasises the initial support of the Polyglot, before the arrival of Montano, by *'ce collaborateur et mécène de la première heure'*. Lindanus subsequently became a fierce opponent of the Polyglot as we shall see. His dispute with Montano over Montano's *De Psalterii Anglicani Exemplari Animadversio* in Volume VIII of the Polyglot has been discussed above.

[30] P. Theunissen "Arias Montano et la Polyglot d'Anvers" Les Lettres Romanes (Louvain) XIX/3 (1965) pg 231–246 pg 233.

[31] *Loc. cit. 'Et davantage Monsieur Lindanus est d'avis qu'on adjouxtast le Syriac au Nouveau Testament, chose qui me sembleroit fort a propos. Or Monsieur Emmanuel Tremellius professeur*

the end, it would be Guy Lefèvre de la Boderie, a young disciple of Postel, who edited the Syriac of the Antwerp Polyglot, Tremellius's warm relationship with Plantin and his readiness to co-operate *('qu'il ne nous denieroit chose qui fust en lui et a l'advancement de si belle enterprise')* introduce us to the comparative insignificance of confessional divisions in Plantin's business operations. Though there was confessional controversy generated around Tremellius's edition, and academic rivalry (and salesman's puff) with respect to the *editio princeps* on the part of the Antwerp Polyglot scholars, it is worth remembering again just how few Syriac scholars there were. Plantin was not the sort to let such considerations stand in the way of business. In the event Tremellius would produce his edition of 1569 in Heidelberg.[32] Plantin's Polyglot would exploit the expertise of Masius, Postel and de la Boderie. Once again: there was no-one else.

---

d'Hebrieu a Hidelberghe m'a dict en disnant avec moy [coems?] a son retour d'angleterre, ou il estoit ale ce mois de Decembre dernier, qu'il avoit ja traduit trois Evangelistes et toutes les Epistres tant de St. Paul que canoniques et qu'il ne luy restoit plus que sainct Luc et les Actes a traduire, lesquels il esperoit achever bien tost.'
[32] R. J. Wilkinson, "Emmanuel Tremellius' 1569 Edition of the Syriac New Testament" Journal of Ecclesiastical History 58/1 January 2007 pg 9–25.

CHAPTER FOUR

THE NORTHERN SCHOLARS:
THE ROLE OF POSTEL IN THE ANTWERP POLYGLOT

Guillaume Postel was in many ways the most important figure amongst the sixteenth-century Catholic kabbalists. He was an exceptional linguist and acquired unique typographical expertise especially in printing oriental languages. Postel journeyed twice in the East and profited by learning new languages and collecting oriental books. I have argued elsewhere that Postel was the consistent presence behind all the sixteenth-century Catholic editions of the Syriac New Testament as he will be seen also to be the moving force behind the Antwerp Polyglot.[1]

Though a devout Catholic in his own eyes, Postel developed a quite unique and heterodox religious self-awareness which can only be described as messianic. His thought tended towards the synthetic and he was able to find connections between languages, scripts, legends and history in a way that naturally attracted him to Jewish kabbalistic writings. These he was genuinely able to translate, though his 'readings' were hardly those of the authors. Underpinning all of Postel's thought was a strong conviction of providential history and a belief that the End of the World was imminent. This was not an unusual conviction at the time and was held, as we shall see, by several of the orientalists we shall consider. Such eschatological convictions were frequently linked to notions of the historical and providential role of certain countries whose rulers became possible candidates for the role of the Final Emperor in the emerging end-time scenario. In Postel's case such a role was usually awarded to the French, but we shall see that during the period of the Polyglot he and others were prepared to consider that Spain might fulfil such a role. Moreover, in Postel's case, his eschatological certainties had been corroborated by his relationship with a stigmatic and mystic nun, Mother Joanna, who he met in Venice in 1549.

---

[1] For a comprehensive view of Postel and his orientalism see again my *Orientalism, Aramaic and Kabbalah in the Catholic Reformation. The first printing of the Syriac New Testament* (E. J. Brill, Leiden 2007) upon which the following depends. I do not repeat here bibliography and documentation which is to be found there.

Mother Joanna was for Postel 'the Venetian Virgin' into whose body the Spirit of God had descended and in whose person the Living Christ was present. She was the 'True Mother of the World', the *Shekinah*, the Feminine Spirit of Christ, and (in spite of her sex) the Angelic Pope of the Fourth Age. Postel, her 'son', was to be her Elijah and a male Angelic Pope. It was in Venice at this time that Postel had acquired a copy of the *Zohar*, a work which he was to be the first to print and which he read through the interpretive lens which was supplied for him by Mother Joanna. Though she was without any ancient or oriental language, she was none the less able to expound the mysteries of the Kabbalah in a fashion that became normative for Postel. The heady combination of his relationship with the woman he called *'mia madre'*, the *Zohar*, and his own eschatological role, drove Postel into his mission of preaching universal restitution, penitence, and baptism. 'The restitution of all things' mentioned in the *Zohar* was at hand and it was his job to spread the message.

At this point one may speculate about the influence upon Postel of Francesco Giorgio (1460–1540), one of the *confrères* of San Francesco della Vigna who had been Mother Joanna's confessor before Postel came along. Francesco Giorgio's own subsequent relationship of confessor to the visionary Chiara Bugni probably illustrates the context of female spirituality and its management in which we should place the beginnings of Postel's relationship with Mother Joanna.[2] Georgio was a kabbalist. He wrote his *De Harmonia Mundi* in 1525 and his *Problemata* in 1536 which quotes extensively from the *Zohar*. His major work the *Elegante poema* has recently been edited, and a recent essay upon Giorgio with an up-to-date bibliography by Giulio Busi removes the need for a representation of that material here.[3] Giorgio is important for the aristocratic Franciscan

---

[2] C. Vasoli "Un 'precedente' della 'Virgine Veneziana': Francesco Giorgio Veneto e la clarissa Chiar Bugni" ed. Kuntz, *Postello, Venezia, e il suo Mondo* pg 203–225.

[3] G. Busi "Francesco Zorzi, a methodical dreamer" in ed. J. Dan, *The Christian Kabbalah Jewish Mystical Books and their Christian Interpreters* (Harvard College Library, Cambridge Mass. 1997) pg 97–126. In addition to which I have used C. Wirszubski "Franceso Giorgio's commentary on Giovanni Pico's kabbalistic theses" Journal of the Warburg and Courtauld Institutes XXXVII (1974) pg 145–156; C. Vasoli, *Profezia e Ragione* (Naples 1974) pg 129–403; also his "Da Marsilio Ficino a Francesco Giorgio Veneto" in his *Filosofia e Religione nella Cultura de Rinascimento* (Guida Editori, 1988) pg 233–256 (This is chapter seven of a book paginated only within individual chapters); F. A. Yates, *The Occult Philosophy in the Elizabethan Age* (Routledge, London 1979) pg 29–36. There is also J.-F. Maillard "Sous l'Invocation de Dante et de Pic de la Mirandole: les manuscrits inédits de Georges de Venise (Francesco Zorzi)" Bibliothèque

piety and mystical speculation he exemplifies, and for his search for the Jewish roots of the Christian faith in Kabbalah. He was familiar with Pico's *Conclusiones cabalisticae*, and dependent upon Reuchlin, yet Busi's concern has been to show the extent of Giorgio's own Hebrew reading. Reflections upon Hebrew words and possible combinations of them and play with the letters of the alphabet are among his familiar techniques. One cannot speak with certainty of Giorgio's relationship to Postel, though one may perhaps conjecture plausibly that Mother Joanna had absorbed a little of kabbalistic notions from her previous confessor. We do know however that Postel's pupil Guy Lefèvre de La Boderie who produced the Syriac New Testaments of Antwerp and Paris translated Giorgio's *De Harmonia Mundi* into French in 1578. We shall therefore return to this work a little later.

Postel left Venice to travel to Jerusalem in 1549 leaving behind Mother Joanna yet forever committed to the woman he saw as a symbol of mediation, an embodiment of the Maternal Principle and who had promised to give him the Garment of the Immortal Corporeal Substance of Corporeal Immortality. We have a letter written from abroad by Postel to Cardinal Grevelle 21 August 1549.[4] In the letter Postel develops his recurrent theme of restitution by stressing the role of language in the restoration of human reason and in allowing men to participate in the *Instauration* in which there will be 'but one shepherd and one sheepfold'. Grevelle was to use his influence with Charles V for the training of learned men in knowledge of Hebrew, Chaldaean, Syriac and Arabic in order to enable true religion to become available to all.[5] The importance of knowledge of languages as a means of accomplishing world unity is a fundamental theme of Postel: it is found

---

d'Humanisme et Renaissance XXXVI (1974) pg 47–61. Also his critical edition *Francesco Giorgio Veneto, L'elegante poema & Commento sopra il Poema* (Arche, Milan 1991). Giorgio was consulted by Richard Croke travelling in disguise as 'Giovanni di Fiandra' on the matter of Henry VIII's divorce. See Vasoli, *Profezia e Ragione* pg 181–212.

[4] M. L. Kuntz "A New Link in the Correspondence of Guillaume Postel" Bibliothèque d'Humanisme et Renaissance XLI (1979) pg 575–581. Postel did not know Grevelle when he wrote. Grevelle however was later to be the friend and protector of Plantin. As Bishop of Malines and an advisor to Philip II he was to be involved in the Antwerp Polyglot. Kuntz suggests this correspondence may be further evidence, not merely of the complexities of relationships in sixteenth-century Europe, but also of links between churchmen within the Hierarchy and those we see as less obviously conformist.

[5] Widmanstetter had proposed a similar scheme to Clement VII († 25 September 1534), though the pontiff's death prevented anything being done.

once more for example in *De phoenicum literis, seu de prisco latinae et graecae linguae charactere ejiusque antiquissima origine et usu* (Paris 1552). Postel ends with a request for money. He can get his hands on Syriac and Arabic books if he can pay for them.[6] The impulse to mission (no matter how singular the message) and the importance of languages in evangelisation are essential characteristics of Postel's faith which we must understand if we are to grasp his motives in promoting the Antwerp Polyglot.

When Postel returned to Venice he found that Mother Joanna had died. Postel went to Paris and, in a most productive period between 1551 and 1552, produced some fifteen books, perhaps the most outstanding of which was an annotated translation the kabbalistic Book of Iezirah, *Abrahami Patriarchae Liber Iezirah.*[7] Then, on 6 January 1552 Postel suffered a defining experience—his *Immutation.* Mother Joanna returned to him, purified his body, and infused her spirit into his very bones. He became a new man, his reason restored to pre-lapsarian clarity, his spiritual body a white garment. Whatever the experience was, it now drove Postel into a frenzy of evangelism. He had the power of Christ within him, the indwelling of the Shechinah. He was the Firstborn of the Fourth Age, the Son born of the New Adam (Christ) and the New Eve (Mother Joanna).

Postel plunged into activity, but his message, perhaps not surprisingly, was not welcomed. He travelled to Basle and then back to Venice where he worked on Syriac New Testament manuscripts with Moses of Mardin. In 1554 he was in Vienna where he provided mystical, philological and typographical assistance to J. A. Widmanstetter and Moses of Mardin in the production of the 1555 *editio princeps* of the Syriac New Testament. The story of the production of this remarkable Syriac New Testament has been told elsewhere, but two points may be stressed here: first, that that project is itself to be understood in the context of Postel's kabbalistic and personal convictions; and second, that it provided Postel with invaluable experience in the preparation of such an edition.[8] But before the Vienna *editio princeps* appeared, Postel left Vienna abruptly in May 1554 apparently to go to Venice to stop his books being put on the Index. In Venice he was imprisoned by the

---

[6] *Loc. cit.* pg 581.
[7] W. P. Klein, *Sefer Jezirah ubersetzt und kommentiert von Guillaume Postel* (Frommann-Holzboog, Stuttgart-Bad Cannstatt 1994).
[8] For this see again my *Orientalism, Aramaic and Kabbalah in the Catholic Reformation. The first printing of the Syriac New Testament* (E. J. Brill, Leiden 2007).

Inquisition and incarcerated. On 17 September 1555 he was declared both heretical and insane. Paul IV had been consulted and Postel was moved to the papal prison of Ripetta. He did not emerge until the death of the pontiff on 18 August 1559 when the College of Cardinals freed everyone held in the papal prisons lest they be burned by the angry mobs that attacked the prisons on the death of the unpopular pope. Postel clearly blamed Paul IV for his imprisonment and saw the pontiff's death as a punishment for his resistance to Postel's prophecies. Previously in 1547, François I had died after receiving a personal prophetic message from Postel and Postel interpreted his death as a similar reward for incredulity.[9]

Paul IV had earlier issued upon his election in July 1555 a proclamation that placed severe restrictions upon Jews.[10] As a result of this Postel was to share his prison with Benjamin Nehemia of Civitanova whose diary records life in the papal prison.[11] We learn that Postel both recited the Psalter and prayed in Hebrew. The Pope was to authorise the burning of Hebrew books in Rome in 1559 and this was carried out by Cardinal Ghislieri, the future Pius V. The burning of the Talmud in Rome in 1553 was a symbol of the change from the atmosphere of the High Renaissance to one of suspicion of Hebrew learning and the cause of the departure of Masius and Moses from Rome. We may register here the perpetuation in Rome in subsequent years of that same anti-Judaism that was naturally inimical to an orientalism celebrating Jewish arcana.[12]

---

[9] Kuntz, *Postel*, pg 124 and pg 129.

[10] Kuntz, *Postel*, pg 130. For heightened fear of Jewish marrano espionage at the time of the Cyprus War: B. Pullan, *op. cit.*, pg 19 and 184ff.

[11] F. Secret "Benjamin Nehemia ben Elnathan et G. Postel à la prison de Ripetta en 1559" Revue des Études juives CXXIV (1965) pg 174–176. Also D. Kaufmann "Die Verbrennung der talmudischen Litteratur in der Republik Venedig" Jewish Quarterly Review (original series) XIII pg 533–538.

[12] See: F. Secret "Postel, temoin de la destruction des Talmuds à Rome en 1559" Bibliothèque de Humanisme et Renaissance XXIII (1961) pg 358–9 who cites Bibliothèque nationale fonds 3401 f. 66–68v. Though reflecting the almost inevitable Christian bias against the Talmud, the passage also describes Postel's appreciation of Judaism and is given explicit and helpful treatment, supplemented by other sources, in Kuntz, pg 130–135. Postel imagined a new Christian Judaism, as necessary for Christians as for Jews, consistent with the revelation to Moses and the *Shekinah*, or Christ, in every man. This religion he called Sabbathianism and Postel evidently expected it to take off sometime after 1566. It is perhaps not surprising that he did not get on with the Pope. On Postel's Sabbathianism, see: B. McGinn "Cabalists and Christians: Reflections on Cabala in Medieval and Renaissance Thought" in eds. R. H. Popkin and

In the year of his release from Ripetta, Postel brought out the first printed Aramaic text of the *Zohar* with Vincenzo Conti at Cremona as the printer. Though 1559 had been a difficult year for all Jewish books with Cardinal Ghislieri burning Hebrew books in Rome, Postel had persuaded Rabbi Basola of Ancona that the book should be set first in Aramaic. Postel thereafter worked hard for the printing of his Latin version, but Oporinus, the Basle printer with whom he placed the work, was never persuaded to do it.[13] Nevertheless, the *Zohar* remained of the first importance for Postel, because, as we have seen, it proved all the mysteries revealed by Mother Joanna—especially the Second Coming of Christ in the female person—previously overlooked by Jews and Christians alike.[14]

From Cremona Postel went to Basle, but did not apparently meet Oporinus who may well have been trying to avoid him. Baron Paumgartner was kind to Postel and offered to repurchase from Ottheinrich of Heidelberg, on the latter's death, books which Postel in his poverty had previously sold him: Postel had to send Paumgartner in return other books then in Paris.[15] Postel's eagerness to be reunited with his books is of course connected with his eschatological timetable and the pressing need to publish them. Ironically the Calvinists would end up publishing them.[16]

After six months Postel returned to Venice. Thence, by way of Trent where the Council was in its closing stages and in fear of attacks by Flacius Illyricus he went to Ausburg but was unable to rendezvous with Paumgartner.[17] Then he moved through Germany to France. He was on the run, fearing further charges and imprisonment, and without mate-

---

G. W. Weiner, *Jewish Christians and Christian Jews. From the Renaissance to the Enlightenment* (Kluwer Academic, Dordrecht 1994).

[13] See Kuntz, *Postel* pg 136–137 for the *Zohar* and Postel's two translations neither of which was ever printed. Also A. Rotondo, *Studi e ricerche di storia ereticale* pg 127–147. On Postel's translation of Bahir, Rotando, *op. cit.*, pg 139 and F. Secret "Un Manuscrit retrouvé" Bibliothèque de Humanisme et Renaissance XXV (1973) pg 87–97.

[14] *Le prime Nove* Gii v–G iii.

[15] See: F. Secret "La Correspondance de Guillaume Postel. Une lettre au Baron Paumgartner" Bibliothèque de Humanisme et Renaissance XXV (1963) pg 212–215. Also ibid: "Une lettre à Oporin (1553)" pg 216–221. Reference is made to this at Lossen pg 351–352 (A letter to Masius September 1563).

[16] For the publishing of these Postel manuscripts in Heidelberg see: R. J. Wilkinson, "Emmanuel Tremellius' 1569 Edition of the Syriac New Testament" Journal of Ecclesiastical History 58/1 January 2007 pg 9–25.

[17] See Lossen pg 353 (Letter to Masius from Paris 25 November 1563), Kuntz, *op. cit.*, pg 138–139.

rial support, but his arrival in Lyons early in 1562 was to put an end
to his peregrinations. A Lyons lawyer Matthew Antoine accused Postel
of preferring the predestination of Moslems to that of Christians, of
"*Postellisme*", and finally charged him with seducing some three hundred
persons from the true faith and into rebellion.[18] In the intervention of
the governor the charges were dropped and Postel returned to Paris
only to raise new outcry there. Postel wrote an apology against these
charges of Matthew Antoine that is of interest to us in that it indicates
that he had gone to Lyons because he wanted to get his Arabic Gospels
printed there and that he had discussed a polyglot bible with Antoine
Vincent there.[19] In all this he was driven by his own messianic role,
interpreted in the light of the Kabbalah and the pressing timetable
it came to impose upon him. We shall hereafter be following Postel's
determined efforts to produce this polyglot until the Antwerp project
was well underway.

Postel defended his views in Paris before the Parlement and on 12
December 1562 was detained for three months in the Monastery of
St-Martin-des-Champs until his case was decided. In spite of a new
detention order in June 1563, Postel regained his freedom. Complaints
however were renewed and the teacher of universal concord was again
accused of wishing to form a sect and of judaising. Postel addressed a
long letter to Catherine de Medici, but was finally seized in the house
of Joseph Scaliger and permanently confined to the monastery early
in 1564. Postel remained in the monastery until his death in 1581.[20]
His material conditions were no doubt more secure, but his spiritual
existence was to be no less dramatic than before. He was in no way
relieved of his pressing mission, and the miracle of Laon would pre-
cipitate him more than ever into a frenzy of eschatological activity.

The Miracle of Laon

In 1566 Nicole Obry, a young recently married girl of sixteen or so,
was dramatically cured of demonic possession by the sacrament of

---

[18] Kuntz, *op. cit.*, pg 140–1; F. Secret "L'arrestation de Postel à Lyons" Bibliothèque
de Humanisme et Renaissance XXIII (1961) pg 357–359.

[19] *Apologie de Guillaume Postel aulx calumnies d'un qui se dict Docteur en loix nomme Matthieu
D'Antoine* Bibliothèque nationale fonds latin 3402 f.26 cited in Kuntz, *op. cit.*, pg 141.

[20] F. Secret "Les Détensions de Postel à Saint-Martin-des-Champs" Bibliothèque
de Humanisme et Renaissance XXII (1960) pg 555–557.

the eucharist in Laon. The publicly staged miracle was part of the Catholic reaction to the Edit d'Amboise of 19 March 1563 whereby Charles IX and Catherine de Medici began their second attempt at a moderate confessional *politique de bascule*. The miracle was celebrated as of the first significance by Postel in *De summopere* of 1566 and also by a pupil of Postel, the professor Jean Boulaese in *Le Miracle de Laon* of the same year.[21]

Postel used the *De summopere* to claim the miracle as a vindication of all his teaching: it showed clearly, he thought, that 1566 marked the beginning of the restitution of all things. And on the eve of that great sabbath it was necessary to convert the Moors, and for that an Arabic bible was needed. Jean Boulaese had copied out Postel's *Thresor des propheties de l'univers* in 1564–1565.[22] Chapter XXXV is entitled: *"Qu'il fault que les Ismaelites recoyvent de la mesme gent Gomerike le souverain benefice de l'Euangile en la langue arabike, pour approuuer les raisons sus exposées comme aussi les Israelites et faulx Hebreux"* and showed Postel's long-standing prophetic expectation that France would evangelise the Moslems. But the French royal family was hardly supportive at the time, and so Postel, in a move of decisive importance for the history of the Antwerp

---

[21] Mme A. H. Chaubard, *Le miracle de Laon en Launoys, representé au vif et escript en latin françoys, espagnol et allemand. A Canbray, chees Pierre Lombard 1566* (*Jean Boulaese*) (Sauvegarde historique, Lyons 1955) (this is a facsimile with introduction) was the first to notice the connection between the Boulaese text and the Antwerp Polyglot. Thereafter see F. Secret "Documents pour servir à la histoire de la publication de la Bible d'Anvers" Revista da Sefarad XVIII (1958) pg 121–128 and "L'Opuscule de G. Postel sur le miracle de Laon" Bibliothèque de Humanisme et Renaissance XXVIII (1966) pg 399–405 with documents that show the importance of the Eucharist for Postel. There is a very full treatment of the miracle and the texts in I. Backus, *Le Miracle de Laon* (J. Vrin, Paris 1994) which is now the standard treatment and to which the reader is referred for further details. However both Secret and Backus herself at this time believed that the *De summopere* and *Le Miracle de Laon* were essentially a single work. They are shown to be separate in her subsequent edition *Guillaume Postel et Jean Boulaese De Summopere (1566) et Le Miracle de Laon (1566)* (Droz, Geneva 1995) which I have used above. Secret, *opera cit.* showed that Boulaese was the amanuensis of Postel during his detention at St-Martin-des-Champs. In 1564–1565 he copied the *Thresor ou recueil des propheties de l'univers* that Postel wrote to promote his Angelic Papacy and King of France's role at the head of the Universal Empire. He informed Postel about the miracle, and placed the brochure in five languages in Philip's hands in Madrid when he obtained the promise of money for the Polyglot. Jean Boulaese was ordained priest in 1565 and was Professor of Hebrew and then Principal of the Collège de Montaigu. M. Kuntz, *Postel* pg 143–162 quite erroneously considers Boulaese to be a pseudonym of Postel.

[22] ed. Secret, *Postel, Thresor des propheties de l'univers* (M. Nijhoff, La Haye 1969) pg 163. See pg 6–7 for the two copies we have of this work. The second was made by Guy Lefèvre de la Boderie.

Polyglot, turned to solicit the help of the King of Spain.[23] He did not however send Philip his *De summopere*, which continued to celebrate the French role (and the election of the Low Countries), although it now acknowledged Philip II as a chief of the Gaulish Church, a direct descendant of Noah, and potentially universal monarch. Rather he sent the much briefer presentation of his message *Le Miracle de Laon* with its polyglot presentation of a short text in five different languages. The approach was thus internationalist and Postel's aspirations for the throne of France tactfully suppressed.

Jean Boulaese described the incarcerated Postel's successful attempt to interest Philip II in a polyglot bible in his *Hebraicum Alphabetum* of 1576:[24] "On 5 May 1567 in Madrid we sought as suppliants by word and writing 30,000 gold coins from the good Catholic King Philipp of Spain for an edition of the Complutensian Polyglot with an Arabic version and we obtained from his lips this which Montano, sent by the same king for this fine purpose, Rephalengius and the brothers Guy and Nicolas Lefèvre de la Boderie have achieved by common endeavour in bringing out that Bible *chez* Plantin."[25]

---

[23] Postel's treatise *De ce qui est premier pour reformer le monde* of 1569 (conveniently in C.-G. Dubois, *Celtes et Gaulois au XVIe siècle* pg 170–171) gives evidence of this new enthusiasm for Spain: "...*nous esleverons icy l'estendart Israelogalique ou Celtibérique (i.e. Spanish) telement qu'en tout l'univers s'espandra la Farine et l'Huylle ainsi que l'Espirit et Vertu d'Elie Multipliée que tout l'univers en Vivra et sera la Gaule et Israel, ou la Celtibérie (i.e. Spain) partout estendue.*"

[24] On this work: I. Backus, *Le Miracle de Laon* pg 87, also 45–46. The work proposes a quick method to learn the *lingua omnium prima* relying very much on Postel's *Compendiaria grammatices introductio ad brevissime demonstrandum*...Paris 1552, a flysheet, of which Boulaese brought out a longer edition in 1566. This work is discussed in W. P. Klein, *Am Anfang war das Wort. Theorie- und Wissenschaftsgeschichtliche Elemente frühennuzeitlichen Sprachbewusstseins* (Berlin 1992) pg 82–92 and 263–280. It is reproduced in F. Secret ed. *Guillaume Postel (1510–1581) et son interprétation du "Candélabre de Moyse"* pg 437. After Postel, Boulaese describes the Hebrew script as made up from '*Punctus, Linea et Superficies*' which correspond to vowels, accents and consonants and, inevitably, the persons of the Holy Trinity. Postel's remarks about the mystic yod are however omitted. The cosmological significance of the twenty-two letters of the alphabet is stressed: '...*Unde merito illi antiqui Hebraeorum Theologi dicunt, maxime Zohar, mundum esse fabricatum viginti duabus literis...*' (2 col. A). Though Hebrew was affected by the Fall, it has since been restored by Christ and whosoever now pronounces it with its accents "*totam elementarem et coelestem et supramundanam harmoniam repraesentat*" (3 col. B).

[25] '...*quinto die Maii, anni domini 1567, Madrici, in Complutentium Bibliorum editionem cum Arabica versione triginta aureorum milia a bono illo D. Philippo, Hispaniarum rege catholico, et ore et scripto, nomine reipublicae supplices postulavimus et eius ore tum obtinuimus, quae ab eodem illo ipso missus in hunc finem optimum d. Benedictus Arias Montanus Hispalensis, Franciscus Raphelengius*

Here then is the claim, essential to our argument, that Jean Boulaese's trip to Spain was instrumental in interesting Philip II in what was evidently presented to him as an improved re-edition of the Complutensian Polyglot.[26] In 1578, seven years after the publication of the Antwerp Polyglot, Boulaese recounted the same story to Gregory XIII in the Preface to the *Thresor*, though pointing out that, after all, the Antwerp Polyglot had not had an Arabic text: '…and we placed [an account of] this miracle [i.e. of Laon] into the hands of the Catholic Prince, King Philipp of Spain, from whom and in the name of the commonweal we sought and he promised to give to that same commonweal thirty thousand gold coins for a printing of the Complutensian Bible with an Arabic version for the conversion of the Moors or Turks (who are Hamites or Ismaelites). Thus a bible in Hebrew, Aramaic, Greek, Latin, and, in the New Testament, Syriac has been printed by Plantin, but we are still awaiting the Arabic version. But you are said, Most Holy Father, to be undertaking that truly pontifical task in Rome and to be the man worthy of doing so first.'[27]

This claim of Boulaese and, of course, of Postel to have sought to promote the cause of the Antwerp Polyglot, and particularly of an Arabic Bible, by the small similarly polyglot pamphlet Boulaese placed in the hands of the King of Spain 5 May 1567 is essential to understanding the genesis of the Antwerp Polyglot. We need not imagine that Philip saw matters quite in their light to appreciate the motivation of Postel and his friends as they raced to produce the Polyglot that their eschatologi-

---

Aluetanus et Guido et Nicolaus Fabricii Boderani fratres collato studio effecerunt in illis Bibliis edendis apud Plantinum.'

[26] On this trip Chaubard, *Le miracle de Laon en Launoys* pg 16–18.

[27] '…*et dedimus hoc Miraculum in manus Catholici domini Philippi regis Hispaniarum, a quo et nomine Reipublicae in conversionem Maurorum sive Turcharum, qui sunt Chamitae et Ismaelitae, petivimus et se daturum eidem reipublicae pollicitus est triginta aureorum millia in Complutensium Bibliorum impressisonem cum Arabica versione. Unde Biblia hebraice, chaldaice, graece et latine, ut et Novum Testamentum syriace iam impressa sunt apud Plantinum sed Arabicam versionem adhuc expectamus. Diceris autem, sanctissime pater, hoc ipsum Romae efficere opus vere pontificium et te hominum primo dignum* (8v)' Similarly he wrote 20 May 1575 (Thresor pg 724) again of his efforts in August and September of 1566: "*Ubi (Paris) statim sumptu alieno quinque linguis edidi horum Epitomen, quam in manus Catholicorum Philippi regis et Elisabethae reginae Hispaniarum dedi.*" In this passage he says he had the same résumé printed at Avignon and Lyons in French *alone* for presentation to Charles IX in Paris! See I. Backus, *Le Miracle de Laon* pg 97–100, 111–114. For Boulaese's subsequent but unsuccessful attempts to interest Gregory XIII in his Arabic bible project at a time when the pope was much taken up with the Jesuits and their work, see: I. Backus, *Le Miracle de Laon* pg 93–95.

cal timetable demanded. They failed completely to produce a printed Arabic bible. The task would eventually fall to Thomas Erpenius and Dutch Protestants, scholars quite out of sympathy with Postel's apocalyptic notions.[28] But the rest of their project bore fruit.

---

[28] On Erpenius who first produced an Arabic New Testament: ed. F. de Nave, *Philologia Arabica* pg 139–169 with bibliography and pg 155 for the Arabic New Testament of 1616. Also: A. Hamilton, *William Bedwell the Arabist (1563–1632)* (Sir Thomas Browne Institute, Leiden 1985) pg 12, 24–35, 80–83 again with bibliography.

CHAPTER FIVE

THE NORTHERN SCHOLARS:
GUY LEFÈVRE DE LA BODERIE

Guy Lefèvre de la Boderie was a pupil of Postel and in a sense became his representative in the production of the Antwerp Polyglot. Subsequent to his work on the Antwerp Polyglot, he edited another edition of the Syriac New Testament in Paris in 1584. After we have considered Guy's contribution to the Antwerp Polyglot and considered that bible and its fate in some detail, we shall finally turn to trace the continuity in world-view and scholarship between Guy's two editions, the Antwerp Polyglot and that of 1584, and to observe the afterlife of Postel's kabbalistic legacy even beyond his death.

The progressive editing and publishing of de la Boderie's works and a steady growth in academic interest in him and his work, however, increasingly enable us to appreciate him in his own right and not merely as an *épigone* of Postel and more exactly to contextualise his two editions of the Syriac New Testament.[1]

Guy was born in the family home near Montgommery in Normandy in 1541.[2] He had seven brothers and a sister, Anne, who entered religion. His brother Antoine followed a diplomatic career and was ambassador for Henri IV in Rome, Brussels and at the Court of

---

[1] F. Roudaut, *Le Point centrique contribution à L'Étude de Guy Lefèvre de la Boderie (1541–1598)* (Klincksieck, Paris 1992) pg 13–20 for a brief summary of academic interest in Guy. This work has a systematic bibliography of Guy's works pg 239–246 that allows me to refer to them only by short titles below. His 1993 edition of *La Galliade (1582)* (Klincksieck, Paris 1993) has contributed enormously to the accessibility and intelligibility of Guy. R. Gorris's splendid edition of *Diverses Meslanges Poetiques* was published in the same year by Droz in Geneva. Roudaut also edited *Poésie encyclopédique et Kabbale chrétienne Onze études sur Guy Lefèvre de La Boderie* (Champion, Paris 1999) the papers from the first conference dedicated to Guy held in Rouen 31 May–1 June 1995. These four volumes constitute a serviceable summary of the state of studies on Guy at present.

[2] For the most recent biographic sketches see F. Roudaut, *Le Point centrique contribution* pg 27–58 and R. Gorris ed., *Diverses Meslanges Poetiques* pg 15–35. A delightful history of the family was written by [H. Le Comte de] La Ferrière-Percy, *Les La Boderie. Études sur une famille normande* (Aubrey, Paris 1857: Slatkine Reprints, Geneva 1969). F. Neve wrote "Guy Lefèvre de la Boderie, orientaliste et poète" in Revue Belge et Étrangère XIII (1862) pg 363–372, 413–433, 679–697. The family chateau still stands in the commune of Sainte-Honorine-la-Chardonne (Athis-De-L'Orne).

King James, London.[3] Another brother, Nicolas, was to share Guy's oriental interests and they worked together on the Antwerp Polyglot.[4] Guy studied mathematics and philosophy at the university in Caen in 1556. He made friends to whom he would later dedicate poems, and learned to reject profane poetry for a 'useful' poetry that drew upon the Ancients to illumine modern consciences.[5] At this point he composed the first seven 'circles' of his poem *L'Encyclie* published in 1571 by Plantin. With this production Guy clearly distanced himself from the teaching of the university that was strongly inspired by Erasmus.[6] When he left Normandy for Paris at the age of twenty, Guy was equipped with several fundamental convictions that would not change: he was a reformist Catholic; he was a poet who sought a unification of religion and politics; he was already a linguist, but one for whom languages were a means to an end—the appropriation of the wisdom of ancient sources of diverse provenance in furtherance of his ambitiously broad vision of human significance.[7]

It was from 1563–1568 in Paris at the Collège Trilingue that Guy learned Hebrew. Gilbert Génébrard was at the Collège at the time: no doubt his support of Guy's Syriac New Testament against that of Tremellius is partially explicable by this early acquaintance.[8] To his Hebrew he added Syriac, learning the language without Grammar or Dictionary—αὐτοδίδακτος καὶ Θεοδίδακτος ('self-taught and taught

---

[3] La Ferrière-Percy, *Les La Boderie* pg 29–98.

[4] La Ferrière-Percy, *Les La Boderie*. Pg 26 indicated that after his return from work on the Polyglot to France c.1570, Nicolas published some philological works, but then took up arms under the Maréchal de Bellegarde. Nicolas published a translation of Pico's *Heptaplus* in 1578, following Guy's translation of Georges of Venice (see below) for which he wrote the Preface. He also wrote: *Ad Nobiliores Linguas Communi Methodo Componendas Isagoge: cui accessi, De literarum Hebraicarum laudibus Oratio. Authore Nicolao Fabricio Boderiano Δευτέρας Φροντίδης σφωτέρας Parisiis, Steph. Prevosteau 1588.*

[5] F. Roudaut, *Le Point centrique contribution* pg 31 for *inter alios* Charles Toustain de La Mazurie (1530?–1590). For his connections with Postel, J.-F. Maillard "Postel et ses disciples normands" in *Guillaume Postel 1581–1981* (Guy Trédaniel, Paris 1985) pg 83–91.

[6] F. Roudaut, *Le Point centrique* pg 32.

[7] *Ibid.*, pg 30 for speculations about the origins of Guy's knowledge of Hebrew.

[8] A. Lefranc, *Histoire du Collège de France* (Hachette, Paris 1893) pg 177 and 381. I have discussed Génébrard's quarrel with Tremellius in R. J. Wilkinson, "Emmanuel Tremellius 1569 Edition of the Syriac New Testament" Journal of Ecclesiastical History 58/1 January 2007 pg 9–25.

by God').[9] This remark in the preface to the 1584 Syriac New Testament probably indicates that he thought his linguistic facility a sign of a providential role. Guy would probably not have heard Postel teach publicly: he had by order of the Parlement of Paris 29 January 1564 been confined to the Monastery of Saint-Martin-des-Champs, as we have seen. But they did meet, and this meeting was formative for Guy's development.[10] Guy and his brother became friends of Postel. Just as Boulaese who in 1564–1565 copied out Postel's *Thresor ou recueil des propheties de l'univers* (which we recall was written in support of Postel's Angelic Papacy and France's right by primogeniture to World Empire), Guy did the same in 1566.[11] A note in his *Dictionarium* indicates his intention to bring out a new edition of Postel's *Candelabri typici* that first appeared in Venice in 1548.[12] After the printer Oporinus in Basle failed to return the manuscripts of his first translation of the *Zohar*, Postel entrusted his second translation of the *Zohar* to Guy.[13] Most importantly

---

[9] Preface to his 1584 New Testament pg XVII: *"Cum enim Hebraicae Regiis professoribus tuis Lutetiae Parisiorum ad aliquot menses operam impendissem, illico me ad rudimenta linguae Syriacae contuli, ex quibus literas dignoscere ac pingere didici tantum: necdum enim extabat grammatica neque dictionarium ullum; postea Novo Testamento Syro Viennae impresso exscribendo & vertendo animum appuli."* A copy of Widmanstetter's *Syriacae linguae...prima elementa* (bound with Postel's annotated copy of Teseo's *Introductio*) and left to Guy in the will of Bartholomaeus Grivellus, B.N. (Rés. X. 701) is described by Secret "Notes sur Guillaume Postel" Bibliothèque de Humanisme et Renaissance XXVIII (1966) pg 691–701 pg 698. Secret places Guy's acquisition of this book after the time remembered in the passage above: "Guy Le Fèvre de La Boderie représentant de Guillaume Postel à la Polyglotte d'Anvers" De Gulden Passer XLIV (1966) pg 245–257 pg 247. Guy continues, *ibid.*: *"Huius autem sacrosanctae linguae amplificandae gratia me fausto quodam sidere genuit Natura. Id enim de me citra jactantiam ausim profiteri, in ea addiscenda nullum habuisse praeceptorem, ne in literis quidem pingendis & dignoscendis, sed in ea me plane esse αὐτοδίδακτος και Θεοδίδακτος, ut de se lingua Graeca Budaeus praedicare non erubuit."* Later he speaks of: *"divino tamen adiuvante gratia"*.

[10] Their names appear together for the first time (though Postel's is discreetly reduced to initials) at the end of the poem prefacing Charles de Bourgueville *L'Athéomachie et discours de l'immortalité de l'âme* (Martin Le Jeune, Paris 1564) see: R. Gorris ed. *Diverses Meslanges Poetiques* pg 18–19 for details. For Guy's marginalia in kabbalistic works which evoke Postellian themes: F. Secret, *Les Kabbalistes chrétiens* pg 193–200 where there is a full but succinct summary of Guy as a pupil of Postel. F. Secret "Guy Le Fèvre de la Boderie représentant de G. Postel à la Polyglotte d'Anvers" De Gulden Passer XLIV (1966) pg 245–257 also offers an account of Guy's presentation of Postel's notions.

[11] F. Secret, *L'Esotérisme de Guy Le Fèvre de La Boderie* (Droz, Geneva 1969) pg 17. However in 1974 Secret was more hesitant about this: Bibliothèque de Humanisme et Renaissance XXXVI (1974) pg 67 n. 1.

[12] *"...in candelebro hebraice Venetiis impreso, quod et nos Deo dante auctum et illustratum propediem in lucem emittemus."*

[13] F. Secret, *L'Esotérisme* pg 25.

for us, at the same time as he was learning from Postel, Guy was working on his Syriac New Testament and completed it in 1567.[14]

The miracle of Laon took place on 8 February 1566. Whilst it is strictly true that there is not the attention given to this event in Guy's works as there is in Postel's, we have already explored the importance of the event in Postel's eschatology and Boulaese's mission to Philip II. Guy's New Testament was to be part of the realisation of Postel's missionary strategy.[15]

Postel sent Guy's translation to Plantin at the beginning of March 1568 and also sent it to Masius.[16] Jean Porthaise, *ligueur*, praised passages in the translation in a letter to the printer 22 June 1568.[17] Postel having reassured his correspondents that Guy was Catholic, Plantin summoned Guy and his brother Nicolas to Antwerp.[18]

Guy's arrival was announced to Masius on 26 December 1569, though his precise date of arrival is not known.[19] In another letter of 27 February 1570 Plantin assured Masius of Guy's humility with respect to Masius, and told him that he was discussing his version with

---

[14] *Ad Sacrarum Linguarum Studiosum Lectorem...Praefatio* vii. r: *"Octodecim mensium spatio Novi Testamenti Characteres Syriacos in characteres Hebraicos mutavi, et sermonis Syriaci in sermonem latinum conversionem ante annos tres, anno videlicet domini 1567, absolvi."*

[15] I disagree therefore with F. Roudaut, *Le Point centrique* pg 37 who discounts the miracle as of any great significance for Guy and also excludes the mission to Philip II from his following account of the Polyglot pg 38–39. The miracle was clearly significant for Postel's, Boulaese's and, I would argue, Guy's view of the Polyglot. It was the sign that confirmed the urgency of the Polyglot project that we shall see Guy continued to press Henri III to support and expand even after Postel's death.

[16] Postel recommended Guy to Masius 4 March 1568 (Chaufpié III pg 232): *"Juvenis & supra aetatem doctus laborisque omnino patientissimus et concordiaeque mundi procurandae, cui uni rei insisto iam totis fere 25 annis, admodum idoneus, quem etiam in filii charissimique discipuli loco habeas."* To Theodore Zwinger Postel wrote 19 November 1572 (F. Secret "Notes sur Guillaume Postel: XI: Quatorze lettres à Théodore Zwinger" Bibliothèque de Humanisme et Renaissance XXVI (1964) pg 120–153, pg 134.): *"Unus ex meis praefuit editioni tam Thargumi totius quam Syriaci Novi Testamennti. Nomen eius vobis nondum innotuit. Est enim juvenis admodum et etiam fratre juniore praeditus (Huic Nicolao, seniori autem Guidoni fabricio nomen est) qui ita callet linguam christianam illam ut si auditor uterque Christi docentis fuisset. Sic fungor vice cotis et qui veritate non valeo, occasione, ut dicebat Paulus* (Philippians 1. 18) *doceo."* The letter to Masius accompanying the translation is dated 17 March 1568 at Antwerp (C.P.III pg 39 #354): *"Monseigneur. Ceste sera seulement pour vous adresser l'incluse que j'aye reçue de Monsieur Postel lequel m'a envoyé avec les 4 evangelistes & actes des apostres transcrits des caractères siriens es hebraiques & translatés en latin aussi par un nommé Guido Fabricius ou Faber & promect de m'envoyer de bref les episodes de Sainct Paul & autre reste dud. Nouveau Testament."*

[17] C.P.III pg 42 # 356. On Porthaise: F. Secret, *L'ésotérisme* pg103 n. 154.

[18] C.P.I pg 252 #116 to Zayas, March 1568; C.P.I pg 270 #123 to Cardinal Granvelle (Archbishop of Malines and representative of Philip II) I May 1568.

[19] C.P.III pg 52 #359 previously cited.

the censors at Louvain.[20] In 1570 Guy worked on his *Dictionarium*, and Plantin wrote repeatedly to Masius insisting that Guy was no rival.[21] Having seen that Plantin had probably originally intended that Masius should take a large part in the project, but subsequently was persuaded that Masius's reputation for heterodoxy prohibited this, we can perhaps understand his delicacy in handling Masius's sensitivities. We shall subsequently consider Guy's work on the Polyglot in detail and also thereafter examine his 1584 Paris edition of the Syriac New Testament. Before that however we must return to the Antwerp Polyglot and its printer, Plantin.

---

[20] C.P.III pg 58 #361 previously cited.
[21] C.P.III pg 63–64 #362 1 August 1570 previously cited and #364 22 October 1570.

CHAPTER SIX

PLANTIN AND THE ANTWERP PROJECT

At the time of the Antwerp Polyglot, Christophe Plantin, the Antwerp printer, had considerable experience not only of producing bibles, but also of producing bibles in exotic type. He had printed a Latin bible in 1559, a duodecimo Greek New Testament in 1564 and a Hebrew bible in three different formats at the end of 1566.[1] The Latin and Hebrew texts were used in producing the text for the Polyglot. It had in fact been Postel who had persuaded Plantin in 1563 to establish a Hebrew press like Bomberg's in Venice.[2] Postel had, it seemed, hoped that after the Venetian ban on printing Hebrew was lifted in 1563, his Arabic Gospels might have found a printer there. His subsequent frustration appears to have been instrumental in bringing Plantin to print oriental scripts: a point perhaps that deserves some emphasis, and underlines again just how important Postel was in promoting oriental typography.

---

[1] For Plantin's Bibles: C de Clercq "Les Éditions bibliques, liturgiques et canoniques de Plantin" De Gulden Passer XXXIV (1956) pg 157–92. The Latin bible was a copy of Gravius's 1547 Louvain Vulgate after the recension of Jean Henten. This was probably the best critical edition available at the time. See: C. Clair, *Christopher Plantin* pg 59–60 and pg 255. Plantin added to this the division into verses that Estienne had introduced in his Vulgate of 1555. (The first division of the sacred text into verses appears in Sante Pagnino's Latin version Lyons 1528.) The Hebrew octavo text had vowel points and accents which had been omitted in the Complutensian Polyglot. Plantin's oriental types are described in: H. M. Parker, K. Melis, H. D. L. Vervliet "Typographica Plantiniana: Early inventories of punches, matrices, and moulds in the Plantin-Moretus archives" De Gulden Passer XXXVIII (1960) pg 1–139. See particularly pg 33, 38 (Payments to Granjon) 48, 66.

[2] Lossen pg 351–3; Chaufpié III pg 227 230 (A letter from Postel September 1563 to Masius): *"Sed vero, ut a Plantino intellexi, res est adhuc multa difficultate implicata, antequam possit rursus institui hebraica illa officina, qualis fuit Venetiis, et multo difficilior, antequam arabica possit institui."* The letter indicates that Postel had hoped to get his Arabic Gospels printed in Venice. We may recall that the ban on Hebrew printing was lifted in Venice in 1563. See Amram, *The Makers of Hebrew Books in Italy* pg 338ff. Plantin had brought a copy of Sante Pagnino's *Lexicon hebraicum* from Jérôme Marnef the Parisian bookseller in September 1563. He had Joannes Isaac, a converted German Rabbi, revise it in his house until October 1564. A Hebrew Grammar under Isaac's name came out in 1564.

On February 26 1566 Plantin wrote to Masius, as we have seen, and for the first time there was explicit mention of a Polyglot. He already had some funds: *"et desjà ay je trouvé qui veulent y employer 3000 escus."* Masius we have already had himself been speaking of such a project since 1554.[3] In the spring of 1566 Plantin set up and printed some specimen sheets that he took to the Frankfurt Fair. He was well placed at this point to proceed with the support of Masius for the Syriac and Targum. His son-in-law François de Raphelengien had produced the Hebrew bibles of 1566, and he had Corneille Kiel, Antoine Spitaels, and Théodore Kemp as correctors for the Latin and Greek. The specimen sheets indicate that the types (but not the Syriac) were already cut and in order, and indeed Plantin stated as much in his letter to Zayas of 19 December 1566 mentioned below.[4] The project was ready before Montano arrived.

Evidently a similar project had been afoot in Germany, where the Lutheran Johannes Draconites had been working at Wittenberg on plans for an edition of the bible in Hebrew, Aramaic, Greek, Latin and German that was to be paid for by Augustus, Elector of Saxony. Draconites's death 18 April 1566 had however terminated the project just before Plantin appeared at Frankfurt.[5] At the September Fair in Frankfurt later that year the Duke of Saxony warmly encouraged Plantin: he had renounced his own project on seeing Plantin's sheets in the spring, although he had already *'déboursé quelques grand nombre de daldres pour faire les préparations de telle ouvrage.'* The City of Frankfurt was also prepared to finance the project if Plantin took up residence there. From Heidelberg, the Elector Palatine, Ottheinrich, who had obtained Postel's manuscripts and attracted Tremellius to Heidelberg in 1561

---

[3] See above: Lossen pg 172#140, J. Perles, *Beiträge* pg 229.

[4] Brief summary on the types: C. Clair, *Christopher Plantin* pg 65. Robert Granjon cut the Syriac type and the punches and matrices are still in the Plantin-Moretus Museum. See also letter 28 July 1569 from Postel to Plantin *'de Syriaca typosyna'* Supplement à la *Correspondance de Christophe Plantin* pg 111–112. Postel's suggestion of the Peshitta in Hebrew characters mentioned 1 October 1567 shows, I assume, that the Syriac type was not then ready.

[5] Johannes Drach (1494–1566) published *Proverbia Salomonis. Cum translationibus fontis Ebraici, Chaldaica Graeca, Latina, Germania...* (I. Crato) Wittenberg 1564 (Fol) no doubt as a prospectus for the larger project. One notices that he was unable to include the typographically challenging Syriac or Arabic types: they could not be cut in Germany. Similarly it appears Antoine Rodolphe Le Chevalier, professor of Hebrew at Strasburg was contemplating a four language edition of the bible but died in 1572 without publishing. See: Clair, *op. cit.*, pg 61–62.

(but had not yet seen the first fruits of his investment which would be Tremellius's New Testament of 1569) sought to tempt Plantin to Heidelberg by offering to pay for the printing if only Plantin would reside there.[6] Had he succeeded the face of Heidelberg orientalism may have been very different![7]

But local politics took a decisive turn. After the iconoclast riots in Antwerp in August 1566, the Catholic King, Philip II, put an end to the previous period of tolerance. Plantin's Calvinist partners Corneille and Charles de Bomberge, Goropis Becanus and Jacques de Schotto fled the city. Plantin however wished to remain in Antwerp and save his press. He must have awaited the arrival of the Duke of Alba on 22 August 1567 with trepidation. On 19 December 1566 he wrote his first letter to Gabriel de Zayas soliciting the King's patronage for his polyglot, and pointedly mentioning the interest of other princes in his venture. In what can only be considered a daring public about-turn, he was at pains to emphasise his future loyalty to the King and Catholicism.[8]

Philip II received the printed sheets of the proposed polyglot and considered the plan. He consulted the theologians of Alcalá and Salamanca, including Arias Montano, on the desirability of the project. Montano replied that it would be the glory of the Christian King's reign. The others welcomed the project as the Complutensian Polyglot had been long out of print. They applauded the addition of the whole Targum and of the Syriac New Testament, and suggested that Montano, as an acknowledged expert, should consider the matter in detail.[9] These communications are unfortunately not datable exactly, but we do know that on 5 May 1567 Jean Boulaese placed his pamphlet *Le Miracle de Laon* in the hands of the King and received the promise

---

[6] These approaches are mentioned by Plantin in the crucial letter to Zayas of 19 December 1566 C.P.I pg 48–52 #20.

[7] See my characterisation of Heidelberg orientalism and Tremellius's Syriac New Testament in R. J. Wilkinson, "Emmanuel Tremellius' 1569 Edition of the Syriac New Testament" Journal of Ecclesiastical History 58/1 January 2007 pg 9–25.

[8] "...*comme je suis dédié à imprimer chose catholiques et proffitables à la République chrestienne, je me suis aussi résolu de ne me transporter en autre lieu que sous l'obéissance de la Majesté de nostre Roy catholique auquel j'ay donné le serment de fidélité et de léale obéissance en mains de ses officiers en cest noble et renommé ville d'Anvers.*" (C.P.I pg 48–52) I refrain from listing all the relevant correspondence of Plantin at this time. It is cited in all the standard accounts and readily available in Max Rooses, *Correspondance de Christophe Plantin* (Antwerp 1883; Kraus Reprint, Nendeln-Liechtenstein 1968).

[9] The Antwerp Polyglot is seen consistently in the Spanish sources and by the Louvain censors as a revision and augmentation of the Complutensian Polyglot.

of thirty thousand ducats.[10] At this point, we may consider the royal decision of support in some form effectively taken, and the significance of Postel, his eschatological timetable, and the little pamphlet *Le Miracle de Laon* in the genesis of the Polyglot made clear. At the same time we may also appreciate more fully the context in which the king made his decision: he was not swayed merely by a prophetic word of Postel, but undertook appropriate consultation on what was to be a major project, the success or failure of which would reflect directly upon his own prestige.

Postel had not merely managed the approach to the King. It is clear that he had also both supervised the production of a Syriac New Testament suitable for the Polyglot, and that he was at pains to get this into Plantin's hands. This same year, 1567, Guy Lefèvre de la Boderie, working in Paris under Postel's supervision, completed his eighteen-month project of transcribing the Syriac New Testament into Hebrew letters. He worked from the manuscript Postel had brought back from the East at Bomberg's expense and had used, alongside others, in the *editio princeps* brought out in Vienna under Philip II's uncle, the Emperor Ferdinand, in 1555.[11] He also wrote his Latin translation of the Syriac. In his *Ad Lectorem...Praefatio* (pg 7, no pagination), Guy emphasises that this was a private venture concluded in Paris before he was asked to go to Antwerp.

Postel was in contact with Abraham Ortellius and Plantin in the spring of 1567. On 1 October Plantin told Zayas that Postel had written to him (not that they had ever discussed a polyglot!) suggesting producing a bible that included the Targum and the Syriac New Testament in Hebrew letters.[12] Early in 1568, King Philip's support was formalised through a *cédula* which appointed Montano, and set out the king's financial commitment and procedural instructions. Montano was to be sent to Antwerp '...*a estar presente y asistir en la impression de la dicha Biblia.*' These words should be taken at face value: Montano was not asked to

---

[10] These communications are taken from the manuscripts of the Sparwenfeldt Collection in the Royal Library of Stockholm of which Rekers made first use in his book. Extracts are quoted B. Rekers, *Benito Arias Montano (1527–1598)* pg 140 and 141, but there is no edition and I regret I have not had the opportunity to read these autographs in Stockholm. It may be that close examination of them would bring greater chronological precision here.

[11] For this manuscript see my *Orientalism, Aramaic and Kabbalah in the Catholic Reformation. The first printing of the Syriac New Testament* (E. J. Brill, Leiden 2007).

[12] CP.I pg 186, 190.

undertake or direct the project but *'be present and assist'*.[13] Plantin wrote a suitably ingratiating letter to Montano on 14 February 1568.

At this point the text of the Syriac New Testament came into Plantin's hands. Plantin wrote to Zayas 15 February 1568 saying that he had just received from Postel: *'tout le Nouveau Testament transcrit des anciens charactères syriaque en lettres hébraïques, avec la traduction latine du Nouveau Testament, chose qui à la vérité enrichira merveilleusement l'ouvrage.'*[14] In March 1568 Plantin wrote to Zayas again: *'depuis trois iours en ça, j'ay receu le Nouveau testament transcrit des charactères syriens, peu entendus en charactères hébraïques communs sans toutefois changer un seul mot. Et davantage le version latine du langage syrien, le tout faict par un nommé Guido Fabricius.'*[15] This letter contains Plantin's last mention of the name of Postel in connection with the Syriac New Testament. Postel had supervised its production, and had it delivered to Plantin. Indeed Postel working behind the scenes had been instrumental both in shaping Plantin's aspirations and in gaining royal support for the whole Polyglot project. On the other hand, Postel had been in protective custody for four years, and his reputation as a heretical madman was such that it could only damage the Polyglot. He ceased to be mentioned.

Montano arrived in Antwerp in June 1568. He was evidently enthusiastic about the scholars assembled and appreciative of Plantin's skill.[16] He had initially to effect the King's instruction that the bible contain the Vulgate text. Raphelengius had been emending Sante Pagnino's Latin modern translation and there had initially been no intention of including the Vulgate. Montano compromised diplomatically and

---

[13] The text is in T. Conzales Carvajal, *Elogio histórico español del dr. B. Arias Montano* in Mem. de la Real Acad de la Historia VII 1832 pg 140–144.

[14] C.P.I pg 21. The reference is to the work prepared by Guy mentioned above. We have seen above that Postel had worked on similar transcriptions himself, so it is possible that he provided some assistance.

[15] C.P.I pg 251. Also in the same vein again in March 1568 to Jean Moffin, Philip's chaplain (C.P.I pg 257–258) where Guy is referred to as *'un homme fort sçavant, demeurant à Paris.'* However, writing to Masius 17 March 1568 (C.P.III pg 39–40) he indicates that he in fact received only the Gospels and Acts from Postel and the rest was promised shortly. As Guy claims to have done the work in 1567, perhaps Postel was revising it. C.P.III pg 42–48 is a letter of 22 June 1568 from a Franciscan, F. Joannes Prothesius, who studied oriental languages in Antwerp with books loaned from Plantin. He knew Guy in Paris and had read *'bonam partem versionis eius ex aramaeo testamento in sermonem latinum.'* He proceeded to discuss different translation techniques, and passages of both Hebrew and Syriac well-rendered by Guy. The editors of the letters omit this material as no doubt too boring even for a standard edition.

[16] Rekers, *op. cit.*, pg 141: Letter of Montano to Zayas 23 March 1569.

both versions were included.[17] But the larger question of the Vulgate's authority was not so quickly settled. Montano had now to defend the Polyglot against the reactionary theologians in Spain headed by León de Castro, with whose suspicions of the *judaizantes* we are now familiar. Under such heavy fire, it was understandable that the association of Postel and Masius with the project should be a source of potential embarrassment. Montano, however, was not easily bullied, and his most significant contribution to the Polyglot was his management of the theological battle.[18]

The Spanish scholars at Alcalá who reported to Zayas their opinion of the Polyglot proof-sheets Montano sent them—Pedro Serrano, Ambrosio de Morales and Luís de Estrada—urged caution upon Montano. They advised him that if the Hebrew text was to be incorporated he would run fewer risks if the Pope chose the scholars. (The collaboration of Masius and Guy Lefèvre de la Boderie was, of course, not concealed as now was that of Postel.) The variants appearing from the Targum should be both abbreviated and strongly defended in the Preface.[19] These scholars found so many variants from the text of the Complutensian that they feared that this detail would provide endless opportunities for opposition. But the Antwerp team were in place, even though, as we know, they were hardly to Pius V's taste; the *modus*

---

[17] Additionally in Volume VIII there are twenty-three pages of: *Communes et familiares hebraicae linguae idiotismi, omnibus Bibliorum interpretationibus ac praecipue latinae Xanti Pagnini versioni accomodati, atque ex variis doctorum virorum laboribus et observationibus selecti et explicati.*

[18] That battle has been best told by Rekers, making use of the material he unearthed in Stockholm. In the absence of an edition of Montano's letters, I here follow his account pg 45–69 without further acknowledgement. He gives short extracts from several of the letters in support of his account.

[19] The Targums were being used as messianic readings of the Hebrew Bible, but they were also a witness to the Hebrew text, hence the anxiety expressed by the Alcalá scholars lest variations be inadequately explained. It would seem however that in the case of Esther where both Targums are rich in midrashic material, the text printed in the Antwerp Polyglot is quite different from either. M. H. Goshen-Gottstein "The 'Third Targum' on Esther and Ms. Neofiti I" Biblica LVI (1975) pg 301–329 argues that the Polyglot Esther Targum is in effect an expurgated text with the midrashic material removed (and not therefore a witness to an earlier Targum closer to the Hebrew text). He claims that Zamora's Targum manuscript from the Complutensian Polyglot project (but which was not used in that Bible) shows annotations intended to cut midrashic material out of the Targum to the Prophets, and that the presence of this material (though mostly edited away) was the reason these Targums did not appear in the Complutensian Polyglot. Goshen-Gottstein assumes the Esther cuts were made by Montano. P. Grelot however, Biblia LVI (1975) pg 53–73, considers that the Antwerp Esther Targum is a real unexpurgated Targum.

operandi had been established; and by the time these Spanish scholars got the proofs, of course, the thing had been printed.

Montano was not short of warnings. Luís de León warned Montano on 28 October 1570 that León de Castro had begun a campaign against the as yet unpublished Polyglot, and Montano will not have overlooked the significance of Luís de León's own arrest in 1572. Masius himself urged Montano against gratuitous changes in traditional wording. He sought to keep his name from mention in the preface but Montano was not prepared to do this, and sought rather to praise Masius for his Targum. Montano even had the court grant Masius a gratuity of six hundred guilders and a gold chain for his work. Masius's instincts, however, were right and his collaboration would prove controversial.[20] Guy Lefèvre de la Boderie wrote to Montano about Postel his master, who—whatever had gone before—had, he claimed, retracted his errors and was now orthodox. But he advised sensibly that Postel's collaboration be not mentioned.[21] Montanus was also warned by the Louvain censors Harlemius, Hunnaeus, and Reyneri Goudanus who co-operated closely with him and also sent him their detailed criticisms of the proofs. Their censorship was exceptionally constructive: *inter alia* they pointed out the necessity of including dictionaries and grammar.[22] In the preface

---

[20] Rekers, *op. cit.*, pg 143, Letter of 10 Oct 1568: *'Nosti enim quanti momenti sit vel verbulum unum, praesertim in Pauli epistolis, quod accepta per orbem sententia vel minime discrepet. Et quidem hac temporum diversitate qua tot haereses tam anxie incipiant omnibus occasionibus vetustam ecclesiae consensionem dirrumpendi.'* C.P.III no. 359 pg 51–55 is a letter of 26 December 1569 from Plantin to Masius assuring him that none of his material would go out other than under his own name: he had just received part of the Targum. He mentions Montano's praise of Masius in the *Apparatus Biblicus*. The letter also contains a recommendation of Guy, who he continues: *'...m'ayant communiqué vostre lectre incontinent l'avoir leue, m'a protesté qu'il ne veut aucunement s'attriber le nom de faire autre chose au dictionnaire, dont je vous avois rescrit, chaldaïcque et syriaque, fors que de l'avoir seulement escrit de Munster, de Haruch et des autres et qu'il s'esjoüira grandement, s'il vous plait d'y mectre vostre nom, qui donnera grande auctorité à l'oevre....'*

[21] Rekers, *op. cit.*, pg 143, Letter of 1 July 1571: *'...Tamen vestrae Dominationi morem gerere paratus sum. Sed scrire velim si placet ut euius viri boni cuius consilio votis et opera adiuti fuimus in hac editione honorificam quidem mentionem faciam, sed qud praeceptor meus fuerit aut quod eius censurae commiserim versionem meam, silentio praetermittam ne tali commemmoratione totum opus male audire incipiat.'* This makes Postel's contribution to the Syriac Version clear. For the rest of this interesting letter, see: F. Secret "Guy Lefèvre de la Boderie Représentant de G. Postel à la Polyglotte d'Anvers" De Gulden Passer XLIV (1966) pg 245–257, pg 245–246. For Montano's judgment upon Postel in a letter of 16 February 1568 to Zayas, see pg 246–248.

[22] Masius had evidently warned against the exorbitant costs of dictionaries and grammars, but the King wanted them. And Plantin indicated that he would be grateful for the Syriac grammar before Easter 1570! The letter (C.P.III no. 359 pg 51–55 of

to the fifth volume of the Polyglot Guy Lefèvre de la Boderie wrote
that Harlemius, one of the Louvain censors, had examined the Syriac
version with him word for word for three months and had compared
it with the Greek.[23] These censors advised Montanus not to include his
own treatise *De Arcano Sermone*. Their embarrassment is apparent in the
trivial reasons they suggested for dropping it before getting to the point.
The treatise discusses the difficulties of translating from Hebrew. Were
the simple to learn of the ambiguities inherent in even literal translation, confidence would be undermined.[24] Montanus kept his treatise
in, but they were right. It was severely handled in Rome.

   As we turn then to consider the specifically Syriac parts of the
Polyglot, we should bear in mind the essential continuity between
them and the previous history of Syriac studies. Postel was the driving
force, though in this case much of the work was done by his pupil Guy
Lefèvre de la Boderie working closely with him in Paris.[25] In addition
there was the sympathetic Masius, himself suspected in Rome for his
views on Hebrew and Kabbalah. Neither excessive claims about the
influence of the Family of Love upon the enterprise, nor the Spanish
patronage of the project should be allowed to conceal that continuity.
Indeed in the latter respect we have been able to emphasise appropri-

---

26 December 1569) also indicates that Masius had sent Plantin an Arabic Dictionary.
C.P.III no. 363 pg 63–66 of 27 February 1570 returns to the question of dictionaries
and grammars: for the Aramaic and Syriac Grammars Plantin suggested Caninius's
Institutiones linguarum syriacae, assyriacae et thalmudicae (Paris 1554) which is a grammar of
Aramaic not Syriac, 'Widmanstadius' (*Prima...Elementa*), and whatever Masius could offer.
Fabricius (Guy Lefèvre de la Boderie) had not written a grammar and only Masius was
of the status to write one. As for dictionaries he sought further help from Masius. The
letter is of further interest because Plantin reports that he now has Syriac characters
and will use them in the grammars.

   [23] C.P.III pg 57–59 Plantin to Masius 27 February 1570 informs him that the Louvain
theologians had had Guy's New Testament for six months and that he was currently
conferring with them in Louvain. That they were comparing with the Greek shows
their interest in its textual witness.

   [24] Rekers, *op. cit.*, pg 143, letter of the Censors to Montano 20 August 1570: '*Quod ad
Arcani Sermonis librum attinet, eum post ultimas nostras ad te litteras accuratius multo quam antea
examinavimus, variisque et doctissimis viris legendum dedimus, nec ullus omnino fuit qui eum operi
complutensi addendum putaret. Nam docti cum tanta interpretum copia et textu varietate si habeant
Patrum commentarios facile eo libro carebunt. Indocti vero parum illius lectione ad intelligendum
sacras litteras viderentur*'.

   [25] F. Secret "Guy Lefèvre de la Boderie Représentant de G. Postel à la Polyglotte
d'Anvers" De Gulden Passer XLIV (1966) pg 245–257. The evidence will be discussed
below.

ately the incarcerated Postel's lobbying of the Spanish King through Jean Boulaese and *La Miracle de Laon*. For Postel the Antwerp Polyglot was a part of the same project he had begun in 1536 when during the course of his first Oriental Journey he became convinced of the need for Bibles in Arabic and Syriac.

CHAPTER SEVEN

THE POLYGLOT: THE SYRIAC NEW TESTAMENT AND ASSOCIATED KABBALISTIC MATERIAL

The kabbalistic material found in the apparatuses of Montano has been discussed above and placed in its context within the Spanish tradition of interest in Hebrew and Jewish exegesis. In the following we shall consider the material from our North European Scholars in the Antwerp Polyglot which may be considered as kabbalistic. This material is found primarily in Volume VI with the edition of the Syriac New Testament.

It is important to make clear why the Syriac language and Syriac editions of the New Testament should be treated in this way as privileged vehicles for esoteric speculation.[1] Syriac is a semitic language (in fact, a late dialect of Aramaic) which was held in the sixteenth century to be the language of Christ. As such it was presumed, like Hebrew, to be a particularly efficient carrier of spiritual truths, and in fact the great work of Jewish kabbalah, the Zohar, is written in Aramaic. Syriac arrived in the West at the time of the Fifth Lateran Council and its initial reception was decisively influenced by Cardinal Egidio da Viterbo who was deeply committed to Christian kabbalah, and who valued the Aramaic arcane tradition above the learning of the Greeks. Egidio's writings on the language and the mystical possibilities of Syriac script determined the approach of Teseo Ambrogio whose *Introductio ad Chaldaicam linguam* became the vade-mecum of all subsequent scholars. Teseo met J. A. Widmanstetter, another avid collector and connoisseur of Kabbalah, and gave him a Syriac Gospel manuscript. He also helped Postel with the secrets of cutting type for Syriac. Subsequently Widmanstetter, with help from Postel, published the fine *editio princeps* of the Syriac New Testament in Vienna in 1555. The edition is graced by a fascinating woodcut of the Apostle John receiving the inspiration for his Gospel

---

[1] For a full account of the origins of Syriac study in the West and its kabbalistic content as summarised here, see my *Orientalism, Aramaic and Kabbalah in the Catholic Reformation. The first printing of the Syriac New Testament* (E. J. Brill, Leiden 2007).

which links together both a crucifix and a sephirotic tree, thus neatly
symbolising the confluence of Christian gospel and Jewish mysticism.

The scholars who concerned themselves with Syriac also shared a
prophetic view of the world and its imminent end. The discovery of the
new world in the West and the simultaneous discovery of the new worlds
of oriental languages were for them twinned signs of the approaching
end. Before the end, however, the Gospel would be preached throughout
the world. Arabic achieved its particular importance as the necessary
medium of this final evangelisation and this determined the eagerness
of Postel and others to have an Arabic version in the Polyglot. The
difficulties of cutting moveable type for ligatured script are, however,
considerable and delayed the eventual printing of an Arabic New
Testament. Syriac, however, had been printed and Postel had the necessary linguistic and typographic expertise. Moreover, Syriac was the
language of Christ and His Mother and thus particularly suitable for
conveying spiritual arcana. Nor was it without evangelical potential as
it was hoped that Syriac transcribed into Hebrew letters might convert
the Jews. We turn then to consider the Syriac materials in the Antwerp
Polyglot, bearing in mind their potential for mystical significance.

Volume VI of the Polyglot comprised, in addition to a Greek lexicon
and grammar, Raphelengius's *Thesaurus hebraicae linguae* and a *Grammatica Chaldaea* of twelve pages,[2] a *Dictionarium syro-chaldaicum G. Fabritii
Boderani*, Masius's Syriac grammar and his *Syrorum Peculium*. There is a
page of corrections in the first issue to which the censor Juan Mariana
presumably referred when he suggested this work had been done too
quickly. We shall first review the contribution of Masius. Though his
contribution is not kabbalistic, it does indicate the considerable standards
of scholarship that the Polyglot reached.

Masius's Syrorum Peculium

In contrast to de la Boderie's Aramaic Lexicon to which we shall
shortly turn, Masius's work is specifically confined to Syriac words and

---

[2] This is a short competent work devoted to Biblical Aramaic and the differences
between it and Hebrew. It shows awareness of such similarities to Syriac as there are,
and a familiarity with the Talmud, Targum, manuscripts and editions of the Hebrew
bible, and the Massorah. It discusses both the morphology of the language and,
because of the confined nature of the corpus, is able to explain forms and variants in
specific verses.

the clarification of their usage. Its title declares as much: '... *Vocabula apud Syros scriptores passim usurpata: Targumistis vero aut prorsus incognita: aut in ipsorum vocabulariis adhuc non satis explicate.*'[3] We have seen above how Masius made use of Moses of Mardin in construing the *Anaphora of St. Basil*. He collected the previously unknown lexical items Moses glossed for him and many appear in this little lexicon. The rarity of Syriac books, he explained to Montano in his brief letter of dedication, made this necessary. Short though the work is (54 pages), Masius claims to have glossed all the Syriac words in the Syriac New Testament and also to have made a contribution to Hebrew lexicography.[4]

It is clear that his resources, other than Moses and the New Testament were slender but one can admire the thoroughness with which they are exploited. Masius clearly had a Psalter and his Syro-hexapla texts. A principal source was his Bar-Cepha, whence he was able to observe Syriac usage in both Old Testament quotations and those made from other authors. He refers quite frequently to Ephrem and usage '*in fragmentis Syricis de Christi natura quae Patriarcha quidam Antiochenus scripsit contra Ioannem Grammaticum.*' He may have had access to some of these independently of Bar-Cepha as we have seen above. He refers also to Sulaqa's confession—another valuable source of Syriac usage.[5]

Masius identifies Greek loan-words. For New Testament and Old Testament words he gives the Greek, or the Greek and Hebrew to illuminate the meaning. He offers synonyms in German and Italian and reports Arabic usage '*ut mihi Syri dixerunt*'. He parses difficult forms and refers to his grammar. He discusses cognates. There is little padding but a few short notes on peoples (e.g. Copts) and some remarks about dating from Alexander the Great (pg 54). He gives some Kurdish words

---

[3] '...words found generally in Syriac writers but either totally unknown to the Targumists or up to now insufficiently explained in their dictionaries.'

[4] '*...utilia tamen fore, ad nonnullarum dictionum Hebraicarum veram significationem intelligendam; quas nobis adhuc Iudaei non recte sunt interpretati.*' He had made the point before (see above). Christians' dependence upon Jews for an accurate understanding of the Hebrew Bible made them uneasy. Syriac offered the reassuring potential signalled here for philological correction of Jewish understanding. An introduction to the modern use of Syriac words and others from cognate languages to shed light upon the meaning of unusual words in the Hebrew Bible is J. Barr, *Comparative Philology and the Text of the Old Testament* (OUP, Oxford, 1968).

[5] A Baumstark, *Geschichte der syrischen Literatur mit Ausschluss der christlich-palästinischen Texte* (Bonn 1922: reprint 1968) pg 189 cites Masius as a source for Syriac usage in the sixteenth century.

in what is apparently the first printed reference to that language.[6] The work is taut, well-focused, and clearly shows the systematic gathering of data over several years the better to understand Syriac usage. We can see again how precious from the linguistic point of view was any text in Syriac, whatever the other merits of its content.

Masius's Grammar

Masius's Grammar stands out as one of the great philological achievements of the sixteenth century. It is reasonably considered the first Syriac grammar, superseding both Widmanstetter's *Prima . . . elementa* 1556 that was little more than a guide to reading the script and Tremellius's historical grammar of Aramaic.[7] The work is also entirely without the mystical interest in the script that characterised Teseo Ambrogio's first attempts at describing the language. The work exploits the Antwerp mastery of the script and the typographic capacity to cope with the minutiae of its vocalisation.[8] It draws upon Masius's profound knowledge of the Hebrew grammarians, the work of Münster,[9] and his own manuscripts of parts of the Old Testament, but also upon his contact with and interrogation of Syriac speakers—Moses and Sulaqa.[10] There are detailed textual explanations and full paradigms. Examples are generally taken from the New Testament and Psalter. The work is directed at '*iis qui Hebraice eruditi sunt*' and to that extent is the work of a Hebraist for Hebraists. This is reflected in the use of Hebrew grammatical terminology (the active participle is called *benoni*, the infinitive *makor*), and Hebrew names for the derived themes of the verb. The

---

[6] Levi della Vida, *Ricerche* pg 145. Smitskamp, *op. cit.*, pg 105 gives a plate illustrating the Kurdish entry.

[7] Masius refers to his own work as '*opus et a nostris hominibus adhuc non tractatum.*' He was apparently unaware of Tremellius's work of which he makes no use. Tremellius's philological achievements are discussed in R. J. Wilkinson, "Emmanuel Tremellius' 1569 Edition of the Syriac New Testament" Journal of Ecclesiastical History 58/1 January 2007 pg 9–25.

[8] For Masius's satisfaction with the letters: Lossen pg 446.

[9] *Grammatica hebraica absolutissima* Heidelberg 1525; *Chaldaica Grammatica* Basle, Froben 1527.

[10] He tells us (pg 3) how he wrote the work: '*Quae aliquando hic, illic observabam atque annotarum dispersaque habebam, ea succisivis operis contraxi atque ratione quadam constrixi et ad artem ut cursim potui, redegi.*'

approach has been long-lived: a grammar appeared in 1987 called *Classical Syriac for Hebraists*.[11]

The dedicatory epistle to Montano which prefaces the Grammar offers an account of the origins of Aramaic and the place of Syriac within the language that is commonplace amongst these early scholars. Masius shows a particular awareness of the large number of Greek loan-words in Syriac. Most interestingly he also shows knowledge of the Syriac massorah that is, I think, mentioned here for the very first time in the West.[12] But in spite of all this, in something approaching despair, the hard-working and learned author of both the *Syrorum Peculium* and the *Grammatica Linguae Syricae*, records that Moses of Mardin had brought a Syriac lexicon with him, but that this had escaped Masius: so much work could have been saved, and so much more progress made in Syriac lexicography had he only had that volume.[13] But given its unavoidable limitations, Masius's work stands out as a milestone of achievement in oriental philology. It is moreover entirely free of any mystical or kabbalistic content. It is in the work of Guy Lefèvre de la Boderie that the kabbalistic oriental scholarship that interests us are most clear.

Guy Lefèvre de la Boderie's Lexicon

De la Boderie's Lexicon has 198 pages. It contains references to kabbalistic material—to *Libri de Divino Auditu*—but also to rabbinic authorities and midrash. Reference is made to the Complutensian Polyglot and the

---

[11] T. Muraoka, *Classical Syriac for Hebraists* (Harassowitz, Wiesbaden 1987). For remarks here I have followed R. Contini "Gli Inizi della Linguistica Siriaca nell'Europa rinascimentale" pg 21. On pg 22 he traces the subsequent Grammars that used Masius as a model. Casparus Waserus was to produce an *Institutio Linguae Syriae ex optimis quibusque apud Syros scriptoribus, in primis Andrea Masio…ex Officina Plantiniana apud Francisum Raphelengium* in 1593. It is effectively an abridgement of Masius's work, see: R. Smitskamp, *op. cit.*, # 60b. He also produced a *Grammatica Syra* in 1619, see: A. van Roey, *Les Études syriaque de 1538–1658* (K. U. Leuven, Faculteit der Godgeleerdheid Bibliotheek, Louvain 1988) pg 11. Amira's 1596 *Grammatica syriaca…*complains about Masius's excessive dependence on Hebrew grammar. It is with the later Maronite scholarship that Amira represents that native Syriac grammatical work first comes to the West.

[12] Dedicatory Epistle pg 4. On the Syriac Massorah: G. H. Gwilliam "The Materials for the Criticism of the Peshitto New Testament, with Specimens of the Syriac Massorah" in eds. S. R. Driver, T. K. Cheyne and W. Sanday, *Studia Biblica et Ecclesiastica III* (Clarendon, Oxford 1891)Vol. III pg 47–104; T. Weiss, *Zur ostsyr. Laut- u. Akzentlehre auf Grund der ostsyr. Massorah HS des British Museum* (Stuttgart, 1933).

[13] Dedicatory Epistle Pg 4.

1516 Genoa Psalter of Giustiniani. Controversially, the translations of Sante Pagnino and Sebastian Münster are mentioned. Specifically Syriac material is derived from Guy's New Testament and also *'ex rituali libro Severi Patriarchae'*, a liturgical work we shall consider later. The lemmata are in Syriac script known as serto, which is often used for titles, while the text makes use of the smaller estrangela script.[14]

The kabbalistic material is found scattered through the various entries.[15] Guy shows how the word *'gl'* is one of the hidden names of

---

[14] Other entries of interest in the Lexicon are two references back to Widmanstetter's *Prima...elementa* (pg 6 and 96) and the claim that the word *'Golgotha'* is Syriac (pg 34). In two places the readings of the *editio princeps* are triumphantly corrected: pg 39 נרם *"Et ad Rom. 9 ubi peperam in Viennensi legebatur* נזם *at in antiquo manuscripto Postelli erat* נרם *Confecit etc."*; and, more expansively, pg 9 glossing *'agra'*: *"Tectum. 24 Matth. ubi inter versus deerat in Viennesi, quem nos secuti fidem vetustissimi exemplaris Syri manuscripti ex oriente a Postello allati, cuius fecit nobis copiam vir doctus simul et perhumanus bonae memoriae D. Bombergi filius, restituimus in Regiis Bibliis Antwerp excussis."* A page in Volume VIII has: *Loca restituta in Novi Testamenti Syriaci contextu ope antiquiss. exemplaris manuscripti, cuius in praefatione mentionem fecimus.*

[15] References to kabbalistic material are set out fully in this footnote to relieve the main text of more technical material. Under אגלא we read: *'Est unum nominibus Dei arcanis'*, and an explanation follows: *"Est unum nominibus Dei arcanis, quod sic resolvitur, ut unaquaeque litera, dictionem efficiat. Nam prima quae est Aleph valet* אתה *Tu: secunda Ghimel est* נבור *Potens: tertia Lamed ponitur pro* לעולם *id est, in aeternum: quarta Aleph pro* אדני *Adonai sive Domino accipitur. Quae si simile iungas,* אגלא, *talis prodibit sensus hoc est "Tu es potens in aeternum Dominus" Sic Galatinus Lib. II c.15. Quidam allii sic explicant, ut primo X unitatem innuat,* ג *ternarium sive Trinitatem, Aleph vero & Lamedh sic positi* אל *Deum praepotem significent, ac si Christiane diceres, Deum Triunum, vel Unitrinum"* (pg 3). Under the term אטבח *'atbash'*, a technique for letter manipulation, Guy mentions both Levita and Egidio (pg 5). Also pg 19: *"Et hac literarum commutatione abscondunt multa secreta, ne quibus facile intellegi possint."* ...Sub אידרא (sic) *Manus*...we read about the mysteries of Ten and the Sephiroth and the Cherubim: *"...Daleth vero eiusdem nominis* ד *valet 4, & 4 literas magni & sacrosacti nominis illius* איה *iuxta illud* כי יד יהיה חיה. *Quoniam manus Domini Tetragrammaton et* חייה. *Deinde e omnes omnium rerum quaterniones, quae possunt reperii in scientia de Mercava designat: ut 4 Animaliafacta, 4 Evangelistas, 4 Elementa, 4 plagas sive ventos aut cardines mundi, 4 Aetates tum orbis tum hominis, & alia innumera; quae nunc nimis longum esset recensere. Haec autem obiter hic attingere volui, ut iis qui sectantur mysteria, aliquo modo gratificarer."* On the Sephirotic Tree we find sub אילן (pg 8): *"Seriem quoque decem nominum Dei, sive decem Numerationum, de quibus infra, vocant* אילן *Arborem. Quod eorum alia sint quae vice radium, alia trunc, alia ramorum, alia denique cacuminis ponantur: ut videre est in Candelabro* (Postel's work) *Hebraice Venetiis impresso, quod nos deo dante auctum et illustratem propediem in lucem emittemus."* Postel is also mentioned pg 56 with respect to the Psalms: *"quibus titulus est Al Susanim, ubi fere perpetuo de Ecclesiae instauratione agitur, quos interpretes omnesuno ore de liliis intelligunt, sicut et flores hebraice dicti Perahim quorum fit mentio in Candelabri descriptione."* נבורה *Fortitudo*, one of the Sephiroth, is glossed pg 31 by reference to kabbalistic works and *Orphici Theologii.* It is linked to the divine name אלהים, and the left arm. Sub את: *"Item particula* את *Hebraice, in libris secretioribus ut in Zohar, Portis Lucis, Portis Iustitiae, Bahir et alios, numquam mysterio caret & saepissime idem innuit quod A & Ω in Apocalypsii: nempe, Principium & Finem, Deum videlicet."* Mention of the *Zohar* (pg 58) leads to mention of Postel's version: *"Illud Postellus vertit et interpretationem fascibus illustravit, ut ipse testatur sed nondum in lucem prodiit eius translatio".*

God. He considers it an acronym as each of its letters stands in turn for a different, more common name of God. He also discusses the technique of *'atbash'* which permits the order of letters in a word to be changed to give a different sense and to reveal many mysteries difficult to be understood. Guy is also familiar with the sephiroth or divine emanations and his description of the sephirotic tree makes bold mention of Postel and his work. Guy mentions the angel Raziel and two books named for him as well as standard kabbalistic works like the *Bahir, Portis Lucis, Portis Iustitiae* and the *Zohar.* The last prompts him to mention Postel's interpretation which, we have seen, his brother worked on, as, indeed, he may have himself. All of this material was understood through the perspective of Postel's life and work and was, of course, intended as profoundly Christian. It was, none the less, enough to be controversial, indicating de la Boderie's esteem for kabbalistic material and anticipating more generous exposition elsewhere. The mention of Postel in particular was apparently judged too rash. In a second edition of the Grammar volume of the Polyglot incorporating the list of errata in 1571, upon Montano's request, the names of heretics were suppressed. This led to the partial disappearance of mentions of Postel.[16]

The lexicon is preceded by a three page letter to Montano, dated 12 August 1571, in which Guy writes 'a few remarks on the dignity and antiquity of the Chaldaean and Syriac language', which enable us to grasp the significance Aramaic holds for him. He makes use of the image in Nebuchadnezzar's dream in Daniel 2. Aramaic was the great imperial language of Babylon, the first empire and *'head of gold'* of the image. Had its literature not been lost, Aramaic eloquence would appear in no way inferior to that of Greek or Augustan Latin. Indeed traces of the greatness of the Aramaic legacy are to be found in the vocabulary of many languages. The Medes and Persians when plundering the Babylonian Empire (de la Boderie continues to follow the sequence of Daniel 2: the Medes and Persians are *'the breast and arms of silver'*) took the books 'from the public archives' and those subsequently came (he moves down the image to *'the belly and thighs of*

The entry for Raziel, the Angel, offers an opinion of those *'periti scientiae de divino audito'* and mentions two kabbalistic works that carry his name (pg 179).

[16] L. Voet, *The Plantin-Press (1555–1589) A bibliography of the works printed and published by Christopher Plantin at Antwerp and Leiden* (with J. Voet-Grisolle) (Amsterdam 1980–1983) VI vols., Vol. I, pg 289–290. Levi della Vida, *op. cit.*, pg 305 pointed out the suppression of Postel's name when considering J. Perles, *op. cit.*, pg 78–80. It appears, however, that mentions at f. 40b and 156b may have been overlooked.

brass') into the possession of Alexander. At this point all this knowledge
was effectively plagiarised by Alexander's teacher Aristotle and passed
off under his own name. Guy shows with some etymological virtuosity
how the names of the stars, specifically that of Venus, originated with
'Syrians' who live under a clear sky. He outlines the enormous extent
of this unacknowledged borrowing and Greek deceitfulness in terms
that recall quite clearly the cultural myth of Egidio da Viterbo, who, in
the very beginnings of Syriac studies in Rome, contrasted the veracity
of the Aramaic tradition—the Zohar is of course written in a form of
Aramaic—with the lies of the Greek tradition.[17] Postel himself enthu-
siastically embraced the superiority of the oriental kabbalistic tradition
over the derivative Greek impostures. Guy's point in this brief preface
to the lexicon is to emphasise that Syriac is part of the kabbalistic Aramaic tradition described by Egidio, but this is masked by the change of
script and the very considerable differences in the dialects—differences
which would become even more obvious now de la Boderie's transcription of the Syriac New Testament into Hebrew characters facilitated a
comparison of its language with Targumic Aramaic. Philology here is
forcing recognition of the distinction of the Aramaic dialects, yet Guy
still wishes, even as he displays these differences, to see the Aramaic
Tradition as a whole, because, like the kabbalistic Syriac scholars who
preceded him, he believed in an Aramaic transmission of kabbalistic
secrets. As we follow Guy's work, we shall discover progressively that
he is a loyal, though not unreflective, disciple of Postel and belongs
fully to the distinctive type of kabbalistic oriental scholarship which had
held the field since Teseo Ambrogio first learned Syriac.

Guy has an interesting explanation for the development of the Syriac
script which is, of course, different from Hebrew characters, and which
together with the differences of dialect may conceal Syriac's part in the
kabbalistic Aramaic tradition. The script is the result of a deliberate
change made to distinguish its users, orthodox Syriac-speaking Christians, from Ebionites, who were early Christian Jews later considered
heretical because of their inadequate christology and their observance
of Torah. This is of more than antiquarian interest for it shows that
Guy considered his retroversion of the Syriac New Testament text into
Hebrew characters far from being arbitrary but as a *reconstruction* of its

---

[17] I have treated this extensively in my *Orientalism, Aramaic and Kabbalah in the Catholic
Reformation. The first printing of the Syriac New Testament* (E. J. Brill, Leiden 2007).

original script. Yet the innovative Syriac script is not without its spiritual significance as Guy explained in his *Preface to the Learned Reader,* which we shall consider in more detail below. He draws attention there to how the *ductus* of the Syriac script leads the scribes to make the sign of the Cross. His words here are striking: "...the Syrians in making the shapes of their letters trace the holy mystic shape of the cross in memory of him who, lifted up upon it, *stretched out his hands and drew all the ages unto him*".[18] The final words that I have italicised are, it is essential to note, taken from the plate of the Sephirotic Tree in Widmanstetter's 1555 Vienna *editio princeps.* The passage indicates nicely the continuing awareness of the mystical nature of the Syriac script, the authenticity of the Hebrew retroversion, and the persistent kabbalistic approach to the Syriac New Testament.

The Ad Philippum II...Guidonis Fabritii Boderani Epistola

If Guy's introductory letter to Montano was eager to place Syriac firmly in the tradition of Aramaic kabbalistic arcana, his dedicatory epistle to his New Testament returns us directly to the world of Postel's eschatological timetable and the respective roles of Spain and France.[19] King Philip is assured his involvement in the Polyglot is providential—*"divino plane consilio factum est, ut Catholica M.T. sacrorum Bibliorum hoc tempore talem fieri editionem curaverit".* Nor is this mere flattery, for Guy proceeds to the significance of the moment with an exposition of the Hebrew text of Obadiah verses 20 and 21 that rivals Postel himself in its discovery of the history and destiny of the world in etymology.[20] Guy's Latin gloss indicates by its additions (that I have underlined) the burden of his reading: *"And the migration of this army of the children of Israel, who are Canaanites (that is humiliated and given to merchandise), as far as Zarephath (France) and the migration of Jerusalem, which is in Sepharad (Spain) shall possess*

---

[18] "...*Syri in depingendis suarum literarum notis, sacrosanctam crucis mysticam figuram compleverunt, in memoriam illius qui sublatus in ea, manibus expansis, universa ad se traxit saecula".*

[19] F. Secret "De quelque courants prophétique et religieux sous le règne de Henri III" Revue del'Histoire de Religions CLXXI–CLXXII (1967) pg 1–32 pg 12 with text from ed. F. Secret, *Thrésor:* 'Et de Gaule partira la puissance force et virtu, comme escript le prophete Habdias, qui avec l'Espagne, iron en Jerusalem ou au mont Sion à subduger toute la force du Babilonike Esau, qui jusques aujourd'huy ha chassé les Gauloys de leur première et légitime possession.'

[20] Guy offers the same exposition to Henri III in his *Dedicatio* to the 1584 Paris edition pg VIII where he adds the text of *Paraphrasis Chaldaica Ionathan.*

by inheritance the cities of the South. And they shall go up bringing salvation to *mount Zion, [and] to judge Mount Esau, and the kingdom shall be the Lord's".*[21] The prophecy is fulfilled in part but will be so completely when Spain and France join forces to extirpate the Turks and the Moors (*"Mount* *Esau"*). Charles V's exploits went some way to fulfilment—his name *'Carol'* means *'Potens'* in Armenian, a language that evidently remains in the mystical etymological field of vision much as it did for Teseo.[22] Moreover in Hebrew קוראל (qwr'l) means *'Invocator Dei'* as Charles showed himself to be. Both the French and the Spaniards had resisted the Protestants. Besides, there was the meaning of ספרד *'Sepharad'*, the Hebrew name for Spain: it meant 'extending the port or border'[23] which was what they were destined to do. Moreover (and, appropriately, Guy was writing in the year of the Battle of Lepanto) the Syriac word comes from a word meaning 'skilled at sailing'.[24] Guy cites cognates in Hebrew, Chaldaean, and Arabic 'which denote a ship or a fleet'.[25] He gives us the related Hebrew and Syriac words for *'sailors'*. This double etymology has been fulfilled in the Spanish expansion in the New World. And now the Polyglot itself, which is *'Spanish'*, that is ספרדי (sprdy) or ספר די (spr dy) *'Liber Dominans'* or the 'Dominating Book': 'for as long as the world endures, it will dominate all other books'.[26] For this book will convert the East: 'Jews, Turks, Tartars, False Christians, Heretics and all other barbarian nations will finally, under divine providence, submit to Christ by the means of this dominating book'.[27] We recognise Postel's programme and that these enormous claims are meant literally.[28]

---

[21] *'Et transmigratio exercitus huius filiorum Israel, qui Cananaei sunt, (hoc est, humiliati &* *mercimoniis addicti) usque in Tzarphath, Galliam, & transmigratio Ierusalem, quae est in Sepharad,* *Hispania, haereditate possidebunt civitates Austri. Et ascendent salutem procurantes in montem Tzion,* *ad iudicandum montem Esau, & et erit Domino regum.'*

[22] F. Secret "Guy Le Fèvre de la Boderie, Réprésentant de G. Postel à la Polyglot d'Anvers" De Gulden Passer XLIV (1966) pg 245–25, pg 247 quotes this same observation from Postel. He also notes Postel's annotation against the word *Carol* in Teseo's *Introductio* f. 191v: *'Caroli Regis 9 id nominis nomen deduco.'* The volume is Bib. nat. res. X, 701 in Paris. It is bound with Guy's copy of Widmanstetter's *Syriacae* *linguae...prima elementa* and nicely illustrates the continuities in our scholars' use of each other's work.

[23] *'portum seu limitem extendens'.*

[24] *'navigandi perita'.*

[25] *'quod navim seu navium classem notat'.*

[26] *"Quamdiu enim durabit mundus, caeteris omnibus libris dominabitur".*

[27] *"Istius dominatoris libri adiumento Iudaei, Turcae, Tartari, Pseudo-christiani & haeretici,* *aliaeque Barbarae nationes omnes Christi tandem divina providentia subiicientur".*

[28] The notion of an eight volume polyglot having any missionary significance perhaps strikes us as bizarre, but was meant with absolute seriousness. One might like

צרפת *'Tzarphath'* means *'(Gallia) repurgata'* or '(France) Purged'. Sepharad and Tzarphath together then represent the dominant and purging book going forth to the seventy-two nations of mankind 'with the benefit of its three languages'[29] to gather the elect into one. The acceptable time and the day of salvation are approaching. Christ is to return and be confessed by every tongue. And for his patronage of this *Liber Dominans*, King Philip is to be written in the Book of Life.

Ad Sacrarum Linguarum Studiosum Lectorem... Praefatio

Guy offers his readers yet another learned Preface, impressively decorated with Hebrew, Greek and Syriac script using both Granjon's estrangela and serto fonts. His themes are again ones familiar as commonplaces of the kabbalistic scholars. The diversity of tongues after the Tower of Babel has alienated men one from another. Were that to be overcome—and the Polyglot is to be instrumental here—we would all be *'Cosmopolitani'*, fellow-citizens of the world. We would worship the one God 'in one manner, with one rite, and in one language'. Guy refers here to Zephaniah chapter 3. 8–9, an important text which speaks both of judgment at the day of resurrection, and of the establishment of a single, chosen language.[30] This has yet to happen, but just as the gift of tongues at Pentecost was given to bring men into the One Flock of the True Shepherd, so, in their own day, divine providence has brought the oriental languages to light to establish religious unity. Guy speaks of the seventy-two languages of the world (his text is one form of Deuteronomy chapter 32. 8). He explains the mystical significance of seventy-two and of twelve ($6 \times 12 = 72$) in the numbering of Signs of the Zodiac, the Tribes of Israel, Angels, Elders etc., and in support cites texts of the *Zohar* and Joseph Ben Karmitol in שערי צדק *sive Portae Iustitiae*. Guy also finds a three-fold division in the semitic languages with the original Hebrew branching into Babylonian, Chaldaean and Syriac,

---

to consider the use and reception of this bible (not perhaps quite in the way Guy or Postel imagined) in China: J. D. Spence, *The Memory Palace of Matteo Ricci* (Faber & Faber, London 1980) pg 86–89.

[29] *'ter triplicis linguae beneficio.'*

[30] *'Expectate me, inquit Dominus, in diem resurrectionis meae in futurum: quia iudicium meum, ut congregem gentes, ut colligam regna, ad effundendum super ea indignationem meam, omnem iram furoris mei, quoniam in igne zeli mei devorabitur universa terra: quia tunc convertam ad populos labium electum, ut invocent omnes in nomine Domini, & serviant ei humero uno.'*

and Jerusalemite and Arabic. He shows a similar three-fold division
in Greek and Latin—in each case this division hides 'that divine and
adorable Trinity, Power, Wisdom and Goodness.'[31] Power, Wisdom and
Goodness reflect the first three emanations of the kabbalists' Sephirotic
Tree—Crown, Wisdom and Intelligence—which Guy here links to the
three persons of the Trinity.

Guy goes on to speak of the mysterious arcana and numerical pat-
terns in Hebrew script and the Hebrew Bible, and the natural grasp
Hebrew has upon the ontology of the world. He also offers a learned
account of the reflections of the Arcane Tradition in Greek writers.
What however is new in all this is his explicit assertion that all this is
compatible with the decisions of the Fathers at Trent, which illustrates
perhaps a growing nervousness about papal and other perceptions of
the Kabbalah and its Christian exponents as heterodox.

A similar unease may be detected in Guy's remarks about the canon,
for several books accepted as canonical in the west were not generally
received in the east. Guy remarks that the missing canonical books
were not in the *editio princeps* nor his own ancient manuscript though
they were, he says, found in the east and held both holy and authentic.
We may perhaps detect here also a desire to affirm the canon declared
normative at Trent, in the face of the evidence of the Syriac manuscripts he had seen.

Two other remarks in this learned essay drew the attention of the
censor. Guy considered that the translation into Syriac that constitutes
the Peshitta was made by the Evangelist Mark, and was thus very early.
He mentions Postel as reporting that this was a view held in the East.[32]
Whilst the censor Mariana failed to be convinced by this claim for
the authority and authenticity of the Peshitta, he was however happy

---

[31] '*divina illa & adoranda Trinitas, Potentiae, Sapientiae & Bonitas.*'

[32] '*Deinde eundem ipsum Marcum lingua patria, hoc est, Galilaea Syrave transtulisse, non modo Evangelium suum, sed etiam caeteros omnes novi Testamenti libros. Id mihi literis significavit Guilelmus Postellus, affirmavitque se ita a Syris ipsis accepisse, dum in Oriente praestantissimos linguae Syriacae & Arabicae thesauros diligenter conquireret.*' Not only Mariana was unconvinced. Richard Simon, *Histoire critique des Versions du Nouveau Testament* (Reinier Leers 1690) ch. XIII, pg 159 dismisses Postel's theory as fables and expresses surprise that Guy had followed him. In ch. XIV, pg 174 he wrote: '*La veneration qu'il a pour la Version Syriaque à cause de sa grande antiquité, l'a fait tomber dans des fautes grossieres; comme lorsqu'il produit dans sa Preface quelques mots qui sont purement Syriaques, & qu'il en infere qu'il n'est pas vraisemble que l'Evangile qui a été autrefois a l'usage des Ebionites ait été l'Original de St. Matthieu...Il suppose faussement, que les Apôtres ou leus Disciples ont traduit de Grec en Syriaque le Nouveau Testament dans le dialecte des juifs de Palestine.*'

to concur in Guy's next assertion that the lectionary headings in the Syriac New Testament (that Guy attributes to Mark's 'successors' the Patriarchs of Alexandria) offer proof of the antiquity of the rites of the Roman Church.

Turning finally to his own edition, Guy describes his own rapt encounter with the Syriac version of the New Testament, his own eighteen-month work of transcription and translation completed in 1567 and Plantin's Royal commission to produce the Polyglot. After comments about the technicalities of his edition we shall comment upon below, he salutes the Louvain censors and greets Montano.

The Edition Itself

The New Testament is preceded by Jerome's *Epistle to Pope Damasus*, and his *Prologues* and *Arguments* are found throughout the book. This means, of course, that Jerome's authority appears for the Semitic origin of Matthew—'*primum Evangelium scripsit Hebraice*', a claim the censor would dispute, though not delete. More imitative of the manuscript conventions of Syriac scribes, perhaps, are short notices, such as that for John: '*In nomine Domini Deique nostri Ieschua Christi obsignemus Evangelium sacrosanctum praedicationem Iouchanon praeconis.*' Other notices in Syriac and Latin record Montano's approval, for example: '*Finis libri quatuor Evangelistarum literis & lingua Syrorum, quem approbavit cum accurata diligentia Benedictus Arias Montanus a Philippo rege Catholico delegatus Doctor Theologus.*'

A typical opening of the Volume has four columns. The Syriac text is in the left-hand column of the left page and its Latin translation lies next to it. On the right-hand page are the Vulgate and the Greek Text. The Vulgate text has marginal cross-references, and occasionally alternative renderings and variants (for example, at Acts 9. 14). Chapter and verse divisions are given in all four columns. Within the Syriac text chapters are marked by Syriac numerals but verses by the common Arabic numerals. Lacunae are marked as such: at Acts 23. 25, Guy's Latin translation of the Syriac has: '*Deest 25 versum*'.[33] Where whole books are missing in the Syriac, both the left-hand and

---

[33] In *Ad Lectorem…Praefatio*, Guy writes: '*In nonnullis vero locis, in quibus Syrus codex, aliquid minus quam Graecus habere videbatur, inter ipsius interpretationis Latinae versiculos quid deesset, indicavimus. In ipso etiam Graeco illud diligenter est observatum, ut ubicunque aliquid additum est ex antiquis codicibus Graecis, quod in Complutensi editione non inveniebar, quodque alioqui cum vulgata versione consentiebat, obeliscus praefigeretur.*'

the right-hand pages are given over to the Vulgate and Greek alone.
The lections are marked in the Syriac text and are also translated
in the Latin version of it. This was very much to the taste of Mariana,
the ultimate censor.[34] The Syriac text is partially vocalised, the headings
not. Below the four columns of the opening at the bottom of the page
runs Guy's fully vocalised transcription of the Syriac text into Hebrew
characters, again with transcribed lectionary headings and also Arabic
verse numbers. In the margin of the Hebrew transcription in similar
or smaller Hebrew characters are given 'roots', derived stems, and
Hebrew glosses as a guide to successful parsing.[35]

Plantin's type we know was cut by Granjon at Postel's direction. The
headings are in an estrangela very much like that of Widmanstetter's
editio princeps in size and shape. The text is in a large serto ressembling
the larger Vienna sixteen-point used in Widmanstetter's *Syrae Linguae
Prima Elementa* rather than the *editio princeps*, though it has a more pronounced base-line.[36] Plantin did not use Granjon's small serto, so the
estrangela used for the headings is smaller than the main text which is
perhaps a little odd as the estrangela was surely conceived as a script
for headings—as it were, a capital script—and is used in that way in
the *editio princeps*.[37] The same types are used in Guy's Dictionary. This
type became the model for subsequent German cutting and Erpentius's
Syriacs are almost identical.

The *Interpretatio Syriaca* (that is, Guy's translation of the Syriac into
Latin) sits alongside the Syriac text. It is generally quite literal. Square
brackets are used to explain Syriac idioms.[38] On occasions typographic

---

[34] Guy also has twenty pages in Volume VIII: *G. Fabritii Boderani in tabulam titulorum
Novi Testamenti syriaci* that reproduce in one place these lections of the *editio princeps*
that were found useful in arguments with Protestants and that Tremellius notoriously
omitted. For this debate see R. J. Wilkinson, "Emmanuel Tremellius' 1569 Edition
of the Syriac New Testament" Journal of Ecclesiastical History 58/1 January 2007
pg 9–25.

[35] In *Ad Lectorem ... Praefatio*, Guy writes: '*addidimus praeterea in margine difficiliorum vocum
themata, & obscurirum, aut omnino Syriacarum radicum Hebraicam explicationem, tum ut huius
linguae studiosis consuleremus, tum etiam ut Iudaeos linguae sanctae peritos ad novi Testamenti
lectionem alliceremus.*'

[36] Appropriately: '*serto*' means '*linear*'.

[37] R. Smitkamps, *op. cit.*, pg 106 and pg xlvi for a very useful list of Syriac type.
J. F. Coakley *The Typography of Syriac* (British Library, London 2006) is now the essential
reference point for Syriac type.

[38] Thus: Matt. 20 '*inter se et ipsos [privatim]*'; Matt. 22 '*sicut animam tuam [teipsum]*'; Luke
4 '*a criminatore ... [diabolo]*'; Acts 16. 15 '*Filii domus eius [domestici]*'; Acts 18. 18 '*dedit pacem
[valedixit]*'. Also: John 9. 24–25 '*Dixit ei Mortho, Scio resurrecturum in consolatione [resurrectione]
die illo novissimo. Dixit ei Jeschua, Ego sum Consolatio [Resurrectio] & Vita ...*'

distinctions are used to complete the sense.[39] Proper Names are given in their Syriac form to retain their mystical sound and spelling.[40] We meet: *Jeschua, Nouach, Perischaei & Zadoukaei, Beth-Poghe, Beth-Anio* and *Elischebaa.* Square brackets are also used to gloss proper nouns where clarity is necessary.[41] We shall discuss more features of the *Interpretatio* when we consider the *censura* of Juan de Mariana.[42]

Finally we may turn to consider the text of the edition. In the *Ad lectorem…Praefatio*, Guy tells us that upon his arrival in Antwerp, when he was accommodated partly with Plantin and partly in the Jesuit College in Louvain he revised his whole transcription 'and faithfully compared it with a very old Syriac manuscript (dated 1500 years after Alexander in the Syrian fashion).'[43] This was the manuscript, he says, that Postel had brought back from the East at the expense of the Venetian printer Bomberg and had been made available by the generosity of his heirs. He used this manuscript to revise the text of the *editio princeps*: 'I was helped a great deal by this most accurate manuscript, and, relying on it, I corrected many defective or shortened readings, and others incorrectly and falsely printed in the *editio princeps* as scholars can easily see if they compared my edition with the *editio princeps*.'[44] Guy seeks to

---

[39] Thus: Mark 8 '…*pro quinque millibus hominum.*'

[40] In *Ad Lectorem…Praefatio*, Guy writes: '*Propria vero nomina tam virorum, quam regionum & Locorum ex germana & Syriaca prolatione in peregrinum sonum haud immutanda duximus. Inest enim in nominibus propriis, potissimum Hebraeis, Babyloniis, & Ierosolymitanis, vis quaedam & significatio recondita, quae si semel extraneam prolationem induerit, statim evanescit. Itaque Origines ille undequaque doctissimus contra Celsum scribens, propria nomina hebraica in alienam linguam non esse transferenda, gravissimo iudicio censuit & affirmavit: quod profecto etiam in nominibus Syris locum habere debet, ut quae & mysteriis & religione ad hebraica proxime accedant.*' One could not hope for a clearer statement of the mystic significance of both Hebrew *and* Syriac names, and the importance of preserving their *sound*. This reminds of the continuing kabbalistic interest of our editors.

[41] Thus: Matt 16 '*Tu es Kipho [petra]*' and '*Beatus es, Schcemeoun bere d-Jauno [fili columbae]*'; Acts 13. 6 '*Bar-Schoumo [filius nominis]*' of Bar-Jesus; John 12. 13 '*Ouschano [serva quaeso]*'; John 5. 2 '*Beth-Chesdo [Domus misericordiae]*' or even Acts 21. 7 '*ad Acou [Ptolemaiden] urbem.*'

[42] The version was praised for its accuracy at least by Huet, *De Interpretatione* (Lib. II): '*Egregia fuit illius interpretis diligentia, adeo fides elucet in sententiis, et verba verbis consonant; si voculas solum aliquas, provocabula puta, articulos, eiusve generis minuta quaedam eximas, in quibus retinendis parum laboravit.…*' '*Insignis inter alios Guidonis Fabritii elaborata ad syriacum Novi testamenti exemplar interpretatio idque tam diligenti et exquisita convenientia, ut nihil supra.*'

[43] '*atque cum vetustissimo exemplari Syro, iam ab anno 1500 regni Alexandri, a quo Syri annos suos numerant, manuscripto, religiose contuli.*'

[44] "*Quo emendatissimo codice manuscripto, plurimum sane adiuti fuimus, eiusque fidem secuti, loca plurima partim mutila & detruncata, partim perperam & mendose in Viennensi exemplari scripta, restituimus, ut facile animadvertere potuerint docti lectores si huius editionis exemplar cum Viennensi sedulo contulerint*".

impress upon us the fastidiousness of his textual work: he says he has not changed a jot conjecturally (*'proprio arbitrio'*) but only on the authority of his manuscript 'above all when it agreed with the Greek' (*'cum Graeco apprime congru*[ens]*'*). He provides a folio page of his changes in Volume VIII.[45] Masius had previously alerted him in correspondence that printers' errors were frequent in the Pauline Epistles in the *editio princeps*: he had relied however not only on Masius's scholarship but also his manuscript. It is perhaps uncharitable to point out that these changes give the lie to Postel's earlier claim at the time of the *editio princeps* that his manuscript differed not one jot from Moses's. Postel's manuscript is now in the University Library in Leiden Codd. syr 1188.[46]

---

[45] *Loca restituta in Novi Testamenti Syriaci contextu ope antiquiss.exemplaris manuscripti, cuius in praefatione mentionem fecimus.*

[46] De Goeje, *Catal. Codd. Orient. Biblioth. Acad. Lugd.-Bat.* The manuscript consists of two volumes written in different hands, both about the twelfth century. I do not imagine anyone today is seriously interested in the tabulation of the minor variants and printers' errors in these early printed Syriac New Testaments. They were of interest then however as we have seen most importantly to Tremellius and also here to Guy. A convenient tabulation of consonantal variants and different vocalisations in Syriac New Testaments may be found in Aegidius Gutubrius *Notae Criticae in Novum Testamentum Syriacum*...Hamburg 1667, a copy of which is in the Bodleian. I have no idea how accurate it is. Gutubrius sees the differences as vestiges of dialectal differences.

CHAPTER EIGHT

THE POLYGLOT: THE *CENSURA*

Our consideration of the controversies that arose around the text of the Bible both before and after Trent has prepared us to appreciate the nature of the immediate reception of the Antwerp Polyglot and the Syriac New Testament that it contained. Here we shall consider very briefly the controversy in the Netherlands, Spain and Rome. We shall also attempt to recover as much of the Polyglot's final *censura* in respect of the Syriac edition as is possible at present.

The scholarly work on the Polyglot was completed in May 1570, but it took another six months to set up all the texts. Montano sent the *Praefatio* to be judged by the universities of Paris and Louvain and received their approval. But thereafter its troubles started, and the Bible became caught up in the controversy over the authority of the Vulgate and status of Hebrew learning. The story has been told elsewhere, so we shall attend primarily to the debates about the Syriac text inasmuch as we can recover them.[1]

The King had his new Bible presented before the Cardinals in Rome by the Spanish theologian Pedro de Fuentidueñas. By February 1572 his ambassador Zúñiga had to inform him that the papal Commission had raised so many problems that the Pope could not unconditionally grant a privilege. Montano's *De Arcano Sermone* and *De Ponderibus et Mensuris* were suspected of being kabbalistic, the references to Sebastian Münster and the Talmud (both on the Index) were unacceptable, and the collaboration of Masius shocking. Philip II sent Montano to Rome to clear matters up[2] and Masius busied himself writing letters to justify himself.[3] Then Grajal was arrested by the Inquisition in Spain

---

[1] Rekers, *op. cit.*, pg 58–69.

[2] King to Montano 16 March 1572 and the next day to Alba: *Carv* docs 40 & 42.

[3] He wrote a letter to Cardinal Sirleto (no date: beginning of 1572. The text is found in J. H. Jongkees "Masius in moeilijkheden" De Gulden Passer XLI (1963) pg 161–168 pg 164–5) in which he offered a characteristic defence we have considered above. We recall that he had in 1571 sent his *Joshua* to Rome. Alba also wrote to the King to vouchsafe Masius's orthodoxy: *Carv* doc 43 pg 163 'En cuanto al Massio, él es hombre que sabrá volver por sí, y yo advertí dello á Arias Montano.' H. de Vocht

on 22 March 1572. Five days later Luís de Léon and Martín Martínez de Cantalapiedra were taken: Montano was implicated in two of the charges made against Fray Luís.[4]

By August 1572 however Montano had provisional approval for the Polyglot. Pius V had died and Gregory XIII was looking for closer ties with Spain after the victory over the Turks at Lepanto.[5] This did not help the Bible that much however, for there was also opposition to it in the Netherlands. Wilhelmus Lindanus Bishop of Roermond, who had initially supported the notion of a Polyglot, became a fierce antagonist, though Montano was supported by the Louvain scholars and Génébrard in Paris.[6]

In 1574 Léon de Castro launched an attack. He went to Madrid to denounce the Polyglot, being apparently of the opinion that the Hebrew text should be adjusted to agree with the Vulgate, that the Sante Pagnino version should go, and the Apparatus with it—though he declined to make the objections he had set down in *six folios* known. His first official accusation was made at Court at the end of 1574. He was not successful and so he continued his attacks before the Tribunal of the Inquisition.

A resolution of the problem was needed from Rome, though no doubt the Pope preferred to have the troubles in Salamanca sorted out before making a pronouncement. In the summer of 1575 Montano was in Rome. A letter to the King indicates that he felt Castro had more

---

"Andreas Masius (1514–1573)" Studi e Testi CXXIV pg 425–441, pg 430 seems to me quite to overestimate Masius's reputation for staunch orthodoxy.

[4] F. Cantara "Arias Montano y Luís de Léon" Boletin biblioteca de Men. Pelayo XXII 1946 pg 299–338.

[5] Montano's report to the King 18 December in *Codoin* 41 pg 273 with Rekers's perceptive comments *Benito Arias Montano* pg 57. The Apparatus in various parts bears the date 1571 and 1572.

[6] B. Rekers, *Benito Arias Montano* pg 58 gives references to letters in Stockholm and those more accessible in V of J. Denuce, *Correspondance de Christophe Plantin IV–IX* (Antwerp 1914–1920). Hereafter C.P.IV–IX. Raphelengius asked both Montano and Guy to counter Lindanus. He does not appear however to have noticed the obvious personal reasons for Lindanus's fury: Montano's *Benedicti Ariae Montani de Psalterii Anglicani exemplari animadversio*, discussed above, that had mauled Lindanus's own work was included in Volume VIII of the Polyglot. F. Secret "G. Postel et W. D. Lindan" Bibliothèque de Humanisme et Renaissance XXI (1959) pg 459–461 gives Lindanus's comments on Postel: *'qui estant tres docte iusques à miracle presqu'en toutes disciplines, arts libéraux, et langues estranges, a mis en avant ne scay quelles vaines badineries des resveries des rabins et Talmudistes que P. Palladias estime abominables qu'il est indigne les révéler aux bons Chrestiens.'*

influence there than in Spain.[7] In January 1576 the *Congregatio Concilii* chaired by Cardinal Bellarmine pronounced in favour of the Latin text of the Vulgate: nothing could be changed—not a sentence, a word, a syllable or an iota. As to the Polyglot, leniency would be shown in deference to the King and because it had already been printed at great cost. Otherwise it would have been condemned outright. They advised the Pope however to exempt the Apparatus from his privilege.[8] The Pope however did not want to slight the King so left the final decision to the Spanish theologians. Thus it came about that the Jesuit Juan de Mariana had to pronounce upon the Polyglot for the Spanish Inquisition.

Juan de Mariana[9]

Mariana was born in Castile 1535 and entered the Society of Jesus 1554. He studied at Alcalá and in 1561 was ordained and began to teach at the Collegium Romanum where Robert Bellarmine was his pupil. Thereafter he taught at the Jesuit College in Paris. He returned to Spain to the professed house at Toledo in 1574 where he remained

---

[7] Montano to King 12 August 1575 in Stockholm manuscripts, Rekers, *op. cit.*, pg 147.

[8] H Höpfl, *Beiträge zur Geschichte der sixto-klementinischen Vulgata* (Freiburg 1913) gives text of *Judicium de ratione corrigendi biblia regia* 17 January 1576. An extract is found in Rekers, *op. cit.*, pg 148–149.

[9] For general orientation: G. Cirot, *Mariana historien* (Fontemoing, Paris 1905). On his political philosophy: G. Lewy, *Constitutionalism and Statecraft during the Golden Age of Spain: A Study of the Political Philosophy of Juan de Mariana S. J.* (Droz, Geneva 1960), also D. Ferraro, *Tradizione e Ragione in Juan de Mariana* (Franco Angeli, Milan 1989). On the Biblical question there is a considerable Spanish literature: M. de Los Ríos "El P. Juan de Mariana, escriturio El Tratado 'Pro Editione Vulgata'" Estudios Bíblicos II (1943) pg 279–289. F. Ascensio "Juan de Mariana y la Poliglota de Amberes: censura oficial y sugerencias de M. Bataillon" Gregorianum XXXVI (1955) pg 50–80, also his "Juan de Mariana ante el binomio vulgata-decreto tridentino" Estudios Bíblicos XVII (1958) pg 275–288, and another article of his in the same volume "Huellas bíblicas de Juan de Mariana en sus años de Toledo" pg 393–410. Also relevant is J. Ascensio "Encuentro bíblico entre Juan de Mariana y Francisco de Ribera" Estudios Bíblicos XXVII (1968) pg 129–152. A particularly useful article giving a survey of previous scholarship is E. Rey "Censura inedita del P. J. de Mariana a la Poliglota Regia de Amberes (1577)" Razon y Fe CLV (1957) pg 525–548. This article reported the discovery of a copy of Mariana's lost *censura* that was to be published in a subsequent article. As far as I am able to ascertain, the article never appeared. D. Ferraro supra pg 73 in 1989 had also failed to find it. On the Index specifically: F. Ascensio "Juan de Mariana ante el Indice Quiroguiano de 1583–1584" Estudios Bíblicos XXXI (1972) pg 135–178 and J. M. Bujanda, *Index des Livres interdits VI Index de L'Inquisition espagnole 1583, 1584* (Droz, Quebec, Geneva 1993) especially pg 1–55.

until his death. Mariana was appointed synodial examiner and counsel for the Inquisition and made censor of all Scriptural works. He was a competent biblical scholar and, fortunately for the Polyglot, without sympathy for the views and methods of Léon de Castro. He worked as censor on the 1584 *Index Expurgatorius* with Quiroga. His *History of Spain* was published first in Latin in Toledo 1592 and he worked for Philip II in a team editing Isidore of Seville. In 1599 he brought out *De Rege*, his work on political philosophy that notoriously praised Jacques Clément the assassin of Henri III of France in 1589. His *Seven Treatises* came out in Germany in 1609. He was then himself arrested by the Inquisition and tried with *lèse-majesté* for criticism of Spanish fiscal policies in his *Tractatus VII*. He was released about a year later. The *Tractatus VII* got put on the Index and in 1610 the Paris hangman was burning *De Rege*. A commentary on certain parts of the Old and New Testaments appeared in 1619. He died on 16 February 1624.

Mariana's judgment on the Polyglot appears in a letter to the Tribunal of the Inquisition dated 16 August 1577.[10] Mariana found as follows: Montano should have defended the Vulgate better and not arbitrarily departed from the traditional rendering; the Apparatus tended to quote Rabbis rather than the Church Fathers where these had much to say on the topics in question; Münster should not have been quoted as an authority; the team had been too small and it was a mistake to have employed scholars with such dubious reputations (Masius, Guy Lefèvre de la Boderie and Postel); there were errors that had not been spotted; Masius's Targum relied entirely upon rabbinic authorities; and there were debatable points in de la Boderie's Syriac translation. Numerous mistakes in the vocabularies showed haste and carelessness. But there was no conflict with doctrinal principles and so he approved the bible.

The text of the *censura* was seen in 1783, and again in 1957, but is currently lost.[11] We can however, I believe, recover what Mariana wrote on the Syriac New Testament from his treatise *Pro Editione Vulgata* that appeared in his *Tractatus VII* in 1609 where chapter XII *De editione*

---

[10] G. Cirot, *Mariana historien* (Fontemoing, Paris 1905) pg 399–400. The following pages there give Mariana's censorship of the 1574 Louvain Bible, where he avoided too rigorous an interpretation of Trent. Also relevant is Mariana's frank criticisms of the imprisonment of the Spanish Hebraists quoted H. Kamen, *op. cit.*, pg 127–128.

[11] E. Rey "Censura inedita del P. J. de Mariana a la Poliglota Regia de Amberes (1577)" Razon y Fe CLV (1957) pg 525–548 reports both cases, see footnote above.

syriaca is clearly Mariana's *censura* on the version.[12] I do not believe this has been previously used to discover the reception of Guy Lefèvre de la Boderie's Syriac New Testament.

Mariana's censura *of Guy Lefèvre de la Boderie's Syriac New Testament*

Mariana was well informed on Syriac matters. He knew of the relation of Syriac to Hebrew and its difference from 'Chaldaean'. He was aware that it was currently spoken by Christians around Jerusalem and in Syria and that the most famous Syriac writer was Saint Ephrem. He was also aware that there are two versions of the Old Testament, one from the Greek (the Syro-Hexapla) and one from the Hebrew (the Peshitta). He had learned this from Masius's translation of Bar-Cepha's *De Paradiso* that we have seen first made mention of the Syro-Hexapla. He knew also no one had seen a complete Syriac Old Testament and certainly not a printed one.

He, however, had seen both the 1555 *editio princeps* of the Syriac New Testament and Guy's translation. He found the Syriac version useful for illuminating obscurities in both Latin and Greek manuscripts. Particularly helpful did he judge the liturgical material in the *editio princeps*, and subsequently in the Polyglot, for demonstrating the antiquity of the Church's rites when refuting Protestants. Mariana considered the possibilities of the Peshitta version of Mark being the work of the Evangelist himself, and of the originals of Matthew and Hebrews being written in Syriac. He believed, however, (no doubt, correctly) that the whole Syriac New Testament version was produced from the Greek text long after Mark. The Syriac, he argued, follows the Greek even when the Greek has been corrupted from agreement with the Vulgate.[13] Care should therefore be taken not to use the Syriac, made from a corrupt Greek, in turn to corrupt the Vulgate.

---

[12] M.de Los Ríos "El P. Juan de Mariana, escriturio El Tratado *Pro Editione Vulgata*" Estudios Bíblicos II (1943) pg 279–289. I have used the text in Migne, *Cursus Scripturae* I pg 737–876. See Lewy, *supra* pg 27–32 for the problems the *Tractatus VII* caused Mariana. M. de los Ríos in the article just cited pg 281 describes the censorship of the copy of *Pro Editione Vulgata* in the Biblioteca Provincial de Toledo that dates from both 1609 and 1632. The treatise was effectively gutted.

[13] Thus: '*1 ad Corinth. 15: Non omnes dormiemus, sed omnes immutabimur; Joan ultimo: Sic eum volo manare donec veniam; Math 1, vers 13: quia tuum est regnum et potentia et gloria in secula, Amen.*' These words Mariana did not find in his Vulgate.

Unfortunately for us Mariana in his treatise passed over minor faults in the Latin translation but offered only major ones. At Galatians 4. 26 the Vulgate has *'Sina mons est in Arabia, qui conjunctus est Hierusalem'*, whereas Guy has *'confinis est autem ipsi Hierusalem'* which Mariana finds inexact.[14] In Hebrews 11. 34, where, in characterising Rahab, the Vulgate has *'Per fidem Rahab meretrix'*, Guy has *'caupona'*, thus saving the lady's reputation by making her merely an inn-keeper. He commented that *'Nimirum voluit vocem meretricis non a turpi quaestu deduci, sed ab honesto victus quaerendi genere.'* And he did the same at James 2. 25. Here Mariana objected to the fact the ambiguity of the original is removed in the translation. Both the Syriac and Hebrew terms could mean *harlot*. There is a question of the Church's understanding here, and Mariana knew that not only the Targum but, more weightily, Gregory of Nazianzus, wished to save Rahab's reputation. He remained open-minded, but his point that the translator should not prejudice the outcome is fair: it is, he said, a violation of the laws of translation. The same type of violation appeared more seriously in Matthew 26. 28 where for *'Hic est sanguis meus novi Testamenti'* we find *'novi foederis.'* The usage of διαθήκη in Hebrews 9. 16 in the same context shows it must mean *'testamentum'*. Such an error when heretics were accustomed to speak of *'la nouvelle alliance'* was foolish. That in other places in Mark, Luke, and 1 Corinthians 11, Guy reverted to *'testamentum'* argued incredible ignorance or inconsistency. Romans 5. 12 is an old chestnut with Greek variants. The Vulgate has *'Et ita in omnes homines mors pertransiit, in quo omnes peccaverunt.'* But Guy put *'in eo quod'* for *'quo'*. Why? Such a reading merely appeared to give support to Pelagians, and the Syriac can support the traditional reading perfectly well. Likewise at 1 Corinthians 15. 10, where *'Plus quam omnes laboravi, non ego sed gratia illius qui mecum est'* is a translation much favoured by heretics denying *'vim et cooperationem liberi arbitrii, totumque tribuentis gratiae.'* This latter is clearly the worst error: the version was practically Calvin's.

Mariana concluded by noting the deficiencies of the Syriac canon which might encourage wrong ideas and reminds us that *trident. conc*

---

[14] Mariana explains: *"In quo non satis expressit vim vocis* שלם*; nunquam enim significat confinem esse, quod de agris dicitur, sed potius convenire, affinem esse, similem esse; cum qua significatione verbum graecum* συστοιχει*, mirifice facit, quod de elementis, symbolis eorumque affinitate dicitur, neque ad locorum propinquitatem referri debet, quemadmodum neque vox* conjuncta *est posita in editione nostra vulgata, sed ad conditionem, qualitatem et mysterii similitudinem. Aloqui Sina locorum regionibus procul ab Hierosolyma situs est, quo facile importunas de loci huius explicatione quorumdam disputationes evadimus".* He has, I suppose, a point.

decret. sess. 4, cap 1 included the *historia adulterae* in Scripture.[15] He rather ungraciously noted that Guy *did* mention these dangers in Volume I (Mariana suspected he had been warned: almost certainly!—by the Louvain censors, one would guess) but wanted the warning nearer the poison. Particularly he was upset that 1 John 5. 7 was missing, and at a time when the *Arianorum pestem* was on the increase.[16] Notions that the Version was ancient and made by Mark only made these dangers worse.

The harvest here is not perhaps too exciting: there is validity in Mariana's linguistic points about translation, though his concern for the preservation of sound doctrine is paramount. Guy's translation had been worked through by the censors at Louvain and it is generally sound. It is in fact very literal and in this respect conforms to the norms common to the Latin versions provided in both the Complutensian and Antwerp Polyglots.[17] Mariana's concentration upon the Latin *translation* though was understandable for that is what would generally be read. That he criticised the translation as an inadequate reflection of the Syriac is a mark of his learning. His belief that the Peshitta was a relatively late translation from an already corrupt Greek text inevitably reduced the importance of the version with respect to the Vulgate. It could in no way be a competitor, but might be useful in illuminating obscurities in the authoritative Vulgate.

Mariana's *censura*, especially as we have been able to recover it in respect of the Syriac edition, was both sober and learned. It judiciously conceded some of the criticisms brought against the Polyglot, yet in no way satisfied the Spanish extremists nor condemned the kabbalistic scholarship that lay behind the production of the Bible.

---

[15] On the text of the Pericope: U. Becker, *Jesus und die Ehebrecherin; Untersuchungen zur text- und Überlieferungsgeschichte von Joh. 7:53–8:11* (Beihefte der Zeitschrift für die neutestamentlische Wissenschaft 28: A. Töpelmann, Berlin 1963); K. Aland, *Studien zur Überlieferung des Neun Testaments und seines Textes* (W. de Gruyter, Berlin 1967) pg 39–46; I. A. Moir "Fam. 22 A New Family of Manuscripts in the Pericope Adulterae" in ed. T. Baarda et al., *Texts and Testimony Essays on the New Testament and Apocryphal Literature in Honour of A. F. J. Klijn* (Kok, Kampen 1988) pg 170–176.

[16] We have seen earlier how Cisneros dealt tactfully with this verse, and Erasmus did not.

[17] F. J. Fernandez Vallina and L.V. Montaner "Lengua y Literatura en las Biblias poliglotas españolas: Traducciones latinas y modelos subyacentes" Revista da Sefarad XLII (1982) pg 129–139.

CHAPTER NINE

THE 1584 PARIS SYRIAC NEW TESTAMENT

The 1584 Paris Edition of the Syriac New Testament, also the work of Guy, was in some ways the final flowering of the kabbalistic biblical and oriental scholarship we have been considering. Its consideration belongs here as a tailpiece to the great edition of the Polyglot but, before considering it, we shall find it profitable to examine the mystical content of other works of Guy which precede the 1584 edition.

In spite of Guy's considerable labours on the Syriac for the Polyglot, he also found time to help Raphelengius revise Pagnini's Latin version, and made progress with his own work. Plantin brought out Guy's *L'Encyclie des Secrets de l'Eternité* at the beginning of 1571. The work was dedicated to the Duc d'Alençon who had asked him to write it in 1568.[1] The poem established the axis of all Guy's work, the *point centrique* around which he constructed the mystical circles of his poetic and kabbalistic view of the world.[2] The work was not only kabbalistic but also inspired by the spirit of the Counter-Reformation.[3] It was

---

[1] F. Roudaut, *Le Point centrique* pg 4, 40, 43 is eager to stress the evidence for Guy's closeness to royal circles around the Duc d'Anjou (the future Henri III) and also the Duc d'Alençon from at least the time of his arrival in Paris. On pg 40 he gives evidence that the Queen Mother had sought him as tutor for the Duc d'Alençon. J.-F. Maillard "Postel et ses disciples normands" pg 88 suggests Guy was introduced first to Marguerite de Valois, and then by her to her brother the Duc d'Alençon. For Marguerite's court: S. Ratel "La Cour de la Reine Marguerite" Revue du Seizième Siècle XI (1924) pg 1–29, 193–207, XII (1925) pg 1–43. See pg 197–198 for Guy. Later we shall see Guy became secretary to the Duc d'Alençon (who, of course, became the Duc d'Anjou).

[2] For a full exposition: F. Roudaut, *Le Point centrique* pg 200–202 who describes this immobile point of eternity as *inter alia* the primordial point of the *Zohar*, and the second Person of the Trinity. *L'Encyclie* does not at present enjoy a modern edition and commentary.

[3] Fundamental for any characterisation of Guy's thought is F. Secret, *L'Esotérisme* supplemented by the recent editions and conference papers we have noted above. Guy's thought was complex and these detailed treatments obviate the need for a representation of its intricacies here. Our argument requires merely that we establish the continuities of kabbalistic orientalism behind his two printed editions of the Syriac New Testament, and stress the thematic similarities in eschatology, prophetic-politics, liturgical interest etc. that have so far engaged us. The following have been generally helpful in considering Guy's poetry and thought: A.-M. Schmidt, *La Poésie scientifique en France au seizième siècle* (Albin Michel, Paris 1938) pg 182–214; also his "Guy Le Fèvre de la Boderie, Chrétien,

followed by the *Anagrammatismes*, poems which represent an application of Postel's emithology[4] to the celebration of Guy's friendship with Duc d'Alençon and his circle.[5] During his stay in the Netherlands, Guy had stayed with the Jesuits at Louvain.[6] He had evidently found sympathy there with the censors with whom he worked on the Polyglot, and they granted the imprimatur for his *L'Encyclie*.

In 1571 Guy was in Antwerp in July, and Falaise in August. In 1572 he was in Paris[7] in January but back in Antwerp in July to watch his *De Ritibus Baptismi* through the press.[8]

Poète et Kabbaliste" *Aspects du Genie d'Israel (Cahiers du Sud)* (Finbert, Paris 1950) pg 169–182. F. Secret usefully summarises Guy's relationship to Florentine quattrocento humanism in "L'Humanisme florentin du Quattrocento vu par un Kabbaliste français, Guy Le Fèvre de la Boderie" *Rinascimento* V (1954) pg 105–112 which stresses the continuities in kabbalistic thought: *'Avec Guy LeFèvre de la Boderie, c'était la pensée kabbaliste de Pic de la Mirandole qui se continuait.'* pg 112. M. A. Cromie "Symbolic Imagery in the poetry of a Christian Kabbalist, Guy Le Fèvre de la Boderie" *Australian Journal of French Studies* IX (Sept/Dec) (1972) pg 237–249 is a very general survey. D. Wilson, *French Renaissance Scientific Poetry* (Athlone, London 1974) is a helpful general reader with annotated passages of Guy. Wilson also has "The Quadrivium in the Scientific Poetry of Guy Lefèvre de la Boderie" *French Renaissance Studies 1540–1570 Humanism and the Encyclopedia* (Edinburgh UP, Edinburgh 1976) pg 95–108. P. Quignard "La passion de Guy le Fèvre de la Boderie" Po&sie (sic) III (1977) pg 95–109 adds little for historians. Other works are mentioned below at appropriate points.

[4] We have discussed mystical etymologies above. See: F. Secret "L'émithologie de Guillaume Postel" in ed. E. Castelli, *Umanismo e Esoterismo* (Cedam, Padua 1958) pg 381–437.

[5] R. Gorris ed. *Diverses Meslanges Poetiques* pg 22–24. These poems were *'…la pluspart leus et presentez à Mondict SEIGNEUR LE Duc d'Alençon.'* In his Poem LVI v 129 seq. (Gorris pg 277–284) recounts that François: *'en ses jeunes ans/se delectoit d'ouyr mes Cantiques plaisans/Chantez à son honneur, et les secretz que lie Et ma FIGURE ELUE, et ma ronde Encyclie'*. The court of the very last scion of the Valois, to which we shall return later, was thus a place where esoteric poets might find a warm reception. Clovis Hesteau de Nuysement whom Schmidt, *La Poésie scientifique* pg 140 calls *'plus grand des poètes alchimistes français'* was also part of this circle.

[6] Some of the poems in *L'Encyclie* are dedicated to the Louvain Jesuits: ed. Gorris, *Diverses Meslanges Poetiques* pg 22 n 39.

[7] Guy's host in Paris was Jean Desprez to whom he dedicated *inter alia* his translation of the *Harmonia Mundi* and who was a contact of Plantin. He was first fully identified by R. Gorris ed. *Diverses Meslanges Poetiques* pg 26–27. W. Kirsop "The Family of Love in France" *Journal of Religious History* III (1964–5) pg 103–118, pg 111–112 and J.-F. Maillard "Christophe Plantin et la Famille de la Charité en France" *Mélanges à la Memoire de Verdun-Louis Saulnieré* (Droz, Geneva 1984) pg 235–249, pg 243–244 characterise him as a *'familiste convaincu'*. Maillard *ibid.*, also stresses that the court of the Duc d'Alençon was a centre for Familists. Guy was, of course closely associated with both Plantin and the Duc d'Alençon, but as in the case of the other scholars working on the Polyglot, there is hardly enough evidence to make him a Familist himself.

[8] For these dates: F. Roudaut, *Le Point centrique* pg 46.

De Ritibus Baptismi[9]

The Louvain manuscript Cod 1198 that Postel brought back from the East comprises two volumes. The first, copied in the twelfth or thirteenth century by a certain Simeon Jacobita, contains the Gospels and was used, as we have seen above, in the preparation of the Syriac New Testament in the Antwerp Polyglot. The manuscript then as an appendix offers a Baptismal Order of Severus of Antioch (not Alexandria) translated into Syriac by Jacob of Edessa and used in the Jacobite Churches, and part of the Order of the Mass.[10] The last folio Guy describes in his margin (pg 131) as 'eaten away by age and worms' but is perhaps whence he derived his assertion in the preface to the Polyglot that it dated from 1173 AD. The second volume contains the rest of the New Testament and is in a different hand, with a Syriac colophon that is difficult to read. The first volume has written in italics: *"Hauuto* [= avuto] *di Constan: [tinopoli] del Postello"*. The second has a longer (Latin) note about the date of copying and tells us what we know of its provenance.[11] This is the volume that Postel claimed (perhaps with little accuracy) to have collated with that of Moses for the *editio princeps*; that was then *"procuratione Plantini, opere vero Danielis Bombergi"* brought to Antwerp for the Polyglot; and was subsequently to be the source of Raphelengius's variant readings in his 1574 edition. It also contained liturgical material likely to appeal to our scholars. We can see the interest in Syriac lectionary divisions most clearly in the *editio princeps*, where they are given especial prominence and their usefulness in refuting Protestants stressed. The lections were faithfully

---

[9] *D. Severi Alexandrini quondam Patriarchae de ritibus baptismi, et sacrae synaxis apud Syros Christianos receptis, liber; nunc primum in lucem editus Guidone Fabricio Boderiano Exscriptore & Interpretore.* Plantin Antwerp 1572. For the manuscript see: M. J. de Goeje, *Catalogus Codicum Orientalium Bibliothecae Academiae Lugduno-Batavae* (E. J. Brill, Louvain 1873) vol. V, pg 64–67.

[10] A. Baumstark, *Geschichte der syrischen Literatur* pg 253, 353. The Mass text of the manuscript appeared (in a different order) in E. Renaudot, *Liturgiarum Orientalium Collectio* (Paris 1726) Vol. II pg 15–22. J. L. Assemani, *Codex Liturgicus Ecclesiae Universae* vol. II, pg 261ff reprinted the baptismal text with improvements and offered corrections to the translation. For a modern edition of the Anaphora of Severus of Antioch see: H. W. Codrington 'Anaphora Severi Antiocheni' in *Anaphorae Syriacae* (Pontificium Institutum Orientalium Studiorum, Rome 1939) vol. I, fasc. I pg 58–96.

[11] '...anno...1550 est a Postello Venetias delatum Impensis viri et optimi et doctissimi Danielis Bombergi, res eius curante (una cum eius filio Daniele Bombergo) Ioanne Renialmo qui in peregrinationis impensas muneravit Postello 80 aureos. Attulitque una Evangeliorum volumen et psalmorum in eadem Christi lingua Postellus.'

repeated in all subsequent editions except that of Tremellius and I have considered elsewhere the controversy to which his omission gave rise.[12] Masius had produced his translation of the *Anaphora of St Basil* with Plantin in 1567, and now Guy had a similarly interesting manuscript to hand, and no Syriac manuscript at this time when they were so scarce could be ignored.

Plantin himself showed a shrewd commercial interest in the production of breviaries following the reforms of Pius V, but he also took an interest in oriental liturgies that cannot have promised such returns. In 1560 he printed a Latin translation of Byzantine masses for the Augustinian Claude de Sainctes, a Doctor of the Sorbonne who would become Bishop of Évreux, and in 1588 Lindanus, shortly before his death, had asked Plantin to produce the first edition of the *Liturgy of St. Peter*, a curious mixture of the Byzantine mass and the Latin ordinary in Greek, probably used by Byzantines in Southern Italy and Sicily.[13] He had, of course, printed Masius's *Anaphora of St. Basil* in 1567.

One source of interest in liturgical material we have not so far considered is Postel's own mystical readings of the mass. A manuscript in Paris[14] contains reference to the Syriac liturgy that illustrates how this too was susceptible to Postel's inclusive reading of everything.[15] It evidently concerns the Trisagion: '*En la syriake eglise de la tradition des apostres*

---

[12] For the debate between Gilbert Génébrard and Tremellius over this issue see R. J. Wilkinson "Emmanuel Tremellius' 1569 Edition of the Syriac New Testament" Journal of Ecclesiastical History 58/1 January 2007 pg 9–25.

[13] *Liturgiae sive missae sanctorum patrum Iacobi Apostoli & fratris Domini, Basilii Magni e vetusto codice*... On these liturgies of Plantin see: C. De Clercq "Les Editions bibliques, liturgiques et canonique de Plantin" De Gulden Passer XXXIV (1956) pg 157–194, especially pgs 172 and 181–182.

[14] B. n. F fr. 2115 f. 116v.

[15] Quoted by F. Secret "L'Emithologie de Guillaume Postel" pg 413–414 which see for a deeper contextualisation in Postel's thought. The same material may be found in Postel's *Praefatio in Zoharis secundarium Versionem* printed in F. Secret "L'Hermeneutique de Guillaume Postel" in ed. E Castelli, *Umanismo e Ermeneutica* (Cedam, Padua 1963) pg 91–145, pg 124–145 and at pg 132. The importance of the (very) early liturgical testimony of the Syriac Church is stressed: '*Unde Ecclesia syriaca praeter omnes ecclesias mundi sanctissime servans ad hanc diem ritum apostolicae ecclesiae quamvis quid de qua re cantet, dicat, aut oret hodie non intelligat amplius* (i.e. they do not find Postel's mysteries in their mass!), *tamen adorando musculam cum diviniate sua naturam dicit: Sancte Deus, Sancte fortis, Sancte immortalis masculino nomine miserere nobis, et statim in femineo genere: Sancta Deus, Sancta fortis, sancta immortalis, que etiam et crucifixa pro nobis, ut Joseph ab Arimathia et Nicodemus dixere, miserere nobis.*' Evidently Postel believed, this version makes clear, that the Trisagion was sung first in the masculine and then in the feminine. If Guy had worked on the second translation of the *Zohar*, he would very likely have been familiar with this exposition and estimation of the high antiquity of the Syriac liturgy.

l'hom chante (par la spéciale revelation de Ioseph arimathien et Nicodemus qui seulz librement l'emplissant l'aloe et de myrrhe touchèrent le corps nud de Dieu incarné) Sancta Deus, Sancta fortis, sancta et immortalis quae crucifixa es pro nobis miserere nobis. Car à la vérité Dieu et nature sont une mesme vertu et union, combien que nature soit émanée et créée...Ayant donc chanté la syriake église Sanctus etc....à la divinité de Iesu...en apres ils chantent à la nature ou à maternelle partie...' This reading of course goes straight to the core of Postel's interests in the mass and male and female polarities. The critical feminines (*sancta, crucifixa*), needless to say do not occur in any Syriac liturgies but have arisen by a curious misreading on Postel's part.[16]

The Introductory Epistle to *De Ritibus Baptismi* (pg 3–8) is addressed to Pierre Danès (Petrus Danesius), Bishop of Lavaur near Toulouse.[17] It recounts the provenance of the manuscript and its utility for establishing the antiquity of the Roman rite against Protestants: Guy clearly, like Postel, considered the Syriac Liturgy to be of apostolic origin.[18] He then explains how he had added an edition of Widmanstetter's *Syriacae linguae...prima elementa*, augmented by some Biblical chapters, to help beginners read the script.[19] Throughout he provided a vocalised transcription in Hebrew characters, as the Syriac Christians, like the Jews or Arabs, rarely fully vocalised their manuscripts.

In a more mystical passage, reflecting interests common to Postel, Guy likens the three orders of Angels and their functions to the three orders of dignity within the Church—not inappropriate in a dedication to a bishop who shines like the Sun amongst the other ecclesiastical stars as he offers the sacraments of baptism and the mass—the τελετων τελετη.

---

[16] I am indebted to Dr. Sebastian Brock who observes that the common liturgical form of the Trisagion qdyšh (= qdyš'nh) was almost certainly taken by Postel to be the feminine qdyšt'. Dr. Brock also observes that the fact that the Trisagion is here addressed to Christ (as shown by *quae crucifixa*) and not to the Trinity, as the Greeks do, indicates that the source is almost certainly, given its date, Syrian Orthodox (Jacobite). Though Maronites do address the Trisagion to Christ he considers it unlikely at this date. The attribution of the Trisagion to Joseph and Nicodemus is found in several patristic writers: J. M. Hassens, *Institutiones Liturgicae de Rit. Or.* (Rome 1932) vol. II pg 91ff.

[17] Danesius was at the Collège de France from 1530 where he occupied the first Chair of Greek. He became Bishop in 1557.

[18] Pg 4: *'Nec enim parum valet ad confirmandos receptos in Ecclesia Romana ritus Orientalium Christianorum consensus: apud quos non dissimiles in Sacramentorum administratione ceremonias invenias: quae non heri, aut nudiustertius natae sunt, nec a Pontificibus Romanis adinventae, uti dictitant, sed iam a multis retro seculis inter Apostolicos viros in usu fuerunt.'* Guy indicates clearly here that he considers the Syriac liturgy to be apostolic in origin.

[19] This volume is often found in the same volume as the *De Ritibus*, but appeared separately as *Syriacae linguae...prima elementa* Antwerp 1572 of twenty-three pages in quarto. Notoriously this separate volume does not carry Widmanstetter's name.

Guy is eager to stress the power of the Eucharist in a most Postellian way: the first Apostle of France, Dionysus the Areopagite, by frequent daily taking of the eucharist transformed his weak mortal body into the splendour of Christ's glorious body. This *reformatio* was not unknown to the Jews. Guy offers David Kimchi's gloss on Hosea 14. 7, supported by Zechariah 9. 17, as evidence of a Jewish awareness of power of the eucharist to change our mortal nature as a sign of the Redeemer's presence.[20] This exposition is not offered for Danesius, *'qui secretiora religionis nostrae mysteria aquilinis oculis introspici[t]'*, but to convince those not yet initiated by the unexpected testimony of Jewish books. Such a *tour de force* shows us most clearly the deeply kabbalistic and Postellian presuppositions with which Guy approached his edition of the liturgical texts before him. The eucharist was central in Postel's notions and the miracle of Laon had served only to enhance its importance.

The book itself is attractive. An opening displays a column of Syriac on the outside of the pages. Plantin's estrangela is used for rubrics again and the text appears in the larger serto. The text is partially vocalised, the rubrics not. The inside of each page carries a corresponding column of Latin translation, with the text being in italics to distinguish it from the rubrics. At the bottom of each page is the text in fully vocalised Hebrew characters, with rubrics slightly larger.

After the appearance of this book, Guy returned to France for good in July 1572.[21] Whether he was in Paris on Saint-Barthélemy is uncertain. He never mentions the event. It must however have reinforced his theological convictions of the need for unity in France and Roudaut dates the inception of *La Galliade* to this period.[22] His return was marked

---

[20] It will be observed that both biblical verses mention bread and wine in passages describing future felicity. Guy gave both verses and Kimchi's gloss in Hebrew. He translated the gloss: ויש ספרטים יהוו דנן שיהיה שינוי טבע בדנן לעיד בבא הגואל as follows: *'Et sunt qui exponunt (haec verba) Vivent frumento, Quoniam futura est mutatio naturae per frumentum, cum venerit Redemptor. Et paulo post subdit* רזל בשינוי טבע שיהיה לעתי בהם זכרו *id est, Et meminerunt praeceptores nostri, quorum fausta, felixque sit recordatio, mutationis naturae, quae futura est per triticum.'* Thus he contrives to find in the text the elements of the eucharist, a change of nature, and the presence of the Redeemer.

[21] His return is celebrated in poem XXVI (Gorris pg 152–158) dedicated to the Duc d'Alençon. The poems collected in the first edition of the *Divers Meslanges Poetique* in 1578 derive from this period of Guy's return to France.

[22] F. Roudaut, *Le Point centrique* pg 49–50 arguing for Guy as a *Politique* and supporting his argument about the beginning of work on *La Galliade* from Poem XXVI mentioned in the previous note. He notes that D. P. Walker, *The Ancient Theology*

by the appearance of a supernova 12 November 1572 that was widely interpreted as a heavenly sign. Postel wrote *De nova stella quae iam a XII die Novembris anni 1572 ad XXVI Junii anni 1573 sine parallaxi ulla in eodem statu, excepta magnitudine durat, signumque crucis, cum tribus Cassiopae stellis rhombi instar exprimit: G Postelli Judicium* (Basle 1573),[23] and Guy translated a treatise of Hieronymo Muñoz on the subject and added a sonnet of his own on the new star.[24] Also in 1574 Guy translated from the Italian the *Confusion de la secte de Mahumed* by Jehan André.[25] The two works were not unrelated: the eschatological implications of the appearance of the star are linked naturally to the issue of a crusade against Islam and the implications of both are reflected in the poems of the period. It was of course a difficult period in France as the Wars of Religion raged. Guy lost his brother 10 June 1574 at the siege of Saint-Lô and numerous of his manuscripts as his native region of Falaise fell into the hands of Protestants.[26] These national and domestic troubles perhaps account for the silence of our sources over the next four years. During this period however it would appear that Guy became Secretary to the Duc d'Alençon and his interpreter of foreign languages. After his flight 15 September 1575 and the negotiation at Dreux of the *'Paix de Monsieur'* and after the Edict of Beaulieu-les-Loches 6 May 1576 the Duc

---

(Duckworth, London 1972) pg 131 stressed the links between the *Politiques* and the defenders of the *prisca theologia*.

[23] For Postel and the star: J. Céard "Postel et l'étoile nouvelle de 1572" in *Guillaume Postel 1581–1981* (G.Trédaniel, Paris 1984) pg 349–360. Postel co-operated with Cornelius Gemma: F. Secret "Guillaume Postel et Cornelius Gemma" Bibliothèque de Humanisme et Renaissance XXII (1960) pg 559–560.

[24] *Traicté du Nouveau Comete et du lieu où ils se font comme il se verra par les Parallaxes combien ils sont loing de la Terre, et du Prognostic d'iceluy. Composé premierement en Espagnol par M. Hieronyme Mignoz, professeur ordinaire de la langue hebraïque et des mathematiques, en l'université de Valence. Et depuis traduict en François par Guy Le Fevre de La Boderie. Plus un cantique sur la dite estoile, ou apparence lumineuse.* For the treatise: F. Secret, *L'ésotérisme* pg 58–61 with evidence of Guy's dependency upon Postel in the sonnet. The sonnet is fully treated in R. Gorris "L'UN GUIDE ORFEE: temi esoterici e cabbalistici nelle 'Diverses Meslanges Poetiques' di Guy LeFèvre de la Boderie" in *Le culture esoteriche nella letteratra francese, Acts of XV Colloquim of SUSLLF October 1987* (Schena, Fasano 1989) pg 65–83. F. Secret in his edition of *Thrésor* pg 30–31 suggests Guy may at this time have attempted to introduce a prophet who had foretold the star before the King.

[25] *Confusion de la secte de Muhamed, livre premier composé en langue espagnole par Jehan André jadis More et Alfaqui, natif de la cité de Sciativa et depuis faict chrestien et prestre, et tourné d'italien en françois.*

[26] For the events of the time and their effects upon Guy: F. Roudaut, *Le Point centrique* pg 51.

d'Alençon (who took the title Duc d'Anjou) was by some thought to be a suitable leader of the *Politiques*.[27] Roudaut is eager to assimilate Guy sympathetically to these aspirations.[28] Dame Frances Yates also sought to associate Guy at this time with the '*Académie du Palais*'—Ronsard, Dorat, Goulu, Baïf, Tyardet *et alios*—who favoured religious *détente* and sought to get Huguenots and Catholics to make music together.[29]

1578 saw a flood of publication from Guy. There appeared the first edition of *La Galliade ou de la révolution des Arts et des Sciences*—a vast *summa* of contemporary culture and learning presented in the context of the

---

[27] There is need for some caution here. M. P. Holt, *The Duke of Anjou and the Politique Struggle during the Wars of Religion* (CUP, Cambridge 1986), who offers a very clear political narrative, stresses (pg 4 and 213–214 *et passim*) that whilst François de Valois may have sympathised with the *Politiques* in certain religious matters touching freedom of belief (if not freedom of worship), he distanced himself from their more radical politics. Indeed, Holt suggests that his failure was precisely that he did not vigorously defend their position or the Peace of Monsieur. Holt's comments (pg 16) upon the intelligentsia (including Guy) with whom he surrounded himself also bears repetition: '*There is no evidence...that [he] either read or was interested in their works.*'

[28] *Ibid* pg 52. Incidentally, it may be helpful to note what was happening at this time in Antwerp. Plantin's house was attacked by Spanish soldiers on 4 November 1576 and he fled to Paris and did not return until 1578. He left again for Louvain and did not return until 1585 to take again the direction confided in his absence to Raphelengius. Meanwhile, Guy's works had been published by several Parisian printers.

[29] F. A. Yates, *Astrea The Imperial Theme in the Sixteenth Century* (Routledge, London 1975 pg 263. In her *French Academies of the Sixteenth Century* (London 1947: Kraus Reprint, Nendeln (Liechtenstein) 1973) pg 43 she argues the *Le Galliade* not only shows knowledge of nearly all of this group but 'may be regarded as a mirror of [its] historical imagination.' See also R. J. Sealy, *The Palace Academy of Henry III* (Droz, Geneva 1981) pg 73 for details of Henri III's request of a translation of Cicero's *De Natura Deorum* from Guy who was present at the Academy's activities at Blois from November 1567 to April 1577. Dame F. Yates's more general thesis that there was a connection between scholars committed to hermetic or kabbalistic philosophies and practical efforts to effect a reconciliation between warring Catholics and Protestants at the end of the Sixteenth Century is evaluated and found '*not proven*' by J. Harrie "Duplessis-Mornay, Foix-Candale and the Hermetic Religion of the World" Renaissance Quarterly XXXI/4 (1978) pg 499–514. She returned to test the same hypothesis in J. Harrie "Guy Le Fèvre de la Boderie's Vision of World Harmony and the Policies of François d'Anjou" in ed. J. F. Sweeths, *Proceedings of the XI Annual Meeting of the Western Society for French History Riverside California 3–5 November 1983* pg 25–35. The article is a useful summary of the evidence and her conclusion in this case is that the thesis is not supported by the evidence. Whatever the fantasies of the scholars, there is no evidence that they made the slightest difference to François d'Anjou's policies or behaviour.

distinctive Postellian history of France,[30] the *Hymnes Ecclesiastiques*[31] and also *Diverses Meslanges Poetiques*.[32] The same year saw four translations: Ficino's *De la religion chrestienne*[33] and *Discours de l'honneste amour sur le banquet de Platon*; Pico della Mirandola's *La harangue de la dignité de l'homme*; and Francesco Georgio Veneto's *L'Harmonie du Monde*.[34] These latter display clearly the neoplatonic interests of both Guy and Postel.

[30] This is now magnificently edited with a learned commentary by F. Roudaut, *Guy le Fèvre de la Boderie La Galliade (1582)* (Klincksieck, Paris 1993) which obviates detailed discussion here. We may however also mention S. Maser "Musique et harmonie des quatre mondes ou le cercle IV de la Galliade de G. Lefèvre de la Boderie" Renaissance and Reformation/Renaissance et Reforme XVIII (1982) pg 11–33 to illustrate Guy's whole cosmology of Platonic and kabbalistic parallels between the macrocosm and the microcosm and the harmony in the world man can either produce or destroy; and D. Wilson "La seconde édition de la Galliade de Guy Lefèvre de la Boderie, sa composition et ses sources" in *Mélanges à la mémoire de F. Simone. France et Italie dans la culture européene, I: Moyen-Age et Renaissance* (Slatkine Reprints, Geneva 1980) pg 351–359 (concerning the expansion of the second circle on Architecture); Y. Bellenger "Epopée et peuplement: le premier circle de La Galliade et 'Les Colonies' du Du Bartas" in ed. F. Roudaut, *Poésie encyclopédique et Kabbale chrétienne Onze études sur Guy le Fèvre de la Boderie* (Champion, Paris 1999) pg 15–30; M.-M. Fragonard "Histoire et métaphore: l'histoire de la poésie dans La Galliade" *ibid.*, pg 31–46; J. Dauphiné "Le cercle IV de La Galliade: 'triomphe' de la philosophie musicale" *ibid.*, pg 181–190. R. E. Asher, *National Myths in Renaissance France Francus, Samothes and the Druids* (Edinburgh UP, Edinburgh 1993) pg 156–166 deals specifically with the mythical history of France in *La Galliade*.

[31] There is no modern edition. The best introduction is F. Giacone "Le catholicisme dans les Hymnes ecclesiastiques" in ed. F. Roudaut, *Poésie encyclopédique et Kabbale chrétienne* pg 99–168. Notice in Appendix I pg 141–143, a hymn to the Virgin no. 4, and Zachariah's hymn no. 29, 'tourné de Syrien.' Also N. Lombart "Le statut du poète dans les Hymnes ecclesiastiques: tradition liturgique et poétique chez le Fèvre" *ibid* pg 169–180. Guy declares his purpose (H. E. a ij. R) to produce a Catholic collection to rival the hymn-books of Protestants.

[32] Now to be read in R. Gorris's edition.

[33] F. Secret, *L'Esoterisme* pg 76 notes this was in Postel's library. J.-C. Margolin "Sur quelques ouvrages de la bibliothèque de Postel annotés de sa main" in *Guillaume Postel 1581–1981* pg 112–117.

[34] This was put on the Index *donec corrigatur*, but removed with Génébrard's support: Gorris, *op. cit.*, pg 30. For Nicolas's nineteen-page in-folio introduction to his brother's translation that offers a theoretisation of the discovery of divinity by 'the thirty-two Paths of Wisdom' (that is thirty-two ways of reading developed from the four senses but offering an enormous polysemic complexity) see the lucid exposition in: M.-M. Fragonard "Les Trente-deux Sentiers de Sapience de Nicolas Le Fèvre de la Boderie: Une théorie de l'interprétation polysémique au XVIᵉ siècle" in *Mélanges sur la Littérature de La Renaissance à la mémoire de V-L Saulnier* (Droz, Geneva 1984) pg 217–224. (Thirty-two is the number of the 22 letters of the alphabet added to the 10 Sephirot.)

In 1579 Guy retired to Falaise whence we have a letter to Scaliger 25 January.[35] His *La Nature des Dieux de Cicéron* dedicated to Henri III appeared 12 July 1581[36] and 13 October 1581 *Trois Livres de la Vie* again by Ficino. In 1582 the *Hymnes* and the *Galliade* saw second editions, and *Les Diverses Meslanges Poétiques*, a third.[37]

It was at Falaise in 1583 that Guy wrote his Preface dated 29 May to the *Nouveau Testament Syriaque* dedicated to Henri III. This last work[38] is a spiritual testament to a man who believed, like his master Postel, in the *concordia mundi* and the approaching eschaton and built around them his life's work. Postel himself had died after receiving extreme unction on 6 September 1581. Guy was at his side, Nicolas the universal legatee. Guy sought thereafter in Paris to continue the work of his master by pressing in his Dedication to his Syriac New Testament the matter of the polyglot that Postel had for so long believed essential for the conversion of the world in the Last Days (pg 20). Secret writes

---

[35] Given in F. Roudaut, *Le Point centrique* pg 54–55. The letter is of interest as it mentions Guy's studies in Ethiopic. *'Estant encore à Paris mon jeune frere m'escrivit q'aviez singulier desir de voir pour quelque temps une petite Introduction sur la langue Aethiopique faicte par un appellé Marianus Victorinus Reatinus, dediée à Marcel Cervin & imprimée à Rome des l'an 1552 chez Valerius Doricus Brixiensis, avecques un abbregé de leur chronique en latin deslors je vous fis entendre comme encor de presentque ladicte Introduction estoit tellement manque & confuse que cela me vous devoit faire desister de vostre entreprise. Ladicte Introduction est liée avecques autre Introduction en pleusieurs langues par Albonensius Regulus, & d'icelle je me sers pour faire quelques progres en ceste langue, que vous sçavez avoir grande affinité avecque les quatres premieres orientales. Toutesfoi, telle qu'elle est, si avezencore desir de la voir jela vous feray tenir seurement incontinent que j'en seray adverti. Je n'ay en ceste langue que le Psalterion de Po[t]ken, aux aultres j'ay quelques commentaires ou je passe le temps par deça.'*

[36] The King invited him to Blois a second time in May 1581 and then to the Court as Guy indicates in his Preface to 1583 New Testament XVI: *'Cum autem anno 1581 Regia majestas Tua Blesiis primum, deinde Parisiis in aulam suam istinc evocasset...'.* The Duc d'Anjou was at this time becoming increasingly interested in the crown offered him in the Netherlands. He attempted in 1582–1583 to become Compte de Flandre and Duc de Brabant. It may be at this time he had less time for the scholars in his entourage. Guy was however in favour with Henri III who asked for the new edition of *La Galliade*. Guy believed that the King was a true believer as he remarked in his dedication the *De natura Deorum*: *'Vous croyez fermement en dieu, et qu'il n'estoit point besoin de le vous prover par raisons.'* François de Valois's later adventures in the Netherlands are now re-evaluated in F. Duquenne, *L'Entreprise du Duc d'Anjou aux Pays-Bas de 1580–1584 Les responsabilités d'un échec à partager* (Septentrion, Villeneuve d'Ascq 1998). The Duc d'Anjou met a check in the Netherlands with *'La Furie français'* 17 January 1583 when 1500 Frenchmen were slaughtered in his attempt to enter Antwerp. He died 10 June 1584.

[37] *De l'Enfantement de la Vierge Royne des Vierges. Imité du latin de Jaques Sannazar* (Paris Abel L'Angelier) also belongs to this year: Gorris, *op. cit.*, pg 34 for references and Maillard's discovery of the work in the Municipal Library in Bordeaux.

[38] A second edition of *Discours de l'honneste amour* appeared in 1588 and a second edition of *L'Harmonie du Monde*.

paraphrasing Guy's words: *'[il] propose au Roi de compléter la Polyglotte royale en y ajoutant la paraphrase arabe de Saadia Gaon, et la version persane de Jacob Tavas, publié par ce médicin juif de Soliman, Moses Hamon, qui avait offert à Postel, lors de son premier voyage de Constantinople, un manuscript de kabbale.'*[39] Perhaps, even, Postel's death served only to increase Guy's anticipation of the imminent end that we see reflected in the *Dedicatio* to the 1584 Syriac New Testament. Guy died in 1598, not without having in turn found in Blaise de Vigenère his *'disciple esleu'* and continuator of his work as a kabbalist and translator.

The 1584 Edition

The דיתיקא חדרא *H KAINH ΔΙΑΘΗΚΗ Novum Iesu Christi D.N. Testamentum. Ad Christianiss. Galliae et Poloniae Regem Henricum III. Potentiß. & Invictiß. Principem, Christianae religionis Vindicem & Assertorem unicum* appeared according to the title page: *Parisiis MDLXXXIIII Apud Ioann. Bene natum*, the preface being dated Falaise 29 May 1583. The final page (812) has *Excudebat Steph Prevosteau, Ioan. Bene nati sumptibus & labore. Parisiis, pridie kalend. Novembris, anno Domini MDLXXXIII.*[40] The bible has an initial motto from the letters of John Chrystostom about the widow's mite in Luke 21. 2, likening an undertaking made with all one's powers to her gift of all she had. The *Dedicatio* to which we shall shortly turn runs from pg III (*pro* II) to pg XX.

An opening of the bible has the unvocalised Syriac text together with chapter numbers and the lectionary rubrics, in Hebrew characters on the inner side of each page. The absence of Syriac type is expected—there was none in Paris and Plantin's establishment was undergoing its own problems at this point as we have seen.[41] Absence

---

[39] F. Secret, *L'Esoterisme* pg 157 and *Dedicatio* pg xx. Secret omits from the list: *"integram in vetus testamentum Syriacam, Armenicam & Aethiopicam"*, and New Testaments in these languages that did not already have a printed version.

[40] The work was reissued with a fresh title in 1586.

[41] Reference may be made here to an edition of the Syriac New Testament produced by Plantin in 1574, *Novum testamentum syriace characteribus hebraicis*. It was an octavo volume of 380 pages with the whole text given in unvocalised Hebrew script but without a Latin translation. It contained ten sheets drawn up by Raphelengius of variants between the *editio princeps* and Postel's manuscript, Louvain ms Cod 1198. One may imagine that this was produced for scholars familiar with Hebrew script as far cheaper than the Polyglot. It is just possible that it would also have been thought serviceable in the conversion of Jews.

of vocalisation of the Hebrew characters again is almost certainly due
to the enormous effort of setting this up for printing and the necessity
for skilled proof-readers. The transcribed Syriac is this time, however,
made more accessible by an inter-linear Latin gloss placed above the
Hebrew line that renders the Syriac word for word (and thus cannot
be read coherently from left to right, but is almost tolerable read word-
for-word, or phrase-for-phrase from right to left). Care was necessary
to place the appropriate words clearly above each other and initial but
usually final Hebrew letters (Aleph, He, Mem) of the Syriac line were
extended to twice their length to ensure the fit.

The Latin Version from the Polyglot is then placed in a column down
the outside edge of each page, but rubrics etc. are not here reproduced.
The transcribed Syriac is linked to the column of the Latin Version by
chapter and verse numbers. Across the bottom of each page runs the
Greek text again conveniently numbered by verses. The bible follows
the Syriac canon, and thus where books are missing sets Greek and
Latin texts together without Syriac in columns on a page.

Guy himself in his *Dedicatio* pg XX says that the reason for not having
points on the Hebrew was to enable Jews to read it more as Hebrew
or Jewish Aramaic, and make it as little different as possible from the
language of their Talmud. This is not entirely unconvincing but neither
is it entirely free from *faute de mieux*.

In spite of the unavoidable absence of Syriac type or Hebrew vocalisation it is possible to follow the meaning of the Syriac word for word
and thus compare it accurately at this level with the Greek and Latin
versions. The differences between the versions (whether perceived as a
problem, or celebrated as the richness of the tradition) are thus verbally
totally exposed. For an exegete who was not particularly interested in
learning Syriac, or in placing the language with philological precision
with respect to either Hebrew or the other Aramaic dialects, but wished
merely to know, albeit at a verbal level, what the Peshitta actually said,
this edition was both serviceable and attractive. It may perhaps then be
seen as something of a (still very scholarly) vulgarisation of the linguistic
precision of the vocalised edition that had preceded it, and certainly
less cumbersome and expensive than the Polyglot. Just as one suspects
that Tremellius's work was in fact more widely disseminated by his
Latin Version than his laboriously vocalised Hebrew transcription of
the Syriac, so here we may see that Guy's inter-linear crib was perhaps
a more convenient and useful edition for exegetes whose knowledge of
Semitic languages was neither extensive nor exact.

The scholarly utility of the edition is however overshadowed by the remarkable dedication to the King made in his capacity as *Peregrinarum Linguarum Interpres,* or King's Reader in Foreign Languages, and entitled: *De certis quibusdam signorum coniecturis, quae ultimum Filii hominis Adventum sunt praecessura,* or 'Of Certain Sure Interpretations of the Signs which will precede the Coming of the Son of Man.' The *Dictionnaire de Biographie français* calls it a *'Ramas de fables ridicules'.*[42] For us, however, it enables us to place the edition squarely within the kabbalistic and Postellian tradition.

Concerning Certain Sure Interpretations of Signs Which Will Precede the Second Coming of the Son of Man

Guy began by reminding the King that Christ told us that no man knows 'the day nor the hour' of the second advent and that thus precise calculations of the end are not possible. On the other hand, he also announced signs that would herald the advent. These signs were increasingly apparent at the time of writing, so it was necessary to awake from sleep and pray ceaselessly—precisely because one did not know 'the day nor the hour'.

Certain signs concerning the temple in Jerusalem given by Christ in Matthew 24 cannot refer to the destruction of that temple shortly afterwards by the Roman Emperor Vespasian. It is a principle in dealing with prophetic texts that the events and experiences that befell Israel are properly to be understood as figuratively anticipating events in the life of the later Christian Church—as indeed also do the deeds of the Apostles at the time of the first advent. Thus a single narrative on a Scriptural page may contain juxtaposed references to events of one of these three times (Israelite, Apostolic and Ecclesiastical), though all the events in that narrative need not be true of any one time. This is possible because of the structured cyclical repetition of events.[43] Just as the Spirit proceeds from both the Father and the Son, this patterned repetition unites the

---

[42] S.v. 'Guy Le Fèvre de la Boderie'.

[43] Pg III: *'Quemadmodum enim Spiritus Sanctus, qui tum prophetarum oracula, tum certas firmasque Evangelii promissiones dictavit & revelavit, verax est & aeternus, ac veluti linea infinita trium temporum curricula unico puncto comprehensa prophetis, in Aeternitatis Horizonte demonstrat: Sic etiam ea quae praedixit & praenunciavit, nec ad tempus definitum, nec certae cuiusdam aetatis respectu veniunt intellegenda: quin imo revolvi ac repeti debent in omnes omnium seculorum generationes usque ad finem & durationem mundi.'*

Old Law and the Gospel preached by *Iesu ΘΕΑΝΘΡΩΠΩ* and issues in prophecies for the Church which may thus seek the relevant spiritual and prophetic messages from passages that appear at first sight to be about past events. The cyclical explanation given here is characteristic of Guy, though the exegetic practice is hardly new. When Guy goes on to give a list of his exegetical predecessors he begins with 'those ancient Hebrew sages who heard Moses' and who took it as axiomatic that Torah 'indicates the end from the beginning' (התורה מגידה מראשית אחרית). Origen, Basil, Gregory Nazianzus and John Damascene in the East read like this, as did Latins of impeccable orthodoxy: Jerome, Augustine, Ambrose, Hilary and Bede. Guy then gives his own intellectual pedigree when he lists the moderns. The presence of mystical and kabbalistic writers is striking: *D. Bernardus, Rupertus, Cardinalis de Cusa, Abbas Ioachim. Iohannes Picus Mirandulae Comes, Franciscus Georgius in opere de Harmonia mundi, Liber cui titulus est, Onus Ecclesiae, Revelationes Savanarolae, Brigettae etc.'* Guy then appealed to Psalm 90. 4 and 2 Peter 3. 8 to show that they were approaching the end of the Sixth Millenium.

Having established the rationale of his interpretation, Guy then offers his exegesis of Matthew 24 and the signs of the end. He deals with the *'false Christs'* predicted there and after generous examples concludes by mentioning Joachim of Fiore's warnings that pseudo-prophets would arise at the end of the era to scourge the Church for its sins. Relevantly, Cardinal Osius had estimated more than sixty different contemporary heresies were at that time afflicting the Church. Secondly, he says, it is predicted that Rulers will take back the riches they have given.[44] Third, the corruption of clergy will allow the Turkish Emperor to invade Christian territory, to enter Rome, queen of the whole world, and take the clergy—*'Pontifices praecipuosque ministros Ecclesia'*—captive as Shalmaneser took the Israelites away captive to Babylon. Their punishment will be that promised by Moses in Deuteronomy 28. 47–48, thus displaying the cyclical link between Moses's curse, Shalmanesar's deportation, the Abomination that Desolates in Matthew 24, and the imminent deportation of the curia by the Turks. Guy hopes this is a warning rather than a threat and quotes Psalm 113 (pro 132. 12), and the case of Jonah's unfulfilled prophecy against the Ninevites who subsequently repented

---

[44] I am not certain to which bit of Matthew 24 this is supposed to refer. On page VI, Guy rather coyly decides to leave the question of whether this has been fulfilled to those more expert in worldly matters than he, thereby providing no extra clues of what he was thinking.

to show the conditional nature of God's promises. As Ambrose said: *'Deus mutare sententiam, si tu volueris mutare delictum.'*

The prediction of *'wars and rumours of wars'* (Matthew 24. 7) was certainly true of a Europe convulsed with internecine fighting. To the age-old struggle for territory was now added the fracture of Europe by the Lutheran schism, and the defection of nations—*'Transsilvania, Valachia, Bosnia, Bulgaria, Hungaria, Thraciaque & Macedonia'*—to Islam. In all this France had an important role to play. France had always been the right arm of the Church, remaining unspotted (as Jerome observed) even in the time of Arius. If this the most ancient people whose Kings, Martel, Pipin and Charlemagne, had always defended the Roman Pontiffs had been corrupted, what hope was there for the rest? But there were prophecies: St Briget and Joachim of Fiore. Joachim in his Commentary on Jeremiah showed that Germany and Gaul were respectively to be in the same relationship to the Roman Church as Assyria and Egypt were to the Israelites. Israel's sins were punished by Assyria, whereupon she sought help from Egypt. In the same way, the Holy See had always sought to be defended by the French, yet it was to be feared lest France, upon whom alone the Pontiff relied against the German scourge of Lutheranism, should turn out to be (like Egypt) a broken reed that would pierce his hand.[45] God Forbid! Of the other European nations, Italy was not heretical (though given too much to Aristotle and Averroes) and Spain had her Inquisition as a protection. But Europe beyond the Danube was lost. Europe alone had remained faithful to the Holy See since the Arian heresy. The rest of the world, Asia, and Africa (except for Prester John, the Negus in Ethiopia) had followed his heresy and had been now given over to Islam which was, as it were, *'the filthy remnant of Arianism.'* All of which only demonstrated how far they were from the union of all peoples in the Christian religion, 'with one shepherd and one flock', which God had promised and for which the popes worked. The duty of spreading the Gospel as widely as possible also, however, fell upon Henri III for there are prophecies that proclaim the role of the king of France as the last emperor of the End-Time.

At this point Guy offers his reading of Obadiah 20–21 that he had given in the *Ad Philippum II...Epistola* in the Antwerp Polyglot. From

---

[45] One may wonder whether an awareness that the Protestant Henri of Navarre (later to become the Catholic Henri IV) was in line for the throne reinforced this anxiety.

it he drew the conclusion that it was the role of *Gallia repurata*, purged
France, to lead the crusade to liberate the Holy Sepulchre, remove
the Moslem folly from Africa and Asia, and have the Gospel preached
to all peoples. He supports this with a quotation from Augustine's *De
Antichristo* of a prophecy that a King of the Franks will establish his
empire, come to Jerusalem and lay down his crown and sceptre upon
the Mount of Olives: 'This will be the final consummation of the rule
of the Roman Christians.'

Guy has yet to bring his long exegesis of Matthew 24 around to
the matter of the edition. He makes his connections discursively, but
there is maintained a link between the chapter and his argument. For
the next step, he turns to verse 14: *'And this Gospel of the Kingdom shall be
preached in all the world for a witness to all nations: and then shall the End come.'*
In fulfilment of this, Guy continues, just one hundred years previously,
divine providence had brought more than half the world to the light of
the Gospel with the discovery of the New World that previously knew
nothing of Christ. We recognise here the commonplace found before in
Egidio, Widmanstetter and Postel. The prophetic text for this topos is
Psalm 19. 4 quoted by Paul in Romans 10 of the call of the Gentiles.[46]
Guy summarises the evangelical efforts of the early Apostles precisely
to make the point that the apostolic efforts failed to cross the Equator
or penetrate the frozen North or reach other out-of-the-way places:
their voice had *not* yet gone out into all the world. When Christ spoke
in John 10. 16 of *"other sheep I have which are not of this fold"* he referred
to Gentiles but now at his second Advent *'qui nunc INTRA NOS fit'* the
text refers to those in the Antipodes unknown to the ancients.[47]

---

[46] Guy notices the disagreement between the Hebrew text here and the Septuagint
and the Targum and Apostle. The Hebrew has *'their line* קַו *'*, the others *'their voice
קוֹלָם'*. *"Sed utraque expositio convenit"*, he remarks illustrating an exegesis that rather
than set versions against each other seeks to celebrate the whole tradition. The first
reading tells us that the order of the Universe compels our belief. The second *'ad
sensum anagogicum referri debet.'* The heavens are the Church and the sun is the Father
who passes through the signs of the zodiac (the Apostles). The moon is the Blessed
Virgin who is called *'Schechina, sive gloria cohabitans, quae lumen suum a deo mutuatur.'* The
seventy-two *Dodecatemoria signa* correspond to the seventy-two principle disciples, the
seven planets (or branches on the candelabrum) to the seven deacons in Acts. This is,
of course, quite mediaeval and characteristically assumes that the object referred to
by the text is in itself a sign.

[47] This is pure Postel. See: F. Secret "L'Emithologie de Guillaume Postel" pg 408:
'...*ut vel ipsius Dei incarnatio quae est unicum factum sit figura non tantum unius similis facti sed
innumerabilium videlicet, ut sic INTRA NOS agens formetur in nobis, ut incarnetur etiam multo
charius sibi ipsi qua in seipso sit incarnates.'*

Guy now develops this missionary theme, as he moves another step nearer mention of the edition. He finds 1 Kings 9. 27–28 an important prophecy. The passage tells of Solomon's ships made at Ezion-geber with the help of some of Hiram's sailors which then went to Ophir and brought back 420 talents of gold. Guy offers several possible meanings for *'Ophir'* but clearly would like it to refer to America and produces all (that might possibly be construed as) the ancient profane testimony to America to make this interpretation at least possible.[48] The evangelisation of these exotic regions had had to wait upon the arrival of the Society of Jesus. Guy had we know stayed with the Louvain Jesuits and had many friends amongst them, but it is the prophetic significance of their work that is at issue here. He gives a long list of the places where they had preached making as many Christians there as there are in Europe, spreading the Christian faith and the 'Language of Janus[49] or Latin, consecrated by the *titulus* of the Saviour's Cross'. After Babel, human linguistic unity had been fractured into the seventy-two languages of the world. The reverse process is prophesied in Zephaniah 3.9 ('For then will I turn to the people a chosen language...'). After his Ascension 'beyond the flaming walls of the world'[50] Christ sent the gift of tongues to the Apostles at Pentecost when they preached to all the nationalities gathered in Jerusalem. What was there done on a local scale is being done now on a world-wide scale, using knowledge of languages, and this will bring all people into the one flock and Joel's prophecy (2. 28–32: '...I will pour out my Spirit upon all flesh...') that was but partially fulfilled at Pentecost will then be completely realised. In fact Joel's prophecy was being fulfilled daily: there was Henri's own institution of the Order of the Holy Spirit; balls of fire, armed soldiers, and swift horses had been seen in the heavens throughout Gaul; the heavens over the whole of Germany had rung with the sound of arms; Cornelius Gemma in his *Cosmocriticus* recounted how he personally saw

---

[48] He notes some identified it with Samatra which the Portuguese held; Montano in the Polyglot conjectured פירוא pro אופיר and read *'Perou'*; others noted that amongst the seven Hebrew words for gold there is פרוים with a dual ending to signify *'duas Pervanas Indias.'*

[49] With the mention of Janus we notice a reference to the Etruscan mythology of Annio da Viterbo which both Egidio da Viterbo and Postel had made part of the Aramaic tradition. See R. J. Wilkinson *Orientalism, Aramaic and Kabbalah in the Catholic Reformation. The first printing of the Syriac New Testament* (E. J. Brill, Leiden 2007).

[50] *'extra flammatia moenia mundi.'* I cannot account for this strikingly Lucretian phrase here.

the sun turn to blood in 1567; he also reported the appearance of Christ sitting in judgment in the skies over Misnia, together with earthquakes and floods, heavenly signs and eclipses, and pretty well everything else required by Matthew 24. Of course, neither Peripatetics nor Politiques believe a word of all this, but 2 Peter 3. 3–4 ('...there shall come in the last days scoffers...') is there to refute them.

At this point, finally, the King's attention was turned to the circumstances of the edition. Guy referred to the work he and his brother had done in the production of the Antwerp Polyglot. He listed all his contributions including his Dictionary drawn up 'so that the Syrian language, consecrated by the holy lips of the Word, common to the Virgin Mary, Mother of God, vernacular of all the Apostles, and in which Christ himself preached his Gospel might be spread as widely as possible in the universal Church to the benefit of both Christians and Jewish converts.' In 1581 when the King summoned Guy to Blois and then Paris, he learned that the printer Beneventum had begun an edition of his Hebrew transcription of the Syriac without vocalisation and he was delighted and had not serious matters called him home would have been happy to assist in any way in the edition. As it was, the project made Beneventum broke and he had to sell off his workshop and books cheaply to pay for the cost. No doubt part of his reason in asking Guy to write the *Dedicatio* was to draw this circumstance to the notice of the King's generosity.

Guy recounts the history of the printing of the Syriac New Testament: the Emperor Ferdinand was the first to obtain Syriac type and print an edition. Thereafter Philip had commissioned the Antwerp Polyglot from Plantin and upon hearing of the venture Guy had offered his already completed Hebrew transcription and Latin translation. He stresses that he had no teacher, grammar nor dictionary and worked by learning to copy the letters and then translating the words of the *editio princeps*. He clearly thought he had received divine assistance in his labours. He had done the same with Arabic and, hinting heavily about the persistent lack of Arabic Gospels, was ready to cooperate on the production of Arabic type.[51] The reason for it all was to *"provoke Israel to zeal"* as the Apostle said prophetically (Romans 11. 14, 25 and 26).

---

[51] Pg XVII: '*In Arabicis etiam Dictionariolum conquisimi, & propria manu depinxi atque adumbravi sicuti in Syro-Chaldaico & Rabbinico fecerem. Illud autem in Musaeolo meo adhuc delitescit editionem expectans, si quis sit qui Arabicos characteres in usum typographiae effingendos & efformandos curet.*'

One final exegetical exercise interprets the woman in the desert in Revelation 12. 4 as the preaching of the Word in the New World, the 'wings of the eagle' being the minds of them that know truth.[52] This is linked directly to the verse Matthew 24. 28: 'For wheresoever the carcase is, there will the eagles be gathered together.' This in turn evokes Postel's reading of the verse as a reference to the eucharist.[53] Like Postel, Guy cites the Syriac word in Hebrew letters for 'Carcase' 'pgra' which he renders rather as 'Body' with reference to the Sacrifice of the mass *"The eagles will gather there, wherever is the Shekinah or presence of the divine majesty in the mass, the sacrament of his body and blood."*

Guy returns to the question of signs to offer a summary of sorts to which he adds as astronomical evidence the conjunction of the four higher planets in 1583 and the supernova of 1572 that we know had occupied him considerably at the time as it remained fixed in the heavens for fourteen months in violation of the laws of Nature, making havoc of Aristotle's teaching and thus plausibly announcing the Saviour's advent. Guy finds support in a Greek Sibylline text, and Saint Denys's conviction that the star over Bethlehem was a similar violation of natural law. He even quotes his own verse on the supernova. The wise men that came to the first star fulfilled the word of the prophet *'Ab Oriente emittam semen tuum.'* Now there remains the rest of the verse: *'& ab Occidente congregabo te. De Sion quidem exivit Lex & Verbum Domini de Ierusalem.'* That Word was first proclaimed in the Syriac language, eldest daughter of Holy Hebrew. Guy prays the King may now send out that same Word in Syriac and all the other languages of the East, that the souls of the infidels may be won before their bodies are slaughtered in a crusade, for prophecy and typology shows that Islam must be overthrown. The evangelisation of the East, Guy adds, was precisely the motive that inspired Philip II to sponsor the Antwerp Polyglot.

---

[52] Pg XVIII: Guy also quotes a Zoharic text that makes eagles the 72 Angels of the Divine Tabernacle which he finds similarly suitable.

[53] He does so in the context of the miracle of Laon in *De Summopere* f. 52 (Pg 38 of Backus's edition) which is verbally very similar to this passage: *'ut syriace Christus dixit* pagro *corpusve.'* F. Secret "L'Emithologie" pg 422 also cites a letter to Zwinger 29 March 1566: *'Nam alioqui in me ita sponte mori aut iam mortuus esse cuperem, ut in ea qua nunc sum conditione, essem revera illud tale cadaver aut ptoma sive ut syriace docebat Christus Pagro, in quo viverem ego, iam non ego sed viveret in me Christus.'* F. Secret "L'Opuscule de G. Postel sur Le Miracle de Laon" Bibliothèque de Humanisme et Renaissance XXVIII (1966) pg 399–405 has quotations essential for Postel's thinking on the eucharist at this time and the 'Eagles and the Carcase'.

Coming to the point Guy makes pg XX an attempt to get the King
to sponsor another edition of the Polyglot in words we have considered
above. He places stress upon the utility of Arabic and the wide areas
where it is spoken. To encourage a little competition he remarked that
in 1582 he had seen in Paris specimens of the Arabic, Syriac and Armenian that Gregory XIII was printing in Rome. Then finally he concludes
with the wish that Christ may come among the Jews—"INTRA SE
ADVENTUM"—as he is INTRA NOS and find room in his Mansion
for all his saints. The date was the Feast of Corpus Christi.

CHAPTER TEN

FINALE

Writing in 2000 Alexandre Y. Haran described Dynastic Messianism and
the Imperial Dream in France throughout the sixteenth and seventeenth
centuries.[1] He placed the mythology of the last Valois, that we have
been considering, reflected in Guy's long and impassioned eschatological outpouring, in a longer discourse arising in the Middle Ages and
enduring for another century or so. The afterlife of these fancies we
can trace in subsequent references to Postel's exposition of Zaraphat
and Sepharad in Obadiah 20–21 that we found used here in Guy's
Dedication to the 1584 Paris edition.[2] Jacques Barret cites the sermon
of the King's almoner before the Duc de Pasterña 6 December 1612
that repeats Postel's exposition.[3] Claude Villette in 1616 was unwilling
to wait to the end for the fulfilment of the prophecy: *"Dieu vueille que
toutes ces salutaires prophéties s'accomplissent par la main puissante et invincible
de nostre Roy tres chrestiens Louys 13 assistés de la Catholique Espagne".*[4] More
fervent than all, was the fanatic *ligueur* Jean Bouchier (1548–1644 or
1646). Having published pamphlets calling for the murder of Henri III
and Henri IV he was subsequently pardoned and wrote *Couronne mys-
tique ou Armes de Piété contre toute sorte d'Impiété, Hérésie, Athéisme, Schisme, et
Mahométisme* in 1643. There we read (pg 759ff) of the destiny of these
two powerful Christian monarchies, made complementary and united
for their sacred work. Thereafter he reinforces his exposititon with a
mythical history after the fashion of Postel that goes back to Noah.

[1] A. Y. Haran, *Le Lys et le Globe Messianisme dynastique et Rêve impérial en France aux
XVIᵉ et XVIIᵉ siècles* (Champs Vallon, Paris 2000). An important comparative typology
of sixteenth-century messianism is to be found in M. Idel *Messianic Mystics (Yale UP,
New Haven 1998).*
[2] Here I follow A. Y. Haran "L'Espagne dans l'imaginaire français du XVIIᵉ siècle:
entre idéalisation et démonisation" XVII Siècle CXCV Part 2 (1997) pg 305–323, pg
316–318.
[3] *Chant du coq françois* (1621) pg 220: *'De ce passage on tire cette prophétie, que les infidèles
à la fin des siècles seront déffaicts et extermines par un roy de France…'*
[4] *Annales de L'Eglise Catholique, Apostolique et Romaine mariés avec l'Histoire de France en
seize siècles. Paris chez Robert Foüet 1616* pg 959.

He then provides a mystical and eschatological account of this special alliance.

Continuities are, however, to be found more widely. Outliving even French dynastic messianism, Christian kabbalah retained a vitality that it has perhaps even now not entirely lost.[5] Guy's chosen disciple, Blaise de Vignère continued his master's activities as a translator and kabbalist. His *Discours sur l'Histoire de Charles VII jadi escripté par Maistre Alain Chartier* (sine loc. 1594) mixes the mythical politics of France and Spain with the sephiroth and quotations from the Zohar in a manner reminiscent of Postel and Guy.[6] His *Traité de Chiffres* of 1586, though presented as *Secrètes Manières d'Ecrire* perpetuates the interest in alphabets, magic and kabbalah of our scholars, but all now presented as practical code-breaking.[7]

Yet in spite of these continuities Syriac ceased to be located solely within the context of kabbalistic or Postellian interests, however long these continued. The fundamental change in Syriac studies was introduced by the arrival of native scholars in Rome in the second part of the sixteenth century.[8] They founded the discipline upon the scientific principles that continue today to characterise the discipline. Thereafter the story of the kabbalistic passions of the early Syriac scholars was forgotten, and with them both the motives which drove those scholars to petition Philip of Spain for a new polyglot bible and the particular kabbalistic and eschatological views which informed their work in that bible. It is that story which we have attempted to retell in this book.

---

[5] For the seventeenth century alone: K. Reichart "Christian Kabbalah in the seventeenth century" in ed. J. Dan, *The Christian Kabbalah* (Harvard College Library, Harvard 1997) pg 127–148.

[6] See Haran, *Le Lys et le Globe* pg 223–226. Introductory bibliography on Blaise is found in R. Gorris, *op. cit.*, pg 34–35.

[7] Facsimile edition: Guy Trédaniel, Paris 1996.

[8] See R. J. Wilkinson, *Orientalism, Aramaic and Kabbalah in the Catholic Reformation. The first printing of the Syriac New Testament* (E. J. Brill, Leiden 2007).

BIBLIOGRAPHY

Principal Printed Sources before c. 1800

Ambrogio Degli Albonesi, Teseo, Teseo Ambrogio Introductio in Chaldaicam linguam, Syriacam, atque Armenicam, et decem alias linguas. Characterum differentium Alphabeta, circiter quadraginta, et eorundem invicem conformatio, Mystica et Cabalistica quamplurima scitu digna. Et descriptio ac simulachrum Phagoti Afranii. Theseo Ambrosio ex Comitibus Albonesii I.V. Doct. Papień. Canonico Regulari Lateranensi, ac Sancti Petri in Coelo Aureo Papiae Praeposito, Authore MDXXXIX. Linguarum vero, & Alphabetorum nomina sequens pagella demonstrabit. Pavia excudebat J. M. Simoneta, sumptibus & typis auctoris libri.

Annius Viterbiensis, J. Commentaria fratris Joannis Annii Viterbiensis super opera diversorum auctorum de antiquitatibus loquentium. Rome: Eucharius Silber 1498.

Caninius, A., nstitutiones Linguae Syriacae, Assyriacae atque Thalmudicae una cum Aethiopicae atque Arabice collatione.... Paris, Apud Carolum Sephanum 1554.

Chaufepié, Jacques George de, Nouveau Dictionnaire historique et critique pour servir de Supplement ou de continuation au Dictionnaire Historique et Critique de M. Pierre Bayle. Amsterdam/The Hague/Leiden, 1750–1756.

Galatinus, Petrus, Opus toti christianae Reipublicae maxime utile de arcanis catholicae veritatis, contra obstinatissimam judaeorum nostrae tempestatis perfidiam: ex Talmud, aliisque hebraiicis libris nuper excerptum: & quadruplici linguarum genere elegenter congestum, Orthona maris impressum per Hieronymum Suncinum. 1518.

Giustiniani, Agostino, Psalterium Hebraeum, graecum Arabicum, & Chaldaeum, cum tribus latinis interpretationibus & glossis, Genuae P. P. Porro 1516.

Masius, Andreas, Briefe von Andreas und seinen Freunden 1538–1573, ed. M. Lossen Leipzig 1886 (Publication der Gesellschaft f. Rheinische Geschichtskunde, II).

Masius, Andreas, De Paradisio commentarius, scriptus ante annos prope septingenos a Mose Bar-Cepha Syro, episcopo in Beth-Raman et Beth-Ceno ac curatore rerum sacrarum in Mozal, hoc est Seleucia Parthorum. Invenies, lector, in hoc commentario, praeter alia multa lectu et digna et iucunda, plurimos etiam peregrinos scriptores citatos. Adiecta est etiam divi Basili Caesariensis episcopi λειτουργία sive ἀναφορά ex vetustissimo codice syrica lingua scripto. Praeterea professiones fidei duae, altera Mosis Mardenis Iacobitae, legati patriarchae Antiocheni, altera Sulacae sive Siud Nestoriani, designati patriarchae Nestorianorum. Ad haec duae epistolae populi Nestoriani ad Pontificem Romanum, quarum altera ex Seleucia Parthorum, altera ex Ierusalem scripta est. Omnia ex syrica lingua nuper translata per andream Masium Bruxellanum. Antverpiae, ex officina Christophori Plantini 1569.

Masius, Andreas, Josuae Imperatoris Historia, illustrata atque explicata...Antwerp: Plantin 1574.

Müller, A., Symbolae syriacae, sive I Epistolae duae amoebeae...(Berolini s. a.) II Dissertationes duae de rebus itidem Syriacis. Coloniae Brandeburgiciae,1673.

Münster, Sebastian, Chaldaica Grammatica. Basle 1527.

Plantin, Christophe, Correspondence. M. Rooses, *Correspondance de Christophe Plantin I–III* (Antwerp 1883–1911) and J. Denuce, *Correspondance de Christophe Plantin IV–IX* (Antwerp 1914–1920) abbreviated to CP. followed by volume number. M. van Durme, *Supplement à la Correspondance de Christophe Plantin (de Nederlandsche Boekhandel, Antwerp 1955)*.

Postel, Guillaume, Grammatica Arabica. Paris: Petrus Gromorsus (c. 1539–40).

Postel, Guillaume, Candelabrum...Venice 1548. F. Secret, ed *Guillaume Postel et son Interprétation du Candélabre de Moyse* (B. De Graaf, Niewkoop 1966).

Postel, Guillaume, Abrahami Patriarchae Liber Iezirah. Paris 1552. Edition by Wolf Peter Klein, *Sefer Jezirah ubersetzt und kommentiert von Guillaume Postel* (Frommann-Holzboog, Stuttgart-Bad Cannstatt 1994). This includes the text of Liber Rationis Rationum that was printed in the 1552 edition, Omnium Linguarum quibus ad hanc usque diem mundus est usus, origio...

Postel, Guillaume, De Linguae Phoenicis sive Hebraicae excellentia. Vienna: M. Cimmerman 1554.

Schnurrer, C. F. de, Biblioteca Arabica. Auctam nunc atque integram edidit.... Halae ad Salam 1811 (Reprint Amsterdam 1968).

Torres, Francisco de, De Sola lectione Legis, et Prophetarum Iudaeis cum Mosaico Ritu, et Cultu Permittenda, et de Iesu in Synagogis Eorum ex Lege, ac Prophetis Ostendendo, et Annunciando. Ad Reverendidd. Inquisitores. Libri Duo. Rome 1555.

Venetus, Gregorius Georgius, Septem horae canonicae, a laicis hominibus recitandae, iuxta ritum Alexandrinorum seu Jacobitarum Alexandrino Patriarchae subditorum Arabicae, editae a Gregorio Georgio Veneto, sub auspiciis Leonis X Pontificis Maximi in urbe Fano. 1514.

Widmanstetter, Johann Albert, B. Liber sacrosancti Evangelii de Jesu Christo Domino et Deo nostro etc. characteribus et lingua syra, Viennae Austriacae: Mich. Cymbermann 1555.

Widmanstetter, Johann Albert, C. Syriacae linguae...prima elementa, Viennae Austriacae: Mich. Cymbermann 1555 [1556]. Reprint in W. Strothmann, *Die Anfänge der syrischen Studien in Europa* (Otto Harrassowitz, Wiesbaden 1971) pg 63–114.

Widmanstetter, Johann Albert, D. Syriacae linguae...prima elementa, Antwerpiae: Chr. Plantinus 1572.

Ximenez de Cisneros, D. F. F., Biblia sacra, hebraice, chaldaice et graece cum tribus interpretationibus latinis: de mandato ac sumptibus Cardinalis D. F. Francisci Ximenez de Cisneros. Alcalà 1514–1517. Reimpression by the Fundación Biblica Española y Universidad Complutense de Madrid (1984).

Books and Articles after 1800

Abad, J. M., "The Printing Press at Alcalá de Henares" in ed. P. Saenger, K. van Kampen, *The Bible as Book The First Printed Editions* (British Library, London 1995) pg 101–115.

Aland, K., *Studien zur Überlieferung des Neuen Testaments und seines Textes* (W. de Gruyter, Berlin 1967).

Alcalá, A., "Tres notas sobre Arias Montano. Marranismo, Familismo, Nicodemismo" Cuadernos hispanoamericanos CCXCVI 1975 pg 349–357.

Allgeier, A., "Cod. syr. Phillipps 1388 in Berlin und seine Bedeutung für die Geschichte der Peshitta" Oriens Christianus (3rd series) VII (1932) pg 1–15.

———, "Cod. syr. Phillipps 1388 und siene ältesten Perikopenvermerke" Oriens Christianus (N. S.) VI (1916) pg 147–152.

Amram, D. W., *The Makers of Hebrew Books in Italy* (1909. Reprint Holland Press Ltd, London 1963).

Andrés Martin, M., "En torno a un libro sobre Arias Montano" Arbor XXXIV 7 (1974) pg 119–123.

———, *Arias Montano Dictatum Christianum y Pedro de Valencia Lección Cristiana Indroducción y Edición* (Institución Cultural 'Pedro de Valencia', Valencia 1983).

Andrés, G. de, "Historia de las procedencias de los códices hebreos de El Escorial" Revista da Sefarad XXX 1970 pg 9–39.

Apel, K.-O., "The Transcendental Conception of Language-Communication and the Idea of a First Philosophy" in ed. H. Parret, *History of Linguistic Thought and Contemporary Linguistics* (New York 1976) pg 32–62.

Arkin, A. H., *La influencia de la exégesis hebrea en los comentarios de Fray Luís de León* (CSIC, Madrid 1966).

Ascensio, F., "Encuentro bíblico entre Juan de Mariana y Francisco de Ribera" Estudios Bíblicos XXVII (1968) pg 129–152.

——, "Huellas biblicas de Juan de Mariana en suos años de Toledo" Estudios Bíblicos XVII (1958) pg 393–410.

——, "Juan de Mariana ante el binomio Vulgata-Concilio Tridentino" Estudios Bíblicos XVII (1958) pg 129–152.

——, "Juan de Mariana ante el Iudice Quiroguiano 1583–1584" Estudios Bíblicos XXXI (1972) pg 135–178.

——, "Juan de Mariana y la Poliglota di Amberes: censura oficial y sugerencias de M. Bataillon" Gregorianum XXXVI (1955) pg 50–80.

Assfalg, J., *Syrische Handschriften (in Verzeichnis der Orientalischen Handschriften in Deutschland V)* (Franz Steiner Verlag, Wiesbaden 1962).

Baarda, T., "The Syriac Versions of the New Testament" in ed. B. D. Ehrman and M. W. Holmes, *The Text of the New Testament in Contemporary Research Essays on the Status Quaestionis* (Eerdmans, Grand Rapids 1995) pg 97–112.

Backus, I. [ed.], *Guillaume Postel et Jean Boulaese De Summopere (1566) et Le Miracle de Laon (1566)* (Droz, Geneva 1995).

——, "Guillaume Postel, Théodore Bibliander et le 'Protévangile de Jacques' Introduction histrorique, édition et traduction française du Ms. Londres British Library, Sloane 1411 260r–267v" Apocrypha VI (1995) pg 7–65.

——, *Le Miracle de Laon* (J. Vrin, Paris 1994).

Bainton, R. H. "William Postel and the Netherlands" Nederlandsch Archief voor Kerkgeschiedenis XXIV (1931) pg 161–171.

Balagna Coustou, J., *Arabe et Humanisme dans la France des derniers Valois.* (Maisonneuve et Larose, Paris 1989).

Balagua, J., *L'Imprimerie arabe en Occident (XVIᵉ, XVIIᵉ et XVIIIᵉ siècles)* (Maisonneuve and Larose, Paris 1984).

Balmas, E., "*Le prime Nove dell'altro Mondo* di Guglielmo Postel" Studi Urbinati XXIX/2 (1955) pg 334–377.

Bardy, G., "Simple Remarques sur les Ouvrages et les Manuscrits bilingues" Vivre et Penser III (1945) pg 242–267.

Baroni, V., *La Contre-Réforme devant La Bible La Question biblique* (Imprimerie de la Concorde, Lausanne 1943).

Barr, J., *Comparative Philology and the Text of the Old Testament* (OUP, Oxford,1968).

Bataillon, M., *Érasme et l'Espagne* (1st ed. 1937: reprinted Droz, Geneva 1998).

——, "Philippe Galle et Arias Montano. Matériaux pour l'iconographie des savants de la Renaissance" Bibliothèque de Humanisme et Renaissance II (1942) pg 132–160.

Baumstark, A., *Festbrevier und Kirchenjahr der syrischen Jakobiten* (F. Schöningh, Paderborn 1910).

——, *Geschichte der syrischen Literatur mit Ausschluss der christlich-palästinischen Texte* (Bonn 1922: reprint 1968).

Becker, U., *Jesus und die Ehebrecherin; Untersuchungen zur text- und Überlieferungsgeschichte von Joh. 7:53–8:11* (Beihefte der Zeitschrift für die neutestamentliche Wissenschaft 28: Adolf Töpelmann, Berlin 1963).

Bedouelle, G., "Le débat catholique sur la traduction de la Bible en langue vulgaire" in eds I. Backus and F. Higman *Théorie et pratique de l'exégèse* (Droz, Geneva 1990) pg 39–59.

Bell, A. F. G., *Benito Arias Montano* (Hispanic Society of America, Oxford 1922).
——, *Luís de Léon: A Study in the Spanish Renaissance* (Clarendon, Oxford 1925).
Bellenger, Y., "Epopée et peuplement: le premier circle de La Galliade et 'Les Colonies' du Du Bartas" in ed. F. Roudaut, *Poésie encyclopédique et Kabbale chrétienne Onze études sur Guy le Fèvre de La Boderie* (Champion, Paris 1999) pg 15–30.
Beltrán de Heredia, V., "Catedráticos de Sagrada Escritura en la Universidad de Alcalá durante el siglo XVI" Ciecia Tomista XVIII (1918) pg 140–155; XIX (1919) pg 49–55 & 144–156.
Bennett, J. and Mandelbrote, S., *The Garden, the Ark, the Tower, the Temple. Biblical Metaphors of Knowledge in Early Modern Europe* (Museum of History of Science in association with Bodleian Library, Oxford 1998).
Bension, A., *El Zohar en la España musulmana y cristiana* (Ediciones Nuestra Raza, Madrid 1934).
Bentley, J. H., "New Light on the Editing of the Complutensian New Testament" Bibliothèque de Humanisme et Renaissance XLII (1980) pg 145–156.
——, "New Testament Scholarship at Louvain in the early Sixteenth Century" Studies in Mediaeval and Renaissance History (ns) II (1979) pg 51–79.
——, *Humanists and Holy Writ: New Testament Scholarship in the Renaissance* (University of Princeton. Princeton 1983).
Berger, S., "Les anciennes versiones espagnoles et portugaises de la Bible" Romania XXVIII (Jan.1899) pg 306–408.
Bible Society, *Qyama Hadta The New Covenant commonly called the New Testament: Peshitta Aramaic text with a Hebrew Translation* (Aramaic Scripture Research Society in Israel/ The Bible Society, 1986).
Bietenholz, P. G., *Basle and France in Sixteenth Century. The Basle Humanists and Printers in their contacts with Francophone Culture* (Librairie Droz, Geneva 1971).
Bobrinsky, B., "Liturgie et Ecclésiologie trinitaire de sainte Basile" in *Eucharisties d'Orient et Occident II* (Édition du Cerf, Paris 1970) pg 197–240.
Bobzin, H., "Agostino Giustiniani (1470–1536) und seine Bedeutung für die Geschichte der Arabistik" in eds. Werner Diem and Aboli Arad Falaturi, *XXIV Deutscher Orientalistentag (Köln 1988)* (Stuttgart 1990) pg 131–139.
Bogaert, P. M., "Origène et les Hexaples" in *Dictionnaire de la Bible*, Suppl. fasc. 68 (1993) pg 568–573.
Boumans, R., "The Religious views of Abraham Ortellius" Journal of the Warburg & Courtauld Institue XVII (1954) pg 374–377.
Brecker, B., "Pflug" *Allgemeine Deutsche Biographie* XXV (Leipzig 1667) pg 688–690.
Brock, S. P., "A Fourteenth Century Polyglot Psalter" in G. E. Kaddish and G. E. Freeman, *Studies in Honour of M. R. J. Williams* (Society for the Study of Egyptian Antiquites, Toronto 1982) pg 1–15.
——, "Proper Names" in ed. B. Metzger, *The Early Versions of the New Testament* (OUP, Oxford 1977) pg 85–89.
——, "The Development of Syriac Studies" in ed. K. J. Cathcart, *The Edward Hincks Bicentenary Lectures* (Univ. Coll. Dublin, Dublin 1994) pg 94–113.
Brown, A. J., "The Date of Erasmus's Latin Translation of the New Testament" Transactions of the Cambridge Bibliographical Society VIII/4 (1984/5) pg 351–380.
Bujanda, J. M. de, *Index des Livres interdits, Vol. VI, Index de l'Inquisition espagnole 1583, 1584* (Droz, Geneva 1993).
Burkitt, F. C., "The Syriac forms of New Testament Proper Names" Proceedings of the British Academy V (1911–1912) pg 377–408.
——, "A Note on some Heidelberg Autographs" Proceedings of the Cambridge Antiquarian Society XI (1906) pg 265–268.
Burmeister, K. H., *Sebastian Münster: Versuch eines biographischen Gesamtbildes* (Basel und Stuttgart 1963).

Burnett, C. G. F., "Arabic into Latin in twelfth century Spain: The Works of Hermann of Carinthia" Mittellatein Jahrbuch XIII (1978) pg 100–134.

Burnett, S. G., *From Christian Hebraism to Jewish Studies Johannes Buxtorf 1564–1629 and Hebrew Learning in the Seventeeth Century* (E. J. Brill: Leiden 1996).

Busi, G., "Francesco Zorzi, a methodical dreamer" in ed. J. Dan, *The Christian Kabbalah Jewish Mystical Books and their Christian Interpreters* (Harvard College Library, Cambridge Mass. 1997) pg 97–126.

Cabanelas, D., "Arias Montano y los libros plumbeos de Granada" Miscelanea de estudios árabes y hebraicos XVIII–XIX (1969–1970) pg 7–41.

Cameron, E., *The European Reformation* (OUP, Oxford 1991).

Cantera Burgos, F., "Arias Montano y Fr. Luis de Leon" Boletin de la Biblioteca de Menéndez Pelayo XXII (1946) pg 299–338.

Carreras Artau, J., "La 'Allocutio super Tetragrammaton' de Arnaldo de Vilanova" Revista da Sepharad IX (1949) pg 75–105.

Carvajal, D. T. G., "Elogio Histórico del D. Benito Arias Montano" Memorias Real Academia Historia VII, Madrid (1832) pg 1–199.

Castro, F. P., *El manuscrito apologético de Alfonso de Zamora: Traduccíon y estudio del Séfer Hokmah Elohim* (CSIC, Madrid/Barcelona 1950).

Castro, F. P. and Voet, L., *La Biblia Poliglota de Amberes* (Fundacíon Universitaria española, Madrid 1973).

Castro, F. P., "Un centenar de lecciones del texto biblio hebreo" *Homenaje a Juan Prado*, Miscelánea de Estudios Biblicos y Hebraicos XXIV (1975) pg 43–56.

Cirot, G., *Mariana historien. Études sur l'historiographie éspagnole* (Albert Fontemoing, Paris 1905).

Clair, C., *Christopher Plantin* (Cassell and Co, London 1960).

Coakley, J. F., *The Typography of Syriac. A historical catalogue of printing types 1537–1958* (British Library, London 2006).

Codrington, H. W., *Anaphorae Syriacae quotquot in codibus adhuc repertae sunt, Volumen 1 Fasciculus 1* (Pontifical Institute of Oriental Studies, Rome 1939).

Colomer, E., "La Interpretación del Tetragrama bíblico en Ramón Martí y Arnau de Vilanova" Miscellanea Mediaevalia XIII/2 (1981) pg 937–945.

Combero, C., 'Colonna Pietro'in Dizionario Biografico degli Italiani (G. Ernest and S. Foa, Rome) XXVII pg 402–404.

Conde Prudencio, J., "Arias Montano y la cuestíon bíblica de su tiempo" Revista del Centro de Estudios Extremeños II (1928) pg 403–498.

Contini, R., "Gli studi siriaci" in *Giorgio Levi della Vida nel centenaria della nascita 1886–1967* (Rome 1988) pg 25–40.

——, "Gli Inizi della Linguistica Siriaca nell'Europa rinascimentale" Rivista Studi Orientali LXVIII (1994) pg 15–30.

Cromie, M. A., "Symbolic Imagery in the poetry of a Christian Kabbalist, Guy Le Fèvre de La Boderie" Australian Journal of French Studies IX (Sept/Dec) (1972) pg 237–249.

Dannenfeldt, K. H., "The Renaissance Humanists and knowledge of Arabic" Studies in the Renaissance II (1955) pg 96–117.

Darlow, H. and Moule, H., *Historical Catalogue of the printed editions of Holy Scripture in the Library of the British and Foreign Bible Society* (2 vols in 4) (BFBS: London 1903, reprinted New York, 1963).

Dauphiné, J., "Le cercle IV de La Galliade: 'triomphe' de la philosophie musicale" in ed. F. Roudaut, *Poésie encyclopédique et Kabbale chrétienne Onze études sur Guy le Fèvre de La Boderie* (Champion, Paris 1999) pg 181–190.

De Clercq, C., "Les Editions bibliques, liturgiques et canonique de Plantin" De Gulden Passer XXXIV (1956) pg 157–194.

De Jonge, H. J., "*Novum Testamentum a nobis versum*: the essence of Erasmus's edition of the New Testament" Journal of Theological Studies XXXV (1984) pg 394–413.

De La Fontaine Verwey, H., "Trois Hérésiarques" Bibliothèque de Humanisme et Renaissance XIV (1954) pg 312–330.

De Los Rios, M., "El P. Juan de Mariana escriturario. El tratado *Pro Editione Vulgata*" Estudios Bíblicos II (1943) pg 279–289.

Dedieu, J.-P., "Le Modèle religieux: Le Réfus de la Réforme et le contrôle de la pensée" in Bartolomé Bennassar, *L'Inquisition espagnole XV–XIX siècles* (Hachette, Paris 1979) pg 263–304.

Del Valle Rodríguez, C., "Die Anfänge der Hebräischen Grammatik in Spanien" Historiographia Linguistica VII (1981) pg 389–402.

Delaruelle, L., "La Séjour à Paris d'Agostino Giustiniani" Revue du Seizième Siècle XII (1925) pg 322–337.

Delitzsch, F., *Studies on the Complutensian Polyglot* (S. Bagster: London 1872).

——, *Complutensische Varianten zum Altest. Text. Ein Beitrag zur Biblischen Textkritik* (Leipzig 1878).

Domenichini, D., "Una nota Escurialense di Benito Arias Montano (Esc. Ms. H.I. 15 f. 5r)" Bibliothèque de Humanisme et Renaissance XLIX (1987) pg 607–610.

Duquenne, F., *L'Entreprise du Duc d'Anjou aux Pays-Bas de 1580–1584 Les responsabilités d'un échec à partager* (Septentrion, Villeneuve d'Ascq 1998).

Ehrman B. D. and Holmes, M. W., [eds.] *The Text of the New Testament in Contemporary Research* (Eerdmans, Michigan 1995).

Engberding, H., *Das eucharistische Hochgebet der Basileosliturgie* (Theologie des christlischen Orients 1) (Aschendorff, Munster 1931).

Fernández Marcos, N., "De *Los Nombres de Cristo* de Luis de Léon y *De Arcano Sermone* de Arias Montano" in *Biblia y humanismo Textos, talantes y controversias del siglo XVI español* pg 133–152.

——, and Fernández Tejero, E., *Biblia y humanismo Textos, talantes y controversias del siglo XVI español* (Fundación Universitaria Española, Madrid 1997).

——, "Censura y Exégesis: las Hypotyposeis de Martín Martínez de Cantalapiedra" in *Biblia y humanismo Textos, talantes y controversias del siglo XVI español* pg 27–33.

——, "El Texto griego de la Biblia Políglota Complutense" in *Biblia y humanismo Textos, talantes y controversias del siglo XVI español* pg 219–228.

——, "El Tratado De Arcano Sermone de Arias Montano" in *Biblia y Humanismo Textos, talantes y controversias del siglo XVI español* pg 177–183.

——, "La Exégesis bíblica de Cipriano de la Huerga" in *Biblia y humanismo Textos, talantes y controversias del siglo XVI español* pg 65–82.

——, "Las Medidas del Arca de Noé en la Exégesis de Arias Montano" in *Biblia y Humanismo Textos, talantes y controversias del siglo XVI español* pg 185–191.

——, and Fernández Tejero, E., "Luis de Estrada y Arias Montano" in *Biblia y humanismo Textos, talantes y controversias del siglo XVI español* pg 193–205.

——, and Fernández Tejero, E., "Biblismo y erasmismo en La España del siglo XVI" in *Biblia y humanismo Textos, talantes y controversias del siglo XVI español* pg 15–26.

——, and Fernández Tejero, E., "Desentrañando el Comentario de Cipriano dela Huerga al Salmo 130" in *Biblia y humanismo Textos, talantes y controversias del siglo XVI español* pg 57–64.

——, and Fernández Tejero, E., "El Ex Libris de Cipriano de la Huerga" *Biblia y humanismo Textos, talantes y controversias del siglo XVI español* pg 47–56.

——, and Fernández Tejero, E., "La Polémica en torno a la Biblia Regia de Arias Montano" in *Biblia y humanismo Textos, talantes y controversias del siglo XVI español* pg 229–238.

——, *The Septuagint in Context* (E. J. Brill, Leiden 2000).

Fernández Tejero, E., "¿'Esposa' o Perfecta casada? Dos personajes en la exégesis de Luis de Léon" in *Biblia y humanismo Textos, talantes y controversias del siglo XVI español* pg 119–132.

———, "Luis de Léon, hebraísta: el *Cantur de los cantares*" in *Biblia y humanismo Textos, talantes y controversias del siglo XVI español* pg 101–118.

———, "Del amor y la mujer en Ciprano de la Huerga y Luis de Léon" in *Biblia y humanismo Textos, talantes y controversias del siglo XVI español* pg 85–100.

———, "Benedicti Ariae Montani…*De Psalterii Anglicani Exemplari Animadversio*" in *Biblia y Humanismo Textos, talantes y controversias del siglo XVI español* pg161–167.

———, "Benedicti Montani…*De Mazzoreth ratione atque usu*" in *Biblia y Humanismo Textos, talantes y controversias del siglo XVI español* pg 155–160. Fernández Tejero, E, "Dos Tratados de Benito Arias Montano" in *Biblia y Humanismo Textos, talantes y controversias del siglo XVI español* pg 169–166.

———, "El Text hebreo de la Biblia Políglota Complutense" in *Biblia y humanismo Textos, talantes y controversias del siglo XVI español* pg 209–218.

Fernandez Vallina, F. J., and Montaner, L. V., "Lengua y Literatura en las Biblias poliglotas espagñolas: Traducciones latinas y modelos subyacentes" Revista da Sefarad XLII (1982) pg 129–139.

Ferraro, D., *Tradizione e Ragione in Juan de Mariana* (Franco Angeli, Milan 1989).

Fitzmaurice Kelly, J., *Fray Luís de Léon* (OUP, Oxford 1921).

Fragnito, G., *La Bibbia al rogo. La Censura ecclesiastica e i volgarizzamenti della Scrittura (1471–1605)* (Il Mulino, Bologna 1997).

Fragonard, M.-M., "Histoire et métaphore: l'histoire de la poésie dans La Galliade" in ed. F. Roudaut, *Poésie encyclopédique et Kabbale chrétienne Onze études sur Guy le Fèvre de La Boderie* (Champion, Paris 1999) pg 31–46.

———, "Les Trente-deux Sentiers de Sapience de Nicolas Le Fèvre de la Boderie: Une théorie de l'interprétation polysémique au XVIᵉ siècle" in *Méslanges sur la Littérature de La Renaissance à la mémoire de V-L Saulnier* (Droz, Geneva 1984) pg 217–224.

Friedman, J., "Jewish Conversion, the Spanish Pure Blood Laws and the Reformation: a Revisionist View of racial and religious Anti-semitism" Sixteeth Century Journal XVIII/1 (1987) pg 3–29.

Fücks, J., *Die arabischen Studies in Europa bis in der Anfang des 20 Jahrhunderts* (Leipzig 1955).

Gandillac, M. de, "Le Thème de la concorde universelle" in *Guillaume Postel Actes du Colloque* pg 192–197.

Giacone, F., "Le catholicisme dans les Hymnes ecclesiastiques" in ed. F. Roudaut, *Poésie encyclopédique et Kabbale chrétienne Onze études sur Guy le Fèvre de La Boderie* (Champion, Paris 1999) pg 99–168.

Gitlitz, D. M., *Secrecy and Deceit The Religion of the Crypto-Jews* (Jewish Publication Society, Philadelphia 1996).

Goeje, M. J. de, *Catalogus Codicum Orientalium Bibliothecae Academiae Lugduno-Batavae* (E. J. Brill, Louvain 1873).

Gorny, L., *La Kabbale. Kabbale Juives et Cabale Chrétienne* (Pierre Belfond, Paris 1977).

Gorris, R., "*L'Un Guide Orfée*: Temi esoterici e cabbalistici nelle *Diverses Meslanges Poetiques* di Guy Le Fèvre de la Boderie" *Le Culture esoteriche nella Letteratura francesca Actes du XV Colloque de la SUSLLF* (Pavia, 1987) pg 65–83.

Gottfarstein, J., [trans.] *Le Bahir Livre de la clarté* (Verdier, Paris 1983).

Graf, G., *Geschichte der christlichen arabischen Literatur* (Vatican City 1947).

Grafton A. and Williams M., *Christianity and the Transformation of the Book* (Harvard UP, London 2006).

Greenspoon, L., "A preliminary publication of Max Leopold Margolis's Andreas Masius, together with his discussion of the Hexapla-Tetrapla" in ed. A. Salvesan, *Origen's Hexapla and Fragments* (Texte u. Studien zum Antiken Judentum 58, Tübingen 1998) pg 39–69.

———, "Max L. Margolis on the Complutensian Text of Joshua" Bulletin of the International Organisation for Septuagint and Cognate Studies XII (1979) pg 43–56.

Gruenwald, I., "A Preliminary Critical Edition of Sefer Yezira" Israel Oriental Studies
    I (1971) pg 132–177.
Gundersheimer, W. L., "Erasmus, Humanism and the Christian Cabala" Journal of
    the Warburg and Courtauld Institute XXVI (1963) pg 38–52.
Gwilliam, G. H., "The Ammonian Sections, Eusebian Canons and the Harmonising
    Tables in the Syriac Tetraevangelium" in ed. S. R. Driver et al. *Studia Biblica II*
    (Clarendon, Oxford 1890) pg 241–272.
——, "The Materials for the Criticism of the Peshitto New Testament, with Specimens
    of the Syriac Massorah" in ed. S. R. Driver, T. K. Cheyne, W. Sanday, *Studia Biblica
    et Ecclesiastica* (Clarendon, Oxford 1891) Vol. III pg 47–104.
Hall, B., " A Sixteenth Century Miscellany" Journal of Ecclesiastical History XXVI/3
    (July 1975) pg 309–321.
——, *Humanists & Protestants 1500–1900* (T&T Clark: Edinburgh 1990).
——, *The Trilingual College of San Idelfonso and the Making of the Complutensian Polyglot*
    (E. J. Brill, Leiden 1969).
Hamilton, A., "From Familism to Pietism The fortunes of Pieter van Borcht's Biblical
    Illustrations and Hiël's Commentaries from 1584–1717" Quaerendo XI/4 (1981)
    pg 271–301.
——, "Hiël and the Hiëlists The Doctrine and Followers of Hendrik Jansen van Bar-
    refelt" Quaerendo VII/3 (1977) pg 243–286.
——, "Seventeen Letters from Hendrik Jansen van Barrefelt (Hiël) to Jan Moretus"
    De Gulden Passer LVII (1979) pg 62–127.
——, "The Family of Love in Antwerp" Bijdragen tot de Geschiednis LXX (1987)
    pg 87–96.
——, *The Family of Love* (James Clarke & Co, Cambridge 1981).
Haran, A. Y., "*L'Espagne dans L'Imaginaire français du XVII siècle: entre Idéalisation et Démoni-
    sation*" *XVIIᵉ Siècle* CXCII/2 (1997) pg 305–323.
——, Le Lys et le Globe Messianisme dynastique et Rêve impérial en France aux
    XVIᵉ et XVIIᵉ siècles (Champs Vallon, Paris 2000).
Harrie, J., "Duplessis-Mornay, Foix-Candale and the Hermetic Religion of the World"
    Renaissance Quarterly XXXI/4 (1978) pg 499–514.
——, "Guy Le Fèvre de la Boderie's Vision of World Harmony and the Policies of
    François d'Anjou" in ed. J. F. Sweeths, *Proceedings of the XI Annual Meeting of the Western
    Society for French History Riverside California 3–5 November 1983* pg 25–35.
Hayek, M. *Liturgie Maronite* (Maison Mame, Paris 1963).
Heiming, P. O., *Syriche 'Eniane und Greichische Kanones. Die Ms Sach 349 den Staatsbibliothek
    zu Berlin.* (Verlag der Aschendorffschen Verlagsbuchhandlung: Münster in Westf.
    1932).
Hendricks, D., "Profitless Printing" The Journal of Library History II (1967) pg
    98–116.
Holt, M. P., *The Duke of Anjou and the Politique Struggle during the Wars of Religion* (CUP,
    Cambridge 1986).
Hossian, A., "The Alexandrine Anaphora of St. Basil" in ed. L. Sheppard, *The New
    Liturgy* (DLT, London 1970) pg 228–243.
Idel, M., *Messianic Mystics* (Yale UP, New Haven 1998).
Jones, J. A., "Arias Montano and Pedro da Valencia: Three further documents" Bib-
    liothèque de Humanisme et Renaissance XXXVIII (1976) pg 351–352.
——, "Censuras acerca de la impresión de la *Paraphrasis Chaldaica* de Andrés de León:
    un aspect de la amistad entre Benito Arias Montano y Pedro de Valencia" *Homenaje
    a Pedro Sainz Rodriguez I Repertorios, textos y comentarios* (Madrid, 1986) pg 339–348.
——, "Les advertencias de Pedro de Valencia y Juan Ramírez acerca de la impresión
    de la "Paraphrasis Chaldaica" de la Biblia Regia" Bulletin hispanique LXXXIV
    (1982) pg 328–344.

——, "Pedro de Valencia's defence of Arias Montano: A note of the Spanish Indexes of 1632, 1640, & 1667" Bibliothèque de Humanisme et Renaissance LVII/1 (1995) pg 83–88.
——, "Pedro de Valencia's Defence of Arias Montano: The Expurgatory Indexes of 1607 (Rome) and 1612 (Madrid)" Bibliothèque de Humanisme et Renaissance XL (1978) pg 121–136.
Jongkees, J. H., "Masius in moeilijkheden" De Gulden Passer XLI (1963) pg 161–168.
Kamen, H., *The Spanish Inquisition. An Historical Revision* (Weidenfeld and Nicholson, London 1997).
Kingdom, R. M., "The Plantin Breviaries: a Case Study in the Sixteenth Century Operations of a Publishing House" Bibliothèque de Humanisme et Renaissance XXII (1960) pg 133–150.
Kirsop, W., "The Family of Love in France" Journal of Religious History III (1964) pg 103–118.
Kish, G., *Erasmus' Stellung zu Juden und Judentum* (Tübingen 1969).
Klein, W. P. [ed.], *Sefer Jesirah. Übersetzt und kommertiert von Guillaume Postel. Neudruck der Ausgabe, Paris 1552. Herausgegeben, eingeleitet, und erläutert von WPK* (Frommann-Holzberg: Bad Connstatt/Stuttgart 1994).
——, *Am Aufang War das Wort* (Berlin 1992).
Kottman, K. A., *Law and Apocalypse: the Moral Thought of Luis de León* (Martinus Nijhoff, The Hague 1972).
Kubler, G., *Building the Escorial* (Princeton UP, Princeton 1982).
La Ferrière-Percy, H. Le Comte de, *Les la Boderie. Etude sur une famille normande* (A. Aubry: Paris 1557. Slatkine Reprint, Geneva 1969).
Levi della Vida, G., *Ricerche sulle Formazione del piu antico fondo dei manoscritti orientali della Biblioteca Vaticana. Studi e Testi 92* (Biblioteca Apostolica Vaticana, Città del Vaticano 1939).
Lewy, G., *Constitutionalism and Statecraft during the Golden Age of Spain: a study of the political philosophy of Juan de Mariana S.J.* (Droz, Geneva 1960).
Llorente, M. de la Pinta, *Procesos Inquisitoriales contra los Catedráticos Hebraistos de Salamanca. I Gaspar de Grajal* (Monasterio de El Escorial, Madrid 1935).
Lombart, N., "Le statut du poète dans les Hymnes ecclesiastiques: tradition liturgique et poétique chez le Fèvre" in ed. F. Roudaut, *Poésie encyclopédique et Kabbale chrétienne Onze études sur Guy le Fèvre de La Boderie* (Champion, Paris 1999) pg 169–180.
Lossen, M., 'Masius' in the *Allgemeine Deutsche Biographie* (Leipzig, 1884) Vol. XX pg 559–562.
——, Briefe von Andreas Masius und Seinen Freunden 1538 bis 1573 (Verlag von Alphons Düre, Leipzig 1886).
Maillard, J.-F., "Postel et ses disciples normands" in *Guillaume Postel 1581–1981* (Guy Trédaniel, Paris 1985) pg 83–91.
——, "Christophe Plantin et la Famille de la Charité en France: Documents et Hypothèses" in *Mélanges sur la Littérature de la Renaissance à la Mémoire de V-L Saulnier* (Droz, Geneva 1984) pg 235–253.
Margolis, M. L., *The Book of Joshua in Greek* (Guether, Paris 1931–8).
Markish, S., *Erasmus and the Jews* (Chicago UP: Chicago 1986).
Marnef, G., *Antwerp in the Age of Reformed Underground Protestantism in a Commercial Metropolis 1550–1577* (John Hopkins: Baltimore 1995).
Marsh, C. W., *The Family of Love in English Society 1550–1630* (CUP: Cambridge 1994).
Maser, S., "Musique et harmonie des quatre mondes ou le cercle IV de la Galliade de G. Lefèvre de la Boderie" Renaissance and Reformation/Renaissance et Reforme XVIII (1982) pg 11–33.

Messina G., *Notizia du un Diatessaran Persiano Tradolto dal Siriaco* (Pontificio Instituto Biblico: Roma 1943).

Metzger, B. M., *The Early Versions of the New Testament* (OUP: Oxford 1977).

Meyer J. F. (tr.), *Das Buch Jezira* [Original edition Leipzig 1830]. New edition by Eveline Goodman (Thom. & Christophe Schulte: Berlin 1993).

Moir, I. A., "Fam. 22 A New Family of Manuscripts in the Pericope Adulterae" in ed. T. Baarda et al, *Texts and Testimony Essays on the New Testament and Apocryphal Literature in Honour of A. F. J. Klijn* (Kok, Kampen 1988) pg 170–176.

Morales Oliver, L., "Avance para una biografiá de obras impresaas de Arias Montano" Revista del Centro de Estudios Extremeños II (1928) pg 171.

——, *Arias Montano y la política de Felipe II en Flandes* (Ed. Voluntad, Madrid 1927).

Morreale, M., "Vernacular Scriptures in Spain" *The Cambridge History of the Bible* (CUP, Cambridge 1963) vol. II pg 465–491 and also "Spanish Versions" vol. III pg 125–129.

Moss, C., *Catalogue of Syriac printed books and related literature in the British Museum* (BM, London 1982).

Moss, J. D., *"Godded with God": Hendrick Niclaes and his Family of Love* (The American Philosophical Society, Philadelphia 1981).

Muraoka, T., *Classical Syriac for Hebraists* (Harrassowitz, Wiesbaden 1987).

Narducci, E. *Catalogus codicum mss praeter orientales qui in Bibliotheca Alexandrina Romae asservantur* (Rome 1877).

Nasrallah, J., *L'Imprimerie en Liban* (Harissa 1949)

Nave, F. de [ed.], *Philologia Arabica. Arabische studiën en drukken in de Nederlanden in de 16de en 17de eeuw* (Publikaties MPM/PK 3, Antwerpen 1986).

——, *Het Museum Plantin-Moretus Te Antwerpen. I: De Bibliothoek* (Publikaties MPM/PK, Antwerpen 1985).

——, *Het Museum Plantin-Moretus Te Antwerpen. II: De Archieven* (Publikaties MPM/PK 2, Antwerpen 1985).

Netanyahu, B., *The Origins of the Inquisition in Fifteenth Century Spain* (American Academy for Jewish Research, New York 1995).

Neve, F., "Guy Lefèvre de la Boderie, orientaliste et poète" in Revue Belge et Étrangère XIII (1862) pg 363–372, 413v433, 679–697.

Nippold, F, "Heinrich Niclaes und das Haus der Liebe. Ein monographischer Versuch aus der Secten-Geschichte der Reformationszeit" Zeitschrift für die historische Theologie XXXII (1862) pg 323v402 and 473–563.

Ortega-Monasterio, M.-T., "Arias Montani List of Qere-Ketiv-Yattir Readings" in ed. A. Dotan, *Proceedings of the Ninth International Congress of the International Organisation for Massoretic Studies 1989* (1992) pg 71–84.

Palandjian, H. and Tonoyan A. et al., *Festschrift Prof. Dr. Dora Sakayan zum 65 Geburtstag* (Diocese of the Armenian Church of Canada, Montreal 1996).

Parker, D. C., "Hexapla" in *The Anchor Dictionary of the Bible* (Doubleday, New York 1992) Vol. III pg 188–189.

Pascoe, L. B., "The Council of Trent and Bible Study: Humanism and Scripture" Catholic Historical Review LII (1966) pg 18–38.

Percival, K. W., "Antonio de Nebrija and the Dawn of Modern Phonetics" Res Publica Litterarum V (1982) pg 221–232.

Perles, J., *Beiträge zur Geschichte der hebräischen und aramaischen Studien* (Theodore Achermann, München 1884).

Pidal y de Miraflores, Les Señores Marqueses de, y Miguel Salvó, D., *Coleccion de Documentos Inéditos para La Historia de España. Tomo XXVII, XLI* (Impresta de La Viada de Calero, Madrid 1862).

Pinta Liorente, M. de la, "Fr. Luis de Léon y los hebraístas de Salamanca" Archivo Augustiniano XLVI (1952) pg 147–169.

Pitt, W. E., "The Origin of the Anaphora of the Liturgy of St. Basil" Journal of Eccle-
siastical History XII (1961) pg 1–13.
Popper. W., *The Censorship of Hebrew Books* (Knickerbocker Press, New York 1899).
Reprinted with introduction by M. Carmilly-Weinberger (Ktav, New York 1969).
Quignard, P., "La passion de Guy le Fèvre de la Boderie", Po&sie (sic) III (1977) pg
95–109.
Ramirez, J. A. [ed.], *Dios arquitecto: J. B. Villalpando y el templo de Salomón* (Madrid
1994).
Ramos Frechilla, P. D., "La Poliglota de Arias Montano" Revista Española de Estudios
Biblicos III (1928) pg 27–54.
Ratel, S., "La Cour de la Reine Marguerite" Revue du Seizième Siècle XI (1924) pg
1–29, 193–207, XII (1925) pg 1–43.
Reeve, A. [ed.], *Erasmus's Annotations on the New Testament The Gospels* (Duckworth,
London 1986).
Reinhardt, K., "Hebraische und spanische Bibeln auf den Scheiterhaufen der
Inquisiton. Texte zur Geschichte des Bibelzensur in Valencia im 1450" Historische
Jahrbuch CI (1981) pg 1–37.
——, *Bibelkommentare spanischer Autoren (1500–1700)* (Madrid 1990).
——, *Die biblischen Autoren Spaniens bis zum Konzil von Trent* (Salamanca 1976).
Rekers B., *Benito Arias Montano (1527–1598)* (The Warburg Institute, University of
London, London 1972).
Rodríguez Moñino, A., "La Biblioteca de Benito Arias Montano: Noticias y documentos
para su reconstruccíon" Revista del Centro de Estudios Extremeños II (Jan/Aug
1928) pg 555–598.
Roey, A. van, "Les début des Études syriaques et André Masius" in ed. René Lav-
enant, *V Symposium Syriacum 1988* (Orientalia Christiana Analecta CCXXXVI) (Pont.
Institutum Studiorum Orientalium, Rome 1990) pg 9–11.
——, "Les Études syriaque d'Andreas Masius" Orientalia Louvansia Periodica IX
(1978) pg 141–158.
Rooses, M., *Correspondance de Christophe Plantin* (Antwerp 1883; Kraus Reprint,Nendeln-
Liechtenstein, 1968).
Rosenau, H., *Vision of the Temple The Image of the Temple of Jerusalem in Judaism and Chris-
tianity* (Oresko, London 1979).
Roth, C., *A History of the Marranos* (Jewish Publication Society of America, Philadelphia
1932).
Rotondo, A., *Studi e Ricerche di Storia ereticale italiano del Cinquecento* (Edizione Giappichelli,
Turin 1974).
Roudaut, F. [ed.], *Poésie encyclopédique et kabbale chrétienne. Onze études sur Guy Le Fèvre de
la Boderie* (Honoré Champion, Paris 1999).
——, *La Galliade. Le Fèvre de la Boderie* (Klincksieck 1993).
——, *Le Point Centrique* (Klincksieck, Paris 1992).
Rummel, E., *Erasmus. Annotations on the New Testament. From Philologist to Theologian* (Uni-
versity of Toronto Press, Toronto 1986).
Sabbe, M., "Les rappports entre Montano et Hiël" De Gulden Passer IV (1926) pg
19–43.
Sáenz-Badillos, A., *La Filología Bíblica en los primeros Helenistas de Alcalá* (Verbo Divino,
Estella (Navarra) 1990).
Saenger, P. and van Kampen, K. [eds.], *The Bible as Book The First Printed editions* (Brit-
ish Library, London 1995).
Schild, M. É., *Abendländische Bibelvorreden bis zur Lutherbibel (Quellen und Forschungen zu
Reformationsgeschichte Band XXXIX)* (Gütersloher Verlagshaus Gerd Mohr, Heidelberg
1970).

Schmidt, A.-M., "Guy Le Fèvre de la Boderie, Chrétien, Poète et Kabbaliste" *Aspects du Genie d'Israel (Cahiers du Sud)* (Finbert, Paris 1950) pg 169–182.
——, *La poésie scientifique* (Paris 1938).
Schwarz, W., *Principles and Problems of Biblical Translation Some Reformation Controversies and their Background* (CUP, Cambridge 1955).
Sealy, R. J. *The Palace Academy of Henry III* (Droz, Geneva 1981).
Secret, F., *L'ésotérisme de Guy le Fèvre de la Boderie* (Librairie Droz, Genève 1969).
——, [ed.] Guillaume Postel, *Apologies et Rétractations. Manuscrits inédits publiés avec une introduction et des notes par François Secret* (B de Graaf, Niewkoop 1972).
——, "'L'Ensis Pauli' de Paulus de Heredia" Revista di Sefarad XXVI (1966) pg 79–102, 253–271.
——, "Benjamin Nehemia ben Elnathan et G. Postel à la prison de Ripetta en 1559" Revue des Études juives CXXIV (1965) pg 174–176.
——, "Documents pour servir à la histoire de la Bible d'Anvers" Revista da Sefarad XVIII (1958) pg 121–128.
——, "Egidio da Viterbo et quelques-uns de ses contemporains". Augustiniana XVI (1966) pg 371–385.
——, "Filippo Archinto, Girolamo Cardano, et Guillaume Postel" Studi francesci XIII (n.37) (1969) pg 73–76.
——, "G. Postel et les études arabes" Arabica IX (1962) pg 36.
——, "L'arrestation de Postel à Lyon" Bibliothèque de Humanisme et Renaissance XXIII (1961) pg 357–359.
——, "L'Opuscule de G. Postel sur Le Miracle de Laon" Bibliothèque de Humanisme et Renaissance XXVIII (1966) pg 399–405.
——, "La Correspondance de Guillaume Postel. Une lettre au Baron Paumgartner" Bibliothèque de Humanisme et Renaissance XXV (1963) pg 212–215.
——, "La Rencontre d'Andreas Masius avec Postel à Rome" Revue d'Histoire ecclésiastique LIX 1964 pg 485–489.
——, "Les Débuts du Kabbalisme chrétien en Espagne et son histoire à la Renaissance" Revista da Sefarad XVII (1957) pg 36–48.
——, "Les Détensions de Postel à Saint-Martin-des-Champs" Bibliothèque de Humanisme et Renaissance XXII (1960) pg 555–557.
——, "Les Grammaires hébraïques d'Augustinus Justinianus" Archivum Fratrum Praedicatorum XXXIII (1963) pg 269–279.
——, "Notes pour une Histoire du Pugio Fidei à la Renaissance" Revista di Sefarad XX (1960) pg 401–407.
——, "Pedro Ciruelo: Critique de la Kabbale et de son Usage par les Chrétiens" Revista da Sefarad XIX (1959) pg 48–77.
——, *Guillaume Postel (1510–1581) et sa Interprétation du Candélabre de Moyse* (B de Graaf, Niewkoop 1966).
——, *Les Kabbalistes Chrétien de la Renaissance. Nouvelle edition mise à jour et augmentée* (Arche, Milano 1985).
Sed, N., "Le Sefer Yesira. L'Edition critique, Le Texte primitif La Grammaire et La Métaphysique" Revue des Etudes juives CXXXIII (1973) pg 513–528.
Seiming, P. O., *Syrische 'Eniane und Griechische Kanones* (Verlag der Aschendorffschen Verlagsbuchhandlung: Münster in Westf. 1932).
Sheppard, L. [ed.], *The New Liturgy* (DLT, London 1970).
Spence, J. D., *The Memory Palace of Matteo Ricci* (Faber and Faber, London 1985).
Spinks, B. D., *The Sanctus in the Eucharistic Prayer* (CUP, Cambridge 1991).
Steinmann, M., *Johannes Oporinus. Ein Basler Buckdrucher um die Mitte der 16 Jahrhunderts.* Basler Beiträge zur Geschichtswissenschaft n. 105. (Helbing and Lichtenhahen, Basel-Stuttgart 1967).

Stow, K. R., *Catholic Thought and Papal Jewry Policy 1555–1593* (Jewish Theological Seminary of New York, 1977).

Swietlicki, C., *Spanish Christian Cabala: the works of Luis de Léon, Santa Teresa de Jesus, and San Júan de la Cruz* (University of Missouri Press, Columbia 1986).

Taylor, R., "Architecture and Magic Considerations on the Idea of the Escorial" in eds. D. Fraser, H. Hibbard, and M. J. Lewine, *Essays in the History of Architecture presented to Rudolf Wittkower* (Phaidon, London 1967) pg 81–109 (with plate IX).

Theunissen, P., "Arias Montano et la Polyglot d'Anvers" Les Lettres Romanes (Louvain) XIX/3 (1965) pg 231–246.

Troncanelli, F., *La Città dei Segreti. Magia, Astrologia e Cultura Esoterica a Roma (XV–XVIII)* (Franco Angel, Milan 1985).

Various, *Guillaume Postel 1581–1981 Actes du Collogne International d'Avranches 5–9 setembre 1981* (Editions de la Maisnie, Paris 1985).

——, *Kabbalistes Chrétiennes*. Cahiers de l'Hermétisme (Albin Michel, Paris 1979).

Vasoli, C., "Da Marsilio Ficino a Francesco Giorgio Veneto" in his Filosofia e Religione nella Cultura de Rinascimento (Guida Editori, 1988) pg 233–256.

——, "Un 'precedente' della 'Virgine Veneziana': Francesco Giorgio Veneto e la clarissa Chiar Bugni" ed. Kuntz, *Postello, Venezia, e il suo Mondo* pg 203–225.

——, *Profezia e Ragione* (Studi sulla Cultura di Cinquecento e del Seicento: Napoli 1974).

Vercruyst, J., "Un humaniste brabançon oublié: Andreas Masius Bruxellanus" Le Folklore Brabançon CLII (1961) pg 615–621.

Vocht, H., de, "Andreas Masius (1514–1573)" in *Miscellanea Giovanni Mercati* (Studi e Testi CXXIV) Rome (1946) pg 425–441.

Voet, L., *The Golden Compasses. A History and Evaluation of the Printing and Publishing Activities of the Officina Plantiniana at Antwerp* (trans. R. H. Kaye, Vangendt and Co, Amsterdam 1972).

——, *The Plantin-Press (1555–1589) A bibliography of the works printed and published by Christopher Plantin at Antwerp and Leiden* (with J. Voet-Grisolle) (Amsterdam 1980–1983) VI vols.

Vööbus, A., *The Apocalypse in the Harklean Version* (CSCO: 400, Subs 56 1978).

Walker, D. P., *The Ancient Theology* (Duckworth, London 1972).

Weiss, T., *Zur ostsyr. Laut- u. Akzentlehre auf Grund der ostsyr. Massorah HS des British Museum* (Stuttgart 1933).

Wesselius, J. W, "The Syriac Correspondence of Andreas Masius" in ed. R. Lavenant, *V Symposium Syriacum 1988* (Orientalia Christiana Analecta CCXXXVI) (Pont. Institutum Studiorum Orientalium, Rome 1990) pg 21–30.

Wilkinson, R. J., *Orientalism, Aramaic and Kabbalah in the Catholic Reformation. The first printing of the Syriac New Testament* (E. J. Brill, Leiden 2007).

——, "Reconstructing Tyndale in Latomus: William Tyndale's last, lost, book" Reformation I (1996) pg 252–285.

——, "Emmanuel Tremellius' 1569 Edition of the Syriac New Testament" Journal of Ecclesiastical History 58/1 January 2007 pg 9–25.

——, *The Origins of Syriac Studies in the Sixteenth Century* (Unpublished PhD University of the West of England 2003).

Wilson, D. [ed.], *French Renaissance Scientific Poetry* (Athlone Press, London 1974).

——, "La seconde édition de la Galliade de Guy Lefèvre de la Boderie, sa composition et ses sources" in *Mélanges à la mémoire de F. Simone. France et Italie dans la culture européene, I: Moyen-Age et Renaissance* (Slatkine Reprints, Geneva 1980) pg 351–359.

——, "The Quadrivium in the Scientific Poetry of Guy Lefèvre de la Boderie" *French Renaissance Studies 1540–1570 Humanism and the Encyclopedia* (Edinburgh U.P., Edinburgh 1976) pg 95–108.

Wolf, P. K., *Am Anfang war das Wort. Theorie und Wissenschaftsgeschichtliche Elemente früh-neuzeitlichen Sprachbewusstseins* (Berlin 1992).
Yates, F. A., *Astrea The Imperial Theme in the Sixteenth Century* (Routledge, London 1975).
———, *French Academies of the Sixteenth Century* (London 1947: Kraus Reprint, Nendeln (Liechtenstein) 1973).
———, *Giordano Bruno and the Hermetic Tradition* (Routledge, London 1971).
———, *The Occult Philosophy in the Elizabethan Age* (Routledge, London 1979).

INDEX

Studies in the History
of Christian Traditions

(formerly Studies in the History of Christian Thought)

Edited by Robert J. Bast

102. Dam, H.- J. van (ed.), *Hugo Grotius, De imperio summarum potestatum circa sacra*. Critical Edition with Introduction, English translation and Commentary. 2 volumes. 2001
103. Bagge, S. *Kings, Politics, and the Right Order of the World in German Historiography c. 950-1150*. 2002
104. Steiger, J. A. *Fünf Zentralthemen der Theologie Luthers und seiner Erben*. Communicatio – Imago – Figura – Maria – Exempla. Mit Edition zweier christologischer Frühschriften Johann Gerhards. 2002
105. Izbicki, T. M. and Bellitto, C. M. (eds.). *Nicholas of Cusa and his Age: Intellect and Spirituality*. Essays Dedicated to the Memory of F. Edward Cranz, Thomas P. McTighe and Charles Trinkaus. 2002
106. Hascher-Burger, U. *Gesungene Innigkeit*. Studien zu einer Musikhandschrift der Devotio moderna (Utrecht, Universiteitsbibliotheek, MS 16 H 94, olim B 113). Mit einer Edition der Gesänge. 2002
107. Bolliger, D. *Infiniti Contemplatio*. Grundzüge der Scotus- und Scotismusrezeption im Werk Huldrych Zwinglis. 2003
108. Clark, F. *The 'Gregorian' Dialogues and the Origins of Benedictine Monasticism*. 2002
109. Elm, E. *Die Macht der Weisheit*. Das Bild des Bischofs in der *Vita Augustini* des Possidius und andere spätantiken und frühmittelalterlichen Bischofsviten. 2003
110. Bast, R. J. (ed.). *The Reformation of Faith in the Context of Late Medieval Theology and Piety*. Essays by Berndt Hamm. 2004.
111. Heering, J. P. *Hugo Grotius as Apologist for the Christian Religion*. A Study of his Work *De Veritate Religionis Christianae* (1640). Translated by J.C. Grayson. 2004.
112. Lim, P. C.- H. *In Pursuit of Purity, Unity, and Liberty*. Richard Baxter's Puritan Ecclesiology in its Seventeenth-Century Context. 2004.
113. Connors, R. and Gow, A. C. (eds.). *Anglo-American Millennialism, from Milton to the Millerites*. 2004.
114. Zinguer, I. and Yardeni, M. (eds.). *Les Deux Réformes Chrétiennes*. Propagation et Diffusion. 2004.
115. James, F. A. III (ed.). *Peter Martyr Vermigli and the European Reformations*: Semper Reformanda. 2004.
116. Stroll, M. *Calixtus II (1119-1124)*. A Pope Born to Rule. 2004.
117. Roest, B. *Franciscan Literature of Religious Instruction before the Council of Trent*. 2004.
118. Wannenmacher, J. E. *Hermeneutik der Heilsgeschichte*. *De septem sigillis* und die sieben Siegel im Werk Joachims von Fiore. 2004.
119. Thompson, N. *Eucharistic Sacrifice and Patristic Tradition in the Theology of Martin Bucer, 1534-1546*. 2005.
120. Van der KooI, C. *As in a Mirror. John Calvin and Karl Barth on Knowing God*. A Diptych. 2005.
121. Steiger, J. A. *Medizinische Theologie*. Christus medicus und theologia medicinalis bei Martin Luther und im Luthertum der Barockzeit. 2005.
122. Giakalis, A. *Images of the Divine*. The Theology of Icons at the Seventh Ecumenical Council – Revised Edition. With a Foreword by Henry Chadwick. 2005.
123. Heffernan, T. J. and Burman, T. E. (eds.). *Scripture and Pluralism*. Reading the Bible in the Religiously Plural Worlds of the Middle Ages and Renaissance. Papers Presented at the First Annual Symposium of the Marco Institute for Medieval and Renaissance Studies at the University of Tennessee, Knoxville, February 21-22, 2002. 2005.
124. Litz, G., Munzert, H. and Liebenberg, R. (eds.). *Frömmigkeit – Theologie – Frömmigkeitstheologie – Contributions to European Church History*.
125. Ferreiro, A. *Simon Magus in Patristic, Medieval and Early Modern Traditions*. 2005.
126. Goodwin, D. L. *"Take Hold of the Robe of a Jew"*. Herbert of Bosham's Christian Hebraism. 2006.
127. Holder, R. W. *John Calvin and the Grounding of Interpretation*. Calvin's First Commentaries. 2006.
128. Reilly, D. J. *The Art of Reform in Eleventh-Century Flanders*. Gerard of Cambrai, Richard of Saint-Vanne and the Saint-Vaast Bible. 2006.
129. Frassetto, M. (ed.). *Heresy and the Persecuting Society in the Middle Ages*. Essays on the Work of R.I. Moore. 2006.
130. Walters Adams, G. *Visions in Late Medieval England*. Lay Spirituality and Sacred Glimpses of the Hidden Worlds of Faith. 2007.
131. Kirby, T. *The Zurich Connection and Tudor Political Theology*. 2007.
132. Mackay, C.S. *Narrative of the Anabaptist Madness*. The Overthrow of Münster, the Famous Metropolis of Westphalia (2 vols.). 2007.
133. Leroux, N.R. *Martin Luther as Comforter*. Writings on Death. 2007.
134. Tavuzzi, M. *Renaissance Inquisitors*. Dominican Inquisitors and Inquisitorial Districts in Northern Italy, 1474-1527. 2007.
135. Baschera, L. and C. Moser (eds.). *Girolamo Zanchi, De religione christiana fides – Confession of Christian Religion* (2 vols.). 2007.
136. Hurth, E. *Between Faith and Unbelief*. American Transcendentalists and the Challenge of Atheism. 2007.
137. Wilkinson R.J. *Orientalism, Aramaic and Kabbalah in the Catholic Reformation*. The First Printing of the Syriac New Testament. 2007.
138. Wilkinson R.J. *The Kabbalistic Scholars of the Antwerp Polyglot Bible*. 2007.
139. Boreczky E. *John Wyclif's Discourse On Dominion in Community*. 2007.

Prospectus available on request

BRILL — P.O.B. 9000 — 2300 PA LEIDEN — THE NETHERLANDS